EXPLORING AND LOCATING SOCIAL WORK

EXPLORING AND LOCATING SOCIAL WORK

A FOUNDATION FOR PRACTICE

DARREN HILL, LORRAINE AGU,
DAVID MERCER

BLOOMSBURY ACADEMIC
LONDON • NEW YORK • OXFORD • NEW DELHI • SYDNEY

BLOOMSBURY ACADEMIC
Bloomsbury Publishing Plc
50 Bedford Square, London, WC1B 3DP, UK
1385 Broadway, New York, NY 10018, USA
29 Earlsfort Terrace, Dublin 2, Ireland

BLOOMSBURY, BLOOMSBURY ACADEMIC and the Diana logo
are trademarks of Bloomsbury Publishing Plc

First published in Great Britain 2019
This edition published 2024

ISBN: PB: 978-1-1376-0434-7
ePDF: 978-1-1376-0435-4
eBook: 978-1-3503-1380-4

To find out more about our authors and books visit www.bloomsbury.com
and sign up for our newsletters.

CONTENTS

Introduction

> Too much is generally expected of social workers. We load upon them unrealistic expectations and we then complain when they do not live up to them.
>
> (Barclay Committee, 1982: viii)

In reading this book, you will already have decided that social work is of interest to you as a career and profession; or you may be engaged within an undergraduate or postgraduate social work course. In writing this book, we hope to provide for you a foundation in social work education and professional practice. Students and practitioners often feel that social work can only be learned from direct practice, through working within a front-line social work service. There is a kernel of truth in this position. However, social work requires more than just doing; it is more than a technical activity. We as social workers operate in a complex environment, with challenging social presentations. To understand social complexity we must have a solid foundation for practice; a practice that is situated within applied learning, critical thinking and professional practice. Before we begin reading, exploring and locating social work within this text, it is necessary to recognise the enormous task and challenge that social work offers to social work student and practitioners. The opening quote in this introduction, provided by Sir Peter Barclay in his report *The Barclay Report* produced in 1982, offers a timeless insight into the task and expectations social workers face in their daily practice in the community. As a professional activity and institution social work aims to provide the support and protection required for individuals and families who often fall between the cracks in wider welfare, health, criminal justice and education networks. We work with individuals who are socially and economically disadvantaged. The service users we work with are often maligned by the media, and ignored by the political institutions of local and national government. The base and foundation of social work is the teenage mother; the unaccompanied adolescent asylum seeker; the child who has not eaten today; the parental substance misuser; the teenager who has moved around multiple care homes; the older adult with no savings or resources to pay for care; and the homeless individual with complex mental health issues. Everyone has an opinion on the people we work with, but few understand the complexity that brings individuals to social work services. As student social workers and qualified social work practitioners, we often work with social complexity that cannot be resolved with one simple intervention or decision. The decisions we make do not follow a simple outcome, and often they can compound or alleviate the social distress our service users face. The positive results of our practice often go unnoticed, while the negative decisions become public information, consumed within a political discourse that seeks to marginalise and reduce social services.

Despite these complexities and difficulties, the student social worker and the social work practitioner is a privileged role that that few other professions can replicate or provide. We walk with those at the margins of society, and the interventions we provide highlight the complex ethical and practical moral dilemmas we face within society. To provide safety, support and advice to those most in need is truly inspiring and rewarding. In our experience, every prospective social work student comes to the profession wanting to help, to make a difference to the lives of others. It is this sentiment and foundation that drives social work. The bonds of social solidarity and care for others are a fundamental position for our intellectual and practical activity. The contemporary political discourse within our society is centred upon the individualisation of complex social problems. This individualisation of social inequality is further compounded though the breakdown of the welfare state, and the social welfare institutions that seek to alleviate social distress. We are told that business knows best and that market competition supported by privatisation is the best route for delivering social services. It is the position of this book that: collectivity and social solidarity are the foundations for good social welfare and positive social services. The social crises that often bring service users to seek help or be referred to social work support are often too great for one individual to resolve on their own. Social workers as a professional group are one of the last remnants of the welfare state, a concept that is rapidly becoming wilfully redundant within modern society. The ambition to provide social support and care for people from the cradle to grave is a concept that is ingrained within your training and professional status. It is something worth supporting and fighting for. As prospective social workers and students, we must recognise that we have a world to win. Social work is more than a professional activity: it is also a social and political movement. We must be bigger than our individual casework; our strength lies within not only individual action, but also advocating locally, regionally and nationally for improved collective social and material resources. This national action in turn needs to build a global social work vision to secure structural political change to improve welfare provision for all. We hope, by writing this book, we will provide a foundation for your professional practice and critical thinking, and inspire you to connect the micro personal professional practice to the macro economic, social and political context. You, as student social workers, are the future and you have a world to win: the future of our profession is in your hands.

Guide to the chapters

Below is a brief synopsis of each of the chapters in the book. The chapters can be read as interdependent of one another or in an integrated manner. The choice is yours as reader. This is done purposefully, as a student social worker, you may approach this book as a repository to support learning and teaching, seeking each chapter out interdependently, if needed, to support your modular-based learning. It must also be recognised that the chapters in this book have been written from a UK perspective, in particular an English one. While we recognise the unique professional standards, legislation, policy and culture that supports social work practice in Scotland, Wales and Northern Ireland, as England-based social work academics we cannot do these areas justice. The overarching macro themes and commonalities in each chapter will have resonance with our colleagues within different geographic and political communities; but for micro standards, policy and legislation, readers will have to adapt the discussion to suit their geographic and political context.

Each chapter has a flexible case study method that aims to support learning through reflection. This is delivered by in-text boxes that pose careful reflective questions to support student learning. The book includes a glossary and index to support ease of access for student learning. This flexible case study method is supported by clear links, at the beginning of each chapter, between the social work Professional Capabilities Framework (PCF) at entry level and the Health and Care Professions Council (HCPC) Standard of Proficiency (SOP) (BASW, 2017; HCPC, 2017). The ability to map learning to national standard is part of your ongoing learning journey and an excellent preparation for your practice and continuing professional development.

Chapter 1 – The historical development of social work: Making links from the past to the present

This chapter will explore and locate the historical development of social work within the UK, making links to the contemporary role of social work with direct reference to the social, political and economic context that has shaped the professional and institutional development of UK social work.

Chapter 2 – The contemporary role of social work: Working with communities and complexity

This chapter will explore and locate the contemporary role and position of social work within the UK. This section will develop awareness around the professional role and its situation within diverse agencies and multi-disciplinary teams. Through a careful exploration of social work agency and institutional models, the reader will build an awareness of the delivery and practical context of contemporary social work practice.

Chapter 3 – Preparing for social work practice: Models of intervention for social work practice

This chapter will introduce social work models of intervention. Within the chapter, the reader will explore contemporary models of intervention within social work services including key approaches such as risk assessment; care management; and communication skills for direct practice.

Chapter 4 – Working with diversity: Understanding and locating individuals and communities

Building on the models of intervention chapter, this chapter will explore the context of intervention placing individuals and communities within a psychosocial context. A strong emphasis will be placed upon a social model approach to complex situations in the community and individual context. Within this section, the reader will be able to locate that social work intervention is more than a process; it has a social and political context that is intersected by a diverse population base.

Chapter 5 – Global social work: Locating and understanding the impact of globalisation on social work

Building on the diversity chapter, this section will explore social work beyond the UK, but make implicit links to UK practice-locating complex global forces and their impact on local practice. Key themes will be explored locating the context and role of international social work; the impact of global economics on local social work practice; and the experience of migration and conflict as global phenomenon on local social work practice.

Chapter 6 – Preparing for practice: From first placement to final placement

This chapter will cover the stages of student practice placement development. The reader will be given a firm grounding in placement preparation in pragmatic manner including applied values and ethics; professional regulations; the importance of volunteering and transition through the multiple placement opportunities within your course. Central to this will be grounding and preparing the student for the final journey into qualified practice.

Chapter 7 – Summary

Here we briefly review the main points outlined in the rest of the book with some suggestions for what may come next. In broad terms, we suggest that the foundation for good social work practice is a blend of pragmatic activity that is clearly located in an awareness of a larger socio-political context. To prepare for practice the reader will need a broad understanding of society past and present and an acute focused attention to individual detail and social complexity.

1

The historical development of social work: Making links from the past to the present

In this chapter, we will examine the role of social work within our society, and locate the historical development of social work within broader social, political and economic frameworks. The role of social work as a professional activity can be considered as contingent on the overarching historical, political and economic periods it is located within, and it is from this perspective that we will explore the historical development of social work within the UK.

Key concepts within this chapter include:

➢ The role and context (political and economic) of social work within the UK.

➢ Social work as a process of social order and social justice.

➢ The exploration of social work through its key historical moments as shaped by social, political and economic forces.

The discussion in this chapter is also situated alongside the 'Readiness for Direct Practice Level' of the **Professional Capabilities Framework for Social Work (PCF)** developed by the British Association of Social Workers (BASW).

Through reading Chapter 1 students should be able to:

Professionalism

➢ Describe the role of the social worker.

Knowledge

➢ Demonstrate an initial understanding of the legal and policy frameworks and guidance that inform and mandate social work practice.

Building on the PCF we would also like you to familiarise yourself with the **standards of proficiency (SOPs)** for social workers in England (2017) by the **Health and Care Professions Council (HCPC)**. The discussion that develops in this chapter has congruence with the following **HCPC SOPs (6, 6.1 and 6.2)**:

➢ 6. Be able to practise in a non-discriminatory manner.

➢ 6.1 Be able to work with others to promote social justice, equality and inclusion.

➢ 6.2 Be able to use practice to challenge and address the impact of discrimination, disadvantage and oppression.

Throughout this chapter, we will explore the role, history and development of social work in the UK. This discussion raises questions around social work's role as a profession that promotes social justice, equality and inclusion, while seeking to challenge discrimination disadvantage and oppression.

Shaping the role and context of social work: Social order and social justice

As potential social workers, we must acknowledge that social work as a profession has a tradition and heritage that is both commendable and questionable, for reasons that will be explored further in this chapter. The role of social work as a professional activity and institution can be observed through the development of the social welfare state within the UK. In turn, the development of social welfare as a framework can be located and explored in response to the dual processes of urbanisation and industrialisation within the UK. Social work as a professional activity and role within society may be considered as contingent on wider social, economic and political forces. This contingency is highlighted succinctly by Jordan (1984: 31):

> In simple societies there are no social workers. Orphans, widows, handicapped people and the elderly are looked after within the extended family or tribe. Unconventional behaviour is either tolerated, venerated or punished by retributive methods. The notion of having specialists in planning the care of dependents, or in changing the non-conformist behaviour of other people is largely the creation of modern industrial societies.

The historical development of social welfare and social work within the UK and the political and economic forces that have shaped it are situated within a broad historical social context that is enshrouded in political, economic, moral and social frameworks that can often leave the observer and reader feeling uncomfortable. The foundations of social welfare and social work are built on some difficult and uncomfortable truths. These uncomfortable social truths are locked within the social, economic and political framework that surrounded industrialisation and urbanisation within the UK during the nineteenth century. In creating a new urban-technological society that was driven by economic production, new systems of governance arose and evolved to support the **social order** of that period and can be considered cruel and degrading by modern standards. These systems of governance include the confinement and exploitation of the working poor in workhouses; no historian has yet counted or provided a clear estimate of those who died in workhouses from poverty and hard work. We must also never forget the barbaric detention and treatment of mental patients in the asylum, and learning disabled patients in the special hospital; the degrading physical treatments, ritual humiliation and their confinement and exclusion should be remembered forever. Social work has had a role to play in all these situations; our territory and professional domain is the marginalised, neglected and discriminated against. We have often enforced oppression and discrimination, as well as challenged it. Knowing our history is as important as knowing thyself; as social workers, we must understand and reflect on our past to recognise the contradictions, oppressions and discrimination of the present. One of the key factors that shapes our past and present within social work is the overarching political and economic narrative within UK society. The dominant economic and political order of liberal capitalism has nurtured and created an unequal social and economic context – that has facilitated the need for social work and social welfare. Throughout this book we will be locating social work within its wider political, social and economic context, by doing so we will make reference to the political and economic forces of capitalism and liberalism (in its multiple formats). It is therefore necessary that we have an understanding of that context.

Capitalism

Capitalism can be described as an economic and social system that is based on private ownership and private property, as well as capital accumulation, wage labour and competitive markets. Capitalism can be observed as ordering society within a restrictive socioeconomic hierarchy based on a pyramid system; those who control economic resources and own the means of production maintain primacy over those who do not. The foundations of capitalism rest with the ownership of the means of production and their operation for private profit. The means of production refer to

▶

◄

facilities, tools and infrastructure, as well as natural resources and raw materials, which produce economic value. In a capitalist-led economic system key decisions are made by the owners of the means of production. As a direct result of this, society is often structured around the needs of the market in maintaining and supporting the larger socioeconomic system.

Liberalism

In the UK, capitalism is supported by a political system defined as liberalism. Liberalism as a political philosophy is a dynamic and flexible form of government; it is both fluid in its response to political change and flexible in adapting to rapid social change. Liberalism is a political position that is founded on the foundation of liberty and equality. The core principles of liberalism include freedom of speech; a free press; freedom of religion; free markets; civil liberties; and human rights. These principles are underpinned by a secular and democratic government; and the promotion of equality across social groups.

Reflective questions

After reading the brief description of capitalism and liberalism:

- Do you think capitalism is a good way of managing and ordering society?

- What social tensions can you see arising between the processes of political liberalism and economic capitalism?

- How do you think social work and welfare services would develop under liberal capitalism?

Flexibility is a defining feature of social, political and economic liberalism, and it is one of the enduring features of liberal capitalism. However, despite the dynamic nature of liberal capitalism, and its dual processes of industrialisation and urbanisation, the political and economic system has created a situation within western society where social progress and economic stability for citizens are locked into a restrictive socioeconomic hierarchy. As a political and economic system, capitalism creates contradictions in its social and economic conditions; some critics argue that these contradictions are a built-in requirement of the system (Harvey, 2005; Hill et al., 2016; Marx and Engels, [1848] 2016). As Horner (2006: 3) highlights:

> Modern western social democratic capitalist societies are committed to ideals of citizenship, whereby the state offers equality of opportunity but not equality of experience. It is seen to be essentially up to each individual citizen to determine to what extent she or he wishes to take advantage of these opportunities.

Social work as a professional role has developed in the UK in part as a direct response to these social and economic contradictions created by liberal capitalism. For a modern industrial society to function and flourish, it requires, or more appropriately capitalism requires, a stable society that produces consumers and workers to operate its technical and productive institutions (Bailey and Brake, 1975). Social workers are part of the overarching social welfare structures that help maintain a stable society through the promotion of **social order**. Within this restrictive socioeconomic hierarchy, competition and individualism are paramount virtues. As an economic and social process, capitalism can be observed as creating economic 'winners' and 'losers' (Luttwak, 1999). In reality, there are no winners or losers; participation in the economic system is not experienced from a position of equity – many people are socially excluded and marginalised given their location and status within a restrictive political, social and economic hierarchy. This process can be referred to as social and economic inequality. Social work as a professional activity directly supports those individuals that experience social and economic inequality (Sernau, 2013). In providing direct support and social assistance, social work seeks to support those who experience social crises and inequality, moving them back towards social stability and inclusion within mainstream society; this is where conflict and tensions arise. The dominant model of social integration within contemporary UK society is centred on the individual citizen, or the extended family of that citizen, being able to self-support, primarily through employment, but also through informal social support networks to provide for their care and social needs. Working with people who are struggling to care for or support themselves, due to their position within our restrictive social and economic hierarchy, poses difficult ethical questions for social work. These moral and ethical questions can be explored within the reflective case study below.

Case Studies

Below are some case studies that include examples of social crises and social inequality.

Alan is 35 and has been referred to you by the mental health hospital. He is going to be discharged and has no accommodation, social support or access to any financial resources. He has a history of depression and self-harm that is compounded by illicit drug use. Alan has not seen his family for five years due to his drug use and chaotic social situation. Alan wants a fresh start and to be part of the community.

▶

◄

Sharon is 22 and has two children both under five. She has fled her home due to domestic violence by her partner. She is new to your area, has no social support and no possessions. Sharon left residential social care at 18 and is estranged from her family. Sharon wants a new life and a fresh start in a safe area.

George is 87 and has just been diagnosed with dementia. He is happy living at home alone. He has friends in his community housing association. He is estranged from his family. Recently he fell over getting dressed and injured himself; he was admitted to hospital. He couldn't remember what happened. He doesn't have any financial support to pay for help, and won't accept it. George wants to be left alone by professionals.

Reflective questions

- How would you respond to these as a student social worker in the community?
- What would you like to see happen in each situation?
- How would you intervene and improve each situation?
- Would your intervention conflict with the wishes of the service user?

The role of social work: Exploring social order and social justice functions

Social work since its inception has always played a central role in working with those individuals and families who fall between traditional welfare, education and health services. Often the people we work with are categorised as 'problem families' or 'complex cases', and this 'problem'-based discourse is an enduring feature of the operationalisation of social work within the UK (Ferguson, 2011; Jones, 1983). Reflecting on the discussion exercises explored previously, and the 'problem'-based discourse approach of practice, it is the position of this book that the role of social work has two clear themes that have emerged within its tasks and functions within UK society: that of maintaining and supporting **social order**, and the promotion of **social justice**.

Social order

Students entering the social work profession recognise that social work is considered a different role and a distinct profession from wider community, youth, care and support worker roles. While we have a shared history and value base, the role of social work often requires working with individuals who do not want to, or are reluctant to, engage with services or professionals. Social workers operate within a complex social welfare environment that places technical and legal activities within their professional domain. In such a framework, social workers have a duty to intervene, protect, manage and safeguard individuals and communities. Within this **social order** role social workers seek to address the inherent contradictions and inequalities produced by late modern capitalism. In child protection work, social workers often address social and material deprivation as a central feature of practice, alongside physical, sexual and emotional abuse. Children's social workers have a complex task balancing welfare support with safeguarding; this complex task is often delivered through working to obtain better social and material resources to provide a supportive and safe family environment for children and families. The adult social work role often involves the allocation and direct provision of social and material resources to promote independent living in the community. Adult social workers have a very difficult task of balancing adult safeguarding with the management of limited resources, placed alongside a growing 'ageing' population. This **social order**–social work process involves a casework method that places emphasis on the assessment of social need and risk, and the case management of welfare resources. Social workers within their various agencies work towards managing the risk that individuals pose to themselves and the wider community. In doing so social workers apply a range of statutory legislation and social policy to intervene with and promote behaviour adjustment within individuals and families, to promote a safer or better way of living. The role required of contemporary social work within society places great emphasis on self-care and self-improvement, or care of the self, for service users in improving their social and material conditions. Individual responsibility is a core theme within social support – within the **social order** role. In such a role social workers can be observed as maintaining and promoting present social, economic and political conditions: individualism, self-reliance and self-support are core themes that emerge from liberal capitalism, and are diffused throughout society through its supporting welfare provision. However, if individuals do not change or the risk cannot be managed, social workers can apply legislation that seeks to protect and safeguard individuals against their own wishes, if needed, through removal of children and adults to places of safety.

Locating social order–social work

The **social order** role of social work is linked intrinsically to its statutory role and functions within society, and primarily occurs within statutory public agencies within Local Government, Criminal Justice and National Health Services. One notable historical exception is the NSPCC, which has always provided a statutory social work role for children, despite remaining a voluntary association and charity. However, given the market reforms within late modern society that are often introduced as part of the opening up of public services, we are beginning to see the statutory function of social work transition into non-governmental organisations (NGOs) and the private sector.

Social justice

Often the primary motivation for students entering social work is a desire to help, support and promote better social opportunities for those they work with. Social work as a profession has the unique opportunity of working with individuals and communities experiencing some form of social crises. Within the presenting social crises there is a **social justice** opportunity for social workers to promote positive social change – through the administration of direct intervention to provide personal services and advocacy in wider structural welfare services. The overarching aim of **social justice**–social work is to counter some of the worst excesses of modern social work practice; this includes the promotion of:

➢ Spending time with your service users in an attempt to place people before the administrative functions of the social work role.

➢ Listening and advocating for service users within a complex system – placing them at the centre of processes.

➢ Undertaking direct tasks with them through providing direct social support in navigating wider social welfare networks such as housing, education, employment and health services.

In this fast-moving world of increased pressure and demands on social work, **social justice**–social work often starts from a process of slowing professional activity down – to a pace where worker and service user can pause, reflect and work in partnership together.

Locating social justice–social work

The **social justice** role of social work is often located within charities, NGOs (also known as the third sector) and academic think tanks and research units. However, social justice–social work is also a philosophy, approach and methodology for practice within statutory social work services. It can operate on a direct level, providing direct case and community work to service users, but it also advocates and lobbies for individuals and communities at a regional, national and international level.

Exploring social work: A short history of social work in the UK

To understand how social work has developed within its dual themes of **social order** and **social justice**, it is necessary to explore and situate the historical development of social work practice. As we have eluded to previously, social work as a profession is a socially constructed role operating within wider structural welfare services. Both the profession and the services it operates within have developed as a response to the contradictions created by the political and economic structure of society. Social work as a unique and distinct profession has developed in response to the social problems created and nurtured during the development of capitalism, and the processes of industrialisation and urbanisation within the UK. Both the **social order** and **social justice** roles of social work develop as themes in response to the economic cycles of industrial capitalism and political liberalism. Building on our definition of liberalism explored earlier in the chapter, we have further developed the historical moments of social, political and economic liberalism. For the purposes of this textbook, we have defined the key periods of social work development under liberal capitalism within the UK according to the following historical moments or phases:

➤ Social work before capitalism

➤ Classical liberalism (1800s–1945)

➤ Embedded liberalism (1945–1979)

➤ Neo-liberalism (1979–present day)

Each of the phases of liberal capitalism will now be explored in relation to the development of the professional and institutional role of social work. What we are proposing within this text is that each of these key political and economic moments or phases of capitalism creates, develops and supports social work as a profession and institution. Social work as a professional activity is contingent on the social, political and economic conditions we live in. The discussion in this section is not the definitive history of UK social work; it merely serves to highlight key professional and institutional moments.

Social work before capitalism: What did the Tudors and Georgians ever do for us?

While it may be argued that social work as a clear professional role and activity did not exist prior to the era of industrialisation and urbanisation in the Victorian period (Horner, 2006), it may be put forward that social work as a broader activity occurred and was practised in a range of pre-industrial institutions. It is from these monastic, philanthropic and charitable organisations that the moral and practical framework of contemporary social work can begin to be discerned. History informs the modern social work student that their role and position are contingent on the management of political, social and economic distress. The social order prior to industrialisation, urbanisation and capitalism existed within a fixed feudal social hierarchy that offered limited social mobility. Relationships were characterised by either service to an established aristocratic–agricultural elite or progression within strictly controlled craft guilds that provided limited social mobility through mercantile activity (Richardson, 2001). Social work as an activity within the pre-capitalist historical phase was clearly located within local religious and charitable institutions.

During the late Middle Ages, we begin to see early social welfare legislation constructed to manage itinerants and vagabonds through the provision of the Ordinance of Labourers 1349 and the Statute of Labourers 1351 (Horner, 2006). Itinerants and vagabonds can be viewed as a historically socially excluded 'other', or quite simply those who lived beyond the confines of social, political and economic norms. A common theme within all historical social work is **social order**, or the management, control and support of those who live outside the dominant social norms of any given society (Hill et al., 2016). The historic foundations of pre-capitalist social work can be found not only in legislation, but also within religious monastic institutions. The Rule of St Benedict offers a basic social work assessment framework for the care of people (Horner, 2006). This monastic framework divides people into four categories of those who require care and support: the sick, children, guests and the poor (Horner, 2006; Moulin, 1978). This religious framework for the care of the other, or the less socially and economically fortunate within society, provides the embryonic framework for social work as a custom and practice, albeit in a religious rather than secular format.

The Tudor–Elizabethan period of government saw the development of a national social welfare framework for poor relief. Statutes for the provision of poor relief were developed in 1536 and in 1552 which put in place legislation that allowed for the first structural welfare intervention by the state in the form of weekly parish collections for poor relief (McIntosh, 2014). The Tudor–Elizabethan period saw the development of coherent Poor Laws in 1597 and 1601, respectively, with the introduction of the Act for the Relief of the Poor 1597 and the Poor Relief Act 1601. The Elizabethan Poor Laws established a system whereby welfare became a structural tool to manage displaced populations and economic insecurity (McIntosh, 2005). The Elizabethan system embedded the notion of localised relief based on an assessment of need. This process categorised recipients as 'deserving' or 'undeserving' and was administered by Overseers of the Poor (McIntosh, 2005; 2014). The assessment system placed those who were 'deserving' into almshouses or they were given outdoor welfare relief at home. Those considered as 'undeserving', such as adults who could but would not work, were placed into houses of correction, which acted as a prototype workhouse. What we can clearly observe is an intrinsic link between social welfare provision and morality. In developing social welfare and the idea of social work we can discern a form of social morality located between the state, the church and the individual. This contract places emphasis on deterrence from seeking support or help. Those that require help are assessed and categorised as deserving or undeserving of support. This foundational framework has a significant impact on the social and moral development of UK social welfare and social work services.

Key points to remember

This historical moment and period in the development of social work and social welfare has established some coherent themes that remain embedded within contemporary social work practice.

These themes include:

- The role of religious organisations in the form of monastic and church-based institutions has been integral to the development of early social welfare services. This role has continued, with many faith-based institutions remaining key service

▶

◀

providers within the voluntary/third sector, often competing to deliver local govern-ment commissioned services.

- The development of a Tudor social welfare system through poor relief created a structural welfare system based on local parishes. This parish-based system has a historical resonance for the delivery of contemporary social work through local government structures.

- The development of assessment of need. Both the Rule of St Benedict and the Elizabethan Poor Laws categorised and separated those who required support into deserving and undeserving cases. This practice continues in modern social work. Social workers are often asked to assess eligibility and need in the provision of community and residential-based services.

Self-help and bootstraps: Classical liberalism

The birth of social work as a profession and institution can be located more clearly within the historical period defined by the rise of capitalism and the dual processes of industrialisation and urbanisation. This process is concisely summarised in this poignant quote by Trevelyan (1944: 475):

> The age of coal and iron had come in earnest. A new order of life was begin-ning, and the circumstances under which it began led to a new kind of unrest. Immigrants to the industrial and mining districts were leaving an old rural world essentially conservative in its social structure and moral atmosphere, and were dumped down in neglected heaps that soon fermented as neglected heaps will do, becoming highly combustible matter.

The rise of capitalism as a social, political and economic force represented a shift in political, economic and social relationships. Capitalism and the processes of industrialisation and urbanisation transformed society in the UK. This dynamic process saw the UK move from a rural-agricultural society to an urban-industrial one. The previous agricultural-centred society, with its fixed political and economic relationships, was torn apart by the trans-fer of populations from the rural to urban environment (Hobsbawn, 2004). Capitalism required urban-based populations to work in the new emerging industries such as manufacturing. This process of urbanisation and indus-trialisation was not sterile, planned or well managed. As populations were transferred into urban settings, they were often housed in poor and unsanitary conditions that were not conducive to health and well-being. These populations were vulnerable and subject to exploitation by the new emerging industrial capitalists or bourgeoisie, who were an economic and political elite looking to maximise their profit margins. Working conditions were often poor and unregulated, with little attention paid to a safe working environment. The entire family worked from cradle to grave – children and parents often laboured together in the same factories. Life expectancy was short and the living conditions can be considered brutal. One observer of urban living during the period commented:

> Black and noisome, the road sticky with slime, and palsied houses, rotten from chimney to cellar, leaning together, apparently by the mere coherence of their ingrained corruption. Dark, silent, uneasy shadows passing and crossing – human vermin in this reeking sink, like goblin exhalations from all that is noxious around. Women with sunken, black-rimmed eyes, whose pallid faces appear and vanish by the light of an occasional gas lamp, and look so like ill-covered skulls that we start at their stare.
>
> (Morrison, 1889)

This description provides a vivid picture of the social and political context of life for the newly established industrial working class. The dehumanising social conditions had reduced working-class people to a precarious existence. Despite the social and economic contradictions of capitalism, including the production of vast economic wealth and abject poverty – situated side by side – the classic liberal philosophy of the period promoted by the political and economic elite is best summarised by the premise of 'self-help' and the process of 'pulling oneself up by one's own bootstraps'. Classical liberalism as a political and economic phase of capitalism placed emphasis on competition, free markets and minimum state intervention on a macro societal level; on an individual micro level, this resulted in welfare and social work that was focused on individual responsibility, self-care and the deterring of individuals from seeking help (Hill et al, 2016; Rubinstein, 1998). This political and economic narrative or discourse is important for the development of social work practice as it shapes the development of future welfare services and professional roles. This classically liberal concept of self-help and individualism is best summarised by the former social and political activist Samuel Smiles (1812–1904):

> Heaven helps those who help themselves is a well-tried maxim, embodying in a small compass the results of vast human experience. The spirit of self-help is the root of all genuine growth in the individual; and, exhibited in the lives of many, it constitutes the true source of national vigour and strength. Help from without is often enfeebling in its effects, but help from within invariably

invigorates. Whatever is done for men or classes, to a certain extent takes away the stimulus and necessity of doing for themselves; and where men are subjected to over guidance and over government, the inevitable tendency is to render them completely helpless.

(Smiles, [1858] 1997: 1)

The compartmentalisation and individualisation of poverty and inequality by nineteenth-century social structures were not without consequences for the political, economic and social hierarchy. Social and economic inequality can be considered the facilitator of both radical social change and welfare reform.

The history of social work can be regarded as symbiotic with the history of radical social change, with social reform and social work playing a central role in providing relief and stability against upheaval and chaos. In the nineteenth century, working populations within cities were placed in dire social and material conditions that gave rise to political unrest, and in some examples armed struggle. The nineteenth century saw the rise of radical social movements such as Chartism and the Luddites (Marlow, 1969). Chartism as a political force saw the development of mass social movements for political suffrage, as the politically excluded urban poor sought representation and political inclusion (Chase, 2007). The Luddites can be considered a direct consequence of scientific progress stemming from the industrial revolution. The Luddites were often castigated as a reactionary force against technological and social process (Linton, 1992); however, increased technology meant unemployment for the average worker, and unemployment because of industrial progress often led to workers having to place themselves within punitive and degrading social welfare systems. Beyond the UK, the global context of industrialisation and urbanisation had also created social reformist and revolutionary movements throughout Europe. The republicanism of the French Revolution on the European mainland, and the United Irishmen Rebellion closer to home, created a fertile ground for structural social change; this, combined with the subsequent revolutions of 1848 that occurred across mainland Europe, created a potentially explosive situation for the newly emerging economic and political elites. These revolutionary movements threatened the power of the capitalist industrialists by locating the newly emerged working class as the future rulers of society. As Marx and Engels ([1848] 2016) highlighted:

A spectre is haunting Europe – the spectre of communism. All the powers of old Europe have entered into a holy alliance to exorcise this spectre: Pope and Tsar, Metternich and Guizot, French Radicals and German police-spies.

The UK solution beyond political suppression of social movements and geopolitical alliances with conservative power networks across Europe was to enact a range of criminal justice and social welfare responses to manage urban dissent. This dual concession of **social order** measures combined with **social justice** within policy and legislation may well be the compromise that has seen no lasting social revolution happen on the UK mainland during the nineteenth century. While European nations experienced turbulent political relationships, throughout the nineteenth century UK parliamentary democracy and the monarchy remain reformed, but consistent. It is the position of this book that social welfare reforms are pivotal in creating this stability; social welfare reform and the emergence of social work are key factors in promoting and producing **social order**, by managing the expectations of society and mitigating the worst excessing of liberal capitalism through limited concessions to **social justice** via welfare reforms and direct relief.

Rioting for reform: The beginnings of social work and social welfare

The political response to the management of urban distress and political upheaval was to provide a national system of social welfare. The development of a revised and contemporary Poor Law system was a direct consequence of riots and insurrection by agricultural workers in what is known as the Swing Riots (Beckett, 2009). This flashpoint, while a catalyst, must be placed within the wider social context of dissent and upheaval that we have explored previously. The 1832 Royal Commission into the Operation of the Poor Laws, headed by Nassau William Senior (1790–1864), looked into the failing of the historical Poor Laws (Englander, 1998). The report concluded that the historical welfare provision was nurturing dissent, with parish paupers being used as cheap labour, and welfare handouts been used to subsidise poor employment practices (Parliament, 2016). The Royal Commission proposed that the New Poor Law be introduced and governed by the following principles:

Less Eligibility: that those entering the welfare system and workhouse would receive less favourable conditions than those employed outside the workhouse.

Workhouse Test: that an assessment should be made of those who need welfare to decide if they are maintained in the community or in the workhouse.

The Poor Law Amendment Act 1834

The Poor Law Amendment Act 1834 developed the findings of the Royal Commission into a cohesive body of legislation. To implement this system, power was devolved to local Poor Law unions with the role of Poor Law commissioners established to oversee and implement the provision. To meet the requirements of the Poor Law Amendment Act, workhouses were constructed under the provision of Less Eligibility. Conditions within workhouses were harsh, and inmates had to perform labour and tasks to support their interment. This system created resentment, as many labourers had no choice but to enter the workhouse due to the cyclical boom and bust nature of capitalism that led to unpredictable and unfavourable work conditions. Resistance to the workhouse system was sporadic, with key revolts and social protest located within Wales and the north of England (Evans and Jones, 2014). Given the harsh conditions of the workhouse, many Poor Law unions developed the Workhouse Test further and offered either indoor relief at the workhouse or outdoor relief in the community. The original Workhouse Test was meant to end the payment of outdoor relief. Underpinning the Workhouse Test was the premise of the **deserving** and the **undeserving poor**.

The Deserving Poor: included individuals who were widowed, disabled or had a long-term health problem that made them incapable of work.

The Undeserving Poor: included individuals of working age who were capable but unwilling to work.

What we can observe developing within the classically liberal period is a set of institutions, and technical welfare apparatus, that seeks to promote **social order** and distribute some form of limited **social justice** in welfare provision. The political and economic zeitgeist of the period demanded adherence to the principles of self-help and individualism. Welfare was premised on the principle that charity handouts would debase the individual character and the best help was self-help. These political and economic narratives can be observed as a consistent theme of welfare provision since the development of the modern industrial society. The workhouse period was not an isolated institutional development. During this time, we can observe a great enclosure or confinement of individuals who are considered to be deviant, socially unacceptable or non-productive economically (Porter, 1989; 2002). The workhouse period developed a UK welfare response that focused on institutionalisation and containment of social and economic inequality. Initially the workhouses were envisaged as a deterrent to welfare support. Given the reality of the boom and bust nature of liberal capitalism, the workhouse provided a catch-all for those who were marginalised and excluded by the social and material advancements of industrial capitalism. This separation of deserving and undeserving poor did not always fit into a workhouse model, with its limited categorisation of individuals requiring support. As a direct response to this we see multiple institutions develop, including mental health asylums and special hospitals for those with learning disabilities or hearing and visual impairments. Within industrial society those who could not produce economically or conform socially were removed from society. It is during this separation, categorisation and removal of the 'deviant' or 'non-compliant' other from society that a range of social welfare and medical roles emerge to manage these complex individuals, both in the workhouse-asylum and in the community. It is from this period that the forerunners of professional social work emerged within the following institutions:

- The Charity Organisation Society
- The Settlement Movement

We will now explore these key organisations and consider the development and impact on the legacy they have had on social work as a professional activity and institution.

The Charity Organisation Society

Within the UK, the Charity Organisation Society (COS) was led by Helen Bosanquet and Octavia Hill. Bosanquet was a key social reformer and welfare advocate, publishing several works on the conditions of the working poor. Hill was a pragmatic social reformer who believed in self-help and structured social support; her works included the support of good housing with structured social support (Bell, 1942). Hill also championed open green spaces for inner-city workers and structured youth groups such as the Army Cadets. The COS was very much of a classically liberal position – that of self-help, self-reliance and hard work.

    The primary message of the COS was that self-help and individual responsibility were key to reducing poverty and promoting self-reliance from welfare institutions. A key role of COS workers was to administer the Workhouse Test (Smith, 2002; Young, 1956). The Workhouse Test provided a role for charity organisation workers to assess those who required indoor relief at the workhouse and outdoor relief at the home (Horner, 2006; Jordan, 1984). The workers were crucial in deciding who was **deserving** of welfare and who was **undeserving** of support and services (Maltby and Rutterford, 2016). The COS provided the first model for social work practice or 'scientific charity' (Horner, 2006; Payne, 2005). The process of assessment and gatekeeping of welfare become a key function of the COS worker's role and has provided a solid foundation for contemporary social work practice (Gitterman, 2014). It must be noted that the COS also founded the first educational process for social work training and education (Davies, 2008). It advocated for objective and educational training for all welfare practitioners based on its scientific casework method (Hill and Frost, 2018). Prototype social work training courses were formed and the University of Birmingham opened its doors in 1908 with its one-year certificate in social studies (Davies, 2008). The early COS practitioners were great supporters of rigorous training and a standardised methodology for casework with the poor and working classes.

The Settlement Movement

The Settlement Movement was a political and economic social reform movement within the UK that developed in the 1880s and peaked in the 1920s. The Settlement Movement, like its counterpart the COS, developed in response to the process of urbanisation and industrialisation. Whereas the COS developed an individualised scientific casework method in the assessment and relief of poverty, the Settlement Movement developed a collective community-based social education approach to the alleviation of poverty, health inequality and social problems (Scheuer, 1985). This was done through the placement of Settlement Movement houses directly within working-class communities. Despite the difference in approach, it can be observed that the COS and Settlement Movement's primary driving values were that of 'self-help' and 'self-care'. These Settlement Movement houses provided education, welfare relief and health services. However, it may be posited that the collective education provided was a deeper 'collective' embedment of the middle-class values of 'self-help' and 'self-improvement'. The Settlement Movement and the promotion of collective 'self-help' primarily stem from universities and religious organisations. The most famous settlements were Toynbee Hall (Tower Hamlets in East London) founded by Canon Samuel and Henrietta Barnett, and Oxford House (Bethnal Green in East London); both of these projects had strong links to the University of Oxford and the Anglican Church (Barnett, 1918). The Settlement Movement, like the COS, combined welfare with an established and developing bourgeois or middle-class power base within the institutions of the church and the university. Both the COS and the Settlement Movement remained committed to the approach that the welfare service user's problems were centred and located in their behaviour, morality and deficient family relationships. However, despite these individualised beginnings, and promotion of self-help, parts of the Settlement Movement developed a more progressive 'collective' and structurally informed approach to the understanding of poverty and inequality. The real significance of the settlement movement was the idea of 'collective activity' and that self-improvement came from working in groups as a collective. One such collective organisation was Mansfield House located in the East End of London. Mansfield House was organised by Percy Alden. Alden was a key figure in the Settlement Movement, working as both a social worker and a Liberal Member of Parliament. Percy was also a key social reformer of the period maintaining critical support for the developing Independent Labour Party and the socialist Fabian Society. Mansfield House gave young working-class boys an experience of self-organisation and self-determination, providing activities and education for self-improvement and collective advocacy (Bradley, 2007).

Summary

To summarise, social work in the nineteenth and early twentieth centuries can be seen as developing in response to the social complexities caused by industrialisation and urbanisation.

Key points to remember

This historical moment and period in the development of social work and social welfare has established some coherent themes that remain embedded within contemporary social work practice.

These themes include:

- A casework model of social work practice based on a scientific or evidence-based methodology.

- The development of educational training for social welfare professionals.

- The establishment of assessment criteria underpinned by concepts such as 'deserving' and 'undeserving' – this conceptual framework has resonance within

▶

◀

    the care management and eligibility assessment models of contemporary social work practice.

- The further development of a system of welfare services that is managed through local municipal and parish systems. This can be directly linked to contemporary statutory social work practice within local government.

- The development of community-based welfare support, advocacy and social education. This settlement community model can be observed within the contemporary community development models of social work practice.

Collective care – from the cradle to grave: Embedded liberalism (1945–1979)

The nineteenth and early twentieth centuries provided the foundations for the development of professional social work practice. These foundations were deeply rooted in the classically liberal political, economic and moral model of 'self-help' and individualism. However, by 1945 the social, political and economic landscape had changed irreversibly, with far-reaching consequences for social work. The experience of World War II (1939–1945), when placed in context alongside that of the Great War (1914–1918) and the Great Depression (1929–1939), had created a situation where people would no longer accept the classical liberal political and economic premises of individual responsibility and minimum state provision (Hobsbawn, 1999). The economic depression/recession of the 1930s had highlighted that the economic foundations of capitalism were unstable, and that individuals alone could not bear the responsibility of structural financial and economic collapse. The experience of both world wars and the Great Depression created a new political, economic and social discourse. This experience of collective struggle and sacrifice created a context where men and women would no longer return to pre-war roles of subservience and the acceptance of appalling social conditions as the status quo. The state, which had called for collective sacrifice and struggle, had to rethink its position and role in structural social relationships (Sked and Cook, 1979). The social and political conditions of both wars had also created a political and economic challenge to liberal capitalism in the form of Communism in Europe. This, combined with a growing Labour and Trade Union movement, created a social and economic position in which liberal capitalism had to be flexible and adapt to survive (Hobsbawn, 1999; Kowalski, 2006).

Flexibility is one of the enduring features of liberal capitalism. The post-war period saw the classically liberal position of self-help, individualism, minimum state intervention and free enterprise abandoned or diluted with a new approach to political and economic governance. This new embedded liberal model of political and economic practices was theoretically positioned within the economic ideas of John Maynard Keynes; Keynesian economics became the driving force in political and economic thinking during the post-war period (Skidelsky, 2010a). The embedded liberal era was characterised by the use of the state to distribute resources in a more equitable manner. This distribution was pioneered through the implementation of an embedded liberal socio-political framework which included the 1942 report on Social Insurance and Allied Services, better known as the Beveridge Report; this report identified multiple giant evils within society, such as squalor, ignorance, want, idleness and disease (Harris and White, 2013). These identified 'social evils' were addressed by the post-war Labour government, headed by a former social worker and now prime minister, Clement Attlee. Attlee, as prime minster, brought about a seismic programme of collective and state-led social change; this programme of change began to implement multiple social policies in the construction of a 'cradle to grave' welfare state (Thorpe, 2008). These changes were far-reaching and included the Family Allowances Act 1945; National Insurance (Industrial Injuries) Act 1946; National Insurance Act 1946; National Health Service Act 1946; Pensions (Increase) Act 1947; Landlord and Tenant (Rent Control) Act 1949; National Insurance (Industrial Injuries) Act 1948; and the National Insurance Act 1949. These multiple legislative and policy drivers created a state where people received free education from primary school to university level; access to universal social housing with stable rents and tenancies; an excellent range of welfare benefits including national insurance; and free universal health care. The post-war settlement highlighted a clear shift in the discourse from individualism and self-help to a more collective viewpoint in which people were looked after by the state from the 'cradle to the grave' (Hobsbawn, 1999).

Understanding and exploring childhood: Embedded liberalism and social work

The role of social work became more focused during the post-war period. The collective experience of war at a societal level reshaped the traditionally conservative social structures and opened up the hidden world of the family. The collective wartime experience effectively reshaped how the state and society viewed childhood, social class and institutional welfare.

Children from large industrial cities within the UK were often evacuated to the rural countryside and in some case to overseas territories of the British Empire (Mann, 2005). This experience of separation highlighted two key areas of the childhood experience. Firstly, the conditions of the industrial urban working class were exposed, as children were dispersed into rural living, often in middle- or upper-class households (Marwick, 1976). This exposure and diffusion of urban working-class lives with suburban/ rural middle- and upper-class households gave an insight into the poor social conditions of the urban working class (Horner, 2006). These once-separated and closed-off worlds were exposed to one another, highlighting fault lines in the traditional individualised explanations for poverty and inequality. Secondly, the evacuation experience, and also the bereavements of the conflict, highlighted the importance of attachment, separation and loss on the lived experience of both children and adults (Martin, 2011).

The post-war period also demonstrated the failings of the Poor Law model of institutional welfare services. A public examination of children's homes was undertaken, and they were found to be lacking. Children within public care were found to be stigmatised, isolated and repressed (Horner, 2006). Children's residential and community-based care was often managed by overbearing and strict moral guardians, with children often living a life without care or affection (Parker, 2011). The public inquiry into the death of Dennis O'Neill, who at 13 years of age was beaten and starved to death by his foster father, highlighted failings in oversight and administration of looked-after children (Home Office, 1945). Finally, the Curtis Committee in 1946 criticised children's residential care as impersonal, unsupportive and focused on meeting basic survival needs rather than encouraging supportive relationships and encouraging positive individualised child development (Curtis Committee, 1946). With a move away from pre-war institutions and more open, personalised and collective public services, the post-war settlement saw the creation of **Children's Departments** and **Children's Officers**. The new Children's Departments inherited the care of around 16,000 children, some of whom were evacuees, others fostered out or placed within the care of public assistance committees or education departments (Horner, 2006). The new Children's Departments formed a foundation for radical social change in the care of children. Children were viewed as having a defined childhood, and that the experience of care should move beyond basic necessity and moral guidance. The care of children should be personal and centred on developing a sense of individual and collective self-worth (Jordan, 1984). During this period, Children's Social Services were developed on a mixed service provision, with foster care and adoption been used alongside residential nurseries, family group homes, approved schools and separate-sex remand homes for male and female children (Douglas and Philpot, 1998). The later post-war years saw the development of the 1958 Adoption Act that aimed to support the placement of children in homes with adults who could not have children of their own. This period also saw the development of the Children and Young Persons Act 1963; this legislation created a prototype social worker role in the form of Children's Officers. The new Children's Officer role placed a duty on local authorities to help any family whose children were in need but were not in their care. For the first time children's welfare was viewed as been best served where appropriate and when not at risk with the family. This move away from poverty as an admission to care was a key moment in the history of social work. These positive developments in children's social work continued with the 1969 Children and Young Persons Act. This piece of legislation developed and enhanced social work powers. Children and young people would come under the care and control of social workers for a range of diverse reasons including welfare concerns and school non-attendance, as well as moral danger and offending. The broadness of these powers reflect the post-war discourse of 'cradle to grave' care and the confidence in public social welfare institutions.

Caring beyond the institution and the impact of Seebohm

The post-war period was ground breaking in its restructuring of society and institutional care. Social workers were found working across the multiple institutions in various roles. Those working within the adult sector often worked in diverse roles such as mental health officers, hospital almoners, welfare officers and medical social workers (Jordan, 1984). The post-war period began to see a gradual opening up of traditional health and social welfare institutions, as society structurally moved away from warehousing and containing vulnerable populations to resettling them within the wider community. As the institutional role changed so did the professional role of social work. This process of de-institutionalisation within children's and adult services represented a social and cultural shift from the segregation and isolation of socially excluded and marginalised communities. Society was also undergoing vast structural change. The post-war world in the late 1960s saw political and cultural challenges to the traditional socially conservative status quo within the UK. During this period, traditional gender roles, sexuality, youth culture and broader social movements were all challenging the social acceptance of the traditional conservative social hierarchy (Moloney, 2013). The rupture in the social order was also felt in the dismantling of the traditional institutions that warehoused the old, infirm, mentally unwell and socially unacceptable. It is during this period that the great enclosure of the social excluded other was halted and those contained within the system began to be released and resettled back into the community. This process was known as normalisation:

> Social work with people with learning disabilities, long term mental illnesses and physical handicaps moved in the direction of 'normalisation' – treating service users as citizens, whose primary need was for access to the enabling facilities and resources by which all citizens sustain their lives as members of the community.

> (Jordan and Jordan, 2000: 106)

Institutional care in asylums or mental hospitals peaked in 1954 at 148,000 (Gibbins, 1998). During the period 1954–1974, this number was reduced by 60,000. However, this period's rapid closure and move to the community was not supported by the construction of much-needed holistic community-based services to manage this transition. It was not till the late 1970s that a well-planned closure programme was developed with supportive community-based teams established by the white papers *Better Services for the Mentally Handicapped* and *Better Services for the Mentally Ill* in 1975. The process of normalisation was not as rapid as initially envisaged. The dismantling of institutions took time and political commitment. With the shift from institutional silo-managed social work services, a new form of social work was developed that was more generic, holistic and professional. This new social work viewed the social aspect of individuals and communities in a different manner (Horner, 2006; Jordan, 1984). The Mental Health Act (1959) spurred on this new community-based social work; social workers now worked with citizens or clients rather than patients and inmates. This shift towards the social model rather than the medical model of practice was significant. Moving from a bio-deterministic model to a socially orientated community-based practice was at the epicentre of de-institutionalisation. It was around this time that medicine was questioned in its ability to provide a medical cure for physical, learning and mental difficulties (Moloney, 2013). The enclosure of madness, and the marginalised, had not produced a 'cure' or 'fix'; it had merely contained and at worst exacerbated issues through social isolation (Hill et al., 2016). It is a key feature of the history of social care and social work that where medicine is unable to find a cure, it redefines the problem as socially based and moves the medical problem from the hospital or institution to community care. A report by Younghusband (1959) highlighted that the patchwork system of social work services that operated in silo was no longer fit for the comprehensive welfare system. A new type of social work as to be created that was based on a general purpose social worker at its core dealing with those in need from cradle to grave (Younghusband, 1978).

Social work education and training was also developed in a more comprehensive format; historically social workers had done broad social studies courses or were untrained, often learning skills in a vocational setting (Hill and Frost, 2018). The generic training offered in universities was expanded to meet the newly emerging role of community social work, (Jordan, 1984; Younghusband, 1978). The formation of social work in higher education was developed further into the Standing Conference of Organisations of Social Workers (SCOW) in 1963. The once fractured professional identity of social work was brought under the generic and universal umbrella of SCOW. This change in training highlighted a shift in discourse; the concept of separate children's and family departments was challenged within society. Key social policy reformers such as Richard Titmuss (1958) argued for the creation of a social services department that would meet all needs. This debate and discourse was brought forward by the historically important Committee on Local Authority and Allied Personal Social Services, chaired by Frederic Seebohm, also known as the Seebohm Committee, which was formed in 1965 and reported back in 1968 (Seebohm, 1989). The Seebohm Report developed the perspective of Titmuss and concluded that a comprehensive and generic social services was needed for all members of society, young to old (Seebohm, 1989). The Seebohm Report also developed two other key themes. The first theme was a focus on prevention, with a strong emphasis on promoting community-based support and care on the terms of a cost–benefit analysis – then as now the cost of community care for children and adults was less than residential care (Seebohm, 1968). The second key theme was the emergence of community development. The Seebohm Report recognised the limitations of individualised casework and recommended that communities should have intervention and support based on citizen participation. Seebohm recommended that a new local authority department should be:

> A community based and family orientated service, which will be available to all, the new department will, we believe, reach far beyond the discovery and rescue of social casualties; it will enable the greatest possible number of individuals to act reciprocally, giving and receiving service for the well-being of the whole community.
>
> (Seebohm, 1968, para 2)

The confidence and vison of the post-war state in structural intervention into the lives of its citizens reached its peak and zenith in April 1971, following the 1970 Local Authority Social Services Act. The 1970s also saw the formation and regulation of social work education and training. The 1970 Local Authority Social Services Act created the Central Council for Education and Training in Social Work (CCETSW); this central body created the Certificate of Qualification in Social Work which was attached at master's, bachelor's or sub-degree level (Bamford, 2015). The new social services departments would be a hub, providing a range of social services and coordinating wider services provision within health and criminal justice services. They would have a range of staff, with the core worker being a generic social worker able to respond to complex social needs as well as a diverse caseload. The generic social worker was seen as needed to deal with what were called 'problem families', who utilised multiple services and required a single point of access, support and intervention (Philip and Timms, 1962).

However, the new social services departments never seemed to be able to fulfil their potential. The role of generic social worker proved to be a challenge, with social workers struggling to come to terms with working across multiple legal frameworks and social contexts. Social services departments naturally began to specialise and streamline social workers to meet complex social needs. This constant service delivery pressure was also matched by a series of high-profile social services inquiries that portrayed social services in a negative light. The most significant failure was the death of Maria Colwell in 1973. Maria was a 6-year-old girl who was removed by social services from foster carers and placed with her birth family. Maria was subsequently killed by her stepfather. The public inquiry highlighted that social services were not communicating internally and with external agencies; that they did not listen to the wishes of the child; and that family support and family bonds were given greater emphasis than child protection. The reforms from this case led to the establishment of child protection as paramount rather than wider child care or family welfare issues.

Summary

To summarise, the embedded liberal or social democratic period highlighted a significant shift in the discourse surrounding social work and social services. We see the role of social work reimagined within the context of the wider welfare state and post-war consensus.

Key points to remember

This historical moment and period in the development of social work and social welfare has established some coherent themes that remain embedded within contemporary social work practice.   ▶

◀

These themes include:

- The development and creation of an official social worker role that is situated within a local government social services department.

- The creation of a comprehensive social work education that is situated on a national level within further (college) and higher education (polytechnic/university).

- The development of community care and the process of deinstitutionalisation have a profound impact on the provision of social work and its role within contemporary society.

Entrepreneurs of the self: Neoliberalism (1979–present)

The post-war period, with its embedded liberal–social democratic institutions, had developed a comprehensive and thriving welfare state. This level of confidence in centrally planned and nationally regulated universal public services was to come under political and economic critique in the late 1970s and early 1980s. During this period, liberal capitalism reshaped its political and economic narrative into a new model – that of neoliberalism. Neoliberalism as a political and economic philosophy arose as opposition to the Keynesian informed structural interventionism of the post-war period. This new period challenged the notion of public-owned welfare service, utilities and industry. Neoliberalism shared many commonalities with classical liberalism on a macro level, in that it promoted free markets, individualism, private property and the rule of law. Since the late 1970s, neoliberalism on a national and international scale has seen the opening up, or marketisation, of once publicly owned and controlled services (Harvey, 2007). Public utilities such as gas, water and electricity were privatised, and public services have been competitively tendered out to business. This shift in political and economic philosophy has seen one of the greatest transfers of public wealth into private ownership, in a relatively short time period. The process of neoliberalism has become universal, both Conservative and Labour governments in the UK have followed and adhered to the mantra of marketisation.

On a micro level, neoliberalism has moved forward and deployed an ever-increasing business model within social work practice. This neoliberal business model seeks to replicate the 'free market' business and cultural values of capitalism within all our public and private institutions. The business values of professionalism, risk assessment and care management have become integrated ideologies of practice within all areas of contemporary social work practice. The free market has entered our working relationships: we no longer have clients, we have service users or customers; and a consumer experience is a central mechanism of contemporary personalised social work services. While the neoliberal business model has brought great advancements in community care, consumer rights and professionalisation of practice, it has also come at a cost to the provision of universal public services. The neoliberal period has also nurtured a work environment in which social workers are risk-averse. Risk-focused social work often creates a limited silo thinking to social work practice, due to economic cost or time management issues. Often the greatest amount of time in social work is spent making sure we are professional and accountable to the process of risk assessment, care management and the provision of audit information to support good practice. Within modern social work practice we are no longer public servants; we can be seen as active social work entrepreneurs working within a business model to provide services, assess risk and manage structural change in an increasingly complex social context.

The 1980s highlighted a significant cultural and social shift in social work practice. The zeitgeist of neoliberalism under the leadership of the Conservative Prime Minister Margaret Thatcher (1979–1991) had seen a seismic shift in the structure of the state. Nationalised industry and utilities were sold off and the government launched a political struggle for economic control of industry from the trade union movement, which it won in a series of protracted battles with key sectors such as coal mining and ship building (Milne, 2004). This political strategy was also followed by an economic strategy of deindustrialisation of key areas such as steel, textiles and manufacturing. The 1980s saw a huge increase in structural economic and social inequality; during this period, communities were impoverished as unemployment rose, and a widespread increase in problematic drug use was encountered in the areas of deindustrialisation (Parker, 2005). The 1980s saw the embedded liberal or social democratic welfare state come under fierce criticism; social work also came under political and professional attack as a key visible component of the post-war welfare state. This process of reform, or political attack, began with the Barclay Committee. The Barclay Committee produced the Barclay Report in 1982. The report, while critical of current social work practice, was overwhelmingly positive about the need for social work. However, a key critique was the universal nature of generic social work – that the generic community-based model was too ambitious. The report noted that:

> Social Work should be explicitly selective rather than universalist in focus, reactive rather than preventive in approach and modest in its objectives. Social

work should be preventive with respect to the needs which comes to its attention; it neither has the capacity; the resources nor the mandate to go looking for needs in the community at large.

(Barclay, 1982: 237)

The Barclay Report accurately diffused the spirit of the times; welfare and social work were to be scaled back. Towards the end of the 1980s, social work was becoming increasingly specialised, with social work practice contained within fragmented children's, older adults, mental health and youth justice departments (Horner, 2006; Payne, 2005). The vision of generic social service support had become separated and fragmented in responding to complex social needs. The 1989 Children Act attempted to develop the positive aspects of the post-war ideas of the Seebohm Report; the central premise of the Act was based on negotiation with families, involving partnership work. During this period, the concept of prevention was broadened, with local authorities having a duty to provide family support for children in need. However, the legislation was introduced in a difficult political and economic context; with an emphasis on a smaller state remit and reduced funding, many local government social work departments were focusing on child protection rather than broader welfare and prevention (Frost, 1992). During this period, children's social work was becoming increasingly reactive and focused on risk management and care management, both key features of the neoliberal business model that was being diffused into social work service provision in the 1980s (Bamford, 2015). In this context of reduced provision, combined with a conservative rollback of public service provision, children's social work departments were running with high thresholds for intervention and serving provision (Aldgate and Tunstall, 1995).

The rollback of the state during this period also saw a seismic shift in adult social work practice, for older adults, mental health service users and people with learning disabilities. The traditional total institutions of the asylum and special hospital, which had been scaled back since the late 1960s, were now fully opened up the with the National Health Service and Community Care Act (NHS and CCA) 1990. The NHS and CCA saw the introduction of a decentralised model of services from central government, with key concepts of marketisation brought in, such as the buying in of services and care packages. The community care aspect of the NHS and CCA was seen as a great victory for the social model of practice, in that individuals were no longer to be warehoused or segregated; everyone was entitled to live in the community as an active citizen. The NHS and CCA has been noted by critics as having more economic foundations than **social justice** drivers; the cost of institutional care was vast and the provision of community care was more cost-effective (Hill et al., 2016; Means and Smith, 1994). During this period, there was a commitment to community-based support with the construction of adult health and mental health teams combined with social work input. The idea of the multidisciplinary team came to fruition and the social model and social work role were at the heart of this approach. This initial victory for social work, with the removal of oppressed and segregated populations in institutions, was short-lived. In the age of neoliberal economic and political practice, community care was driven by the ideological need to reduce the role and cost of public service provision, and open up the health and social care sector to practices in line with the neoliberal business model. The community care model, with its commissioning of services to the third sector and NGOs, also provided the foundation for the transfer of services to non-state public sector organisations, acting as the catalyst for future free market reforms.

The late 1990s saw the end of the Conservative government administration and the election of a Labour government (1997–2010) under the leadership of Tony Blair (1997–2007). The initial optimism of change and belief that 'things could only get better' were put aside as the pace of neoliberal change remained consistent. The New Labour government had attempted to reconcile the practices of the 'free market' neoliberalism with **social justice** drivers by constructing a third way in parliamentary democracy (Giddens, 1998). Under New Labour public service provision was enhanced and developed. New Labour ensured that public services were well funded, and it was the mission of the labour government to introduce evidence-based practice to social work and social care (Godfrey et al., 2004). Overall the supportive approach to public services such as social work and social care came at a price; the introduction of a deeper managerial and business culture in the New Labour period brought increased audit and surveillance of practice to develop 'best practice' (Bamford, 2015). The modernisation of social work also came with a different approach to professional status and education and training. The title of social worker came to be protected and subject to registration with the General Social Care Council. This professionalisation of social work also came with a new model of education and training. The previously successful Diploma in Social Work course was developed into a bachelor's degree or master's degree system (Hill and Frost, 2018). This shift in policy was a bold move and further implemented central government control in shaping New Labour's modernisation of social work. Critics of the modernisation highlighted that the reforms undermined social work's professional autonomy, and highlighted a mistrust of central government in trusting local government to implement modernisation processes (Jordan and Jordan, 2000).

Children's social work practice saw sweeping changes, and one of the flagship policies of the New Labour government was the development of the Sure Start programme. This development of child care and early years emphasised the importance of a multidisciplinary community-based preventative programme; it was targeted at the 20% most deprived sections of the population (Hall et al., 2015). Local authority social services were expected to participate, but provision was established outside of the local government structure. This central control highlighted the dominance of the New Labour 'third way' in undermining traditional social democratic structures (such as local government social work) (Giddens, 1998). This process of reform and change in broader children's services was developed further in 2001; with the New Labour government re-elected, the government broadened its reform agenda to children's social work services. This transformation was highlighted in the 2002 spending review *Children at Risk*. Once again, a child's death, that of Victoria Climbié, was used to highlight systemic failure in social services and advance an agenda for change (Bamford, 2015; Knowles, 2009). This programme of change was packaged within the framework of the Every Child Matters agenda, and the government centred the change proposals as a response to the *Victoria Climbie Inquiry* (2003). The changes were aimed at strengthening child protection, while at the same time promoting a better prevention or early intervention culture. During this period, a system was created whereby preventative work moved beyond the traditional safety net of social services into wider organisations within health and social care. The aim was to introduce integrated services that combined front-line services that improved outcomes for all children (Parton, 2006).

The legacy for social work after Victoria Climbié and the Laming Report (2003) was the critical view of children's social work due to the high threshold level for intervention. This critique and high threshold for intervention came to a head in a public inquiry surrounding the death of Baby P. Lord Laming was asked to review his previous recommendations and identify what further needed to be done. His recommendations called for the establishment of a national safeguarding unit, the development of performance targets and indicators in children's social work, improvements in children's social work training, and improvements in serious case review procedures – to insure the independence of review chairs (Driscoll, 2009; Laming, 2009). The New Labour years had brought about significant change for social work; the role and vision for social work were to move practice outwards, to be inclusive and to have supportive outreach in the most needed communities; this move was both bold and visionary. However, it came at a price for social work; one of the most visible outcomes of the New Labour era for social work was the separation and breakup of traditional social services departments. Under the Every

Child Matters agenda, a Director of Children's Services was appointed alongside a councillor with lead for children's services, as well as a political role of Children's Commissioner (Bamford, 2015; Horner, 2006). This strategic and managerial move may be viewed as a fait accompli, with social work actually having been specialised and separated many years ago. However, during this period, what we can see is the last vestiges of the generic social services department having become dismantled. Social work education also saw broad reforms, with the development of professional status and post-qualifying experience. The Staying Safe: Action Plan and Social Work Task Force Review (DCSF, 2009a, 2009b) developed a model for post-qualification and supported learning and development in the first year of practice (Newly Qualified Social Worker). The New Labour years also looked at the introduction of children's social work fast-track training aimed at mature graduates, and the establishment of a post-graduate continuing professional development framework introducing an assessed year in practice (the Assessed and Supported Year in Employment, or ASYE). The national College of Social Work was also established, which was a bold yet ultimately doomed initiative that would not survive the next shift in government and political outlook.

Adult social work under the New Labour Years (1997–2010) followed a programme of structural change that saw significant development of adult and mental health services. The key to this change was integration and inclusion with wider health services. The previous reforms had seen the embedment of care management approaches under the 1990 NHS and CCA (Bamford, 2015). The care management approach placed the service user as consumer entitled to choice of services. This practice of free market reforms, consumerism and choice was continued and developed further under the Labour government. The free market care reforms had seen a patchwork of services develop unevenly, and choice often depended on which postcode you lived within. To address this, the Fair Access to Care Services (FACS) (DoH, 2003) was developed. This national framework was given power at local level, and for the first time allowed acre provision thresholds to be observed within a national context. FACS, while positive, clearly located adult social care within a system of rationing: prevention was not of importance; assessment of need at point of intervention was paramount. During the years 1997–2006, the number of those receiving publicly funded home care fell by 25%. A report by the Commission for Social Care Inspectorate (CSCI) found that care was still provided on an organisational need basis rather than needs-led assessment. Supporting community care and adult social work was the introduction of market-based reforms and ideology in the form of personalisation and direct payments; New Labour published *Putting People First* (DoH, 2007). This bold policy called for people to be in charge of their own destinies and to be free from centralised state planning. The key message was that responsibility for care was to become an act of self-management or self-care; the key vison for the service user was to become an entrepreneur of the self. As Bamford (2015: 63) highlights:

> The key changes envisaged by personalisation were mainstream person-centred planning and self-directed support, personal budgets for all those eligible for adult social care support, a universal information advice and advocacy service for those needing services and their carers, and support for vulnerable people to enjoy their rights as citizens.

One of the key features of the neoliberal period has been the transfer of state responsibility for care and structural support to the individual and competitively tendered service providers. It must be noted that all of this change is not negative, and the all-encompassing cradle to grave support of the post-war period often came with limited autonomy, choice and freedom. However, it should be acknowledged that choice, freedom and self-management come at a cost. All service users are not equal and a market-based system is based on economic power; in a system of diminished state funding, service users are often the first to see a reduced provision of funding when the cost of service provision increases. One of the great litmus tests of market reforms came with the Great Recession of 2008 (for more details on the Great Recession, see Chapter 5).

The financial crash of 2008 had its roots within a neoliberal economic framework. The historical deregulation of international banking and finance on a global scale saw the financial and banking sector grow at a fast pace. The unchecked and unregulated global finance system spiralled out of control and this resulted in a systemic global financial crash. To support the banking and financial system national government intervened, providing structural state support for a private financial sector. This massive investment in the banking and financial sector was then used as a platform for a series of austerity measures or cost-savings to redress this cost to government. The financial crash saw the New Labour administration voted out in 2010. The incumbent Conservative–Liberal Coalition government (2010–2015) were elected and promoted an austerity mandate of balancing the books. Adult social work services were one of the first to experience the full weight of the financial cuts. The original vision of FACS (DOH, 2003) did not fit the new economic realities of alleged 'austerity' practices. A revised version of FACS was developed in 2010 (DoH, 2010a; 2010b). The bold strategy of 'putting people first' failed to meet the economic reality of the post-financial crash political and economic context. In reality the neoliberal practices of personalisation and self-care were placing the cost and burden of financial care on the individual. In a world of decreasing health and social care budgets, an increase in care thresholds saw the transfer of cost directly located to the individual. Personal assets, including housing and savings, were the primary resources for many families. The Dilnot Commission (2011) attempted to reconcile this position by introducing a cap on the threshold for support for adult care costs. The process was lengthy and lifetime care costs were capped at £72,000 from 2016. It is widely understood that, despite the cap, families will continue to bear many costs and the thresholds for local authority support continue to be high and the process complex (Age UK, 2017; Bamford, 2015). Adult social care provision has continued to see deep marketisation and neoliberal practices with the development of direct payments; it must be noted that the process of personalisation and direct payments has been popular with both politicians and service users (Bamford, 2015). One of the compelling features of neoliberalism has been to combine the principals of choice, freedom and personal control with a vocal consumer rights and advocacy movement. After a slow initial buy-in from services users, over half a million service users had personal budgets by March 2012 (DoH, 2013). Personal care budgets are now a permanent feature of the social care and social work landscape; they are enshrined within the 2014 Care Act. The popularity of personalisation and direct payments remains high; however, we are yet to see how this transfer of care responsibility and management from the state to the individual will play out and develop in the long term. In a world with shrinking budgets and ideologically driven economic cuts to services, the tendency will be to transfer care into informal unregulated private markets. We may see a race to the bottom in care services to meet reduced financial provision, creating a shadow welfare service for older adults. The challenge for social work is to provide a balance between the paternalism of traditional social democracy and the dynamic move to the individual autonomy of neoliberalism. Care is not a traditional consumer product that is bought and consumed; it is complex, and involves the meeting of multiple needs in both the community and specialist residential care.

The late neoliberal period under the Conservative–Liberal coalition (2010–2015) and Conservative government (2015–present) has seen a shift in service provision for children's social work services. Many of the themes remain consistent with the New Labour (1997–2010) agenda of managerialism supported by an emphasis on child safeguarding in a multidisciplinary and interagency context. Change also came with the coalition government; the Department of Children, Schools and Families was rescinded and social work placed within the Department of Education. The language and lexicon of practice changed, with Every Child Matters having a reduced role within social work practice (Bamford, 2015).

A fresh series of reviews were called including Eileen Munro's (2011a; 2011b) review of children's services. Munro, like her predecessor Lord Laming, made sweeping managerial and technical changes. Many of Laming's previous recommendations (2003, 2009) were removed, including the national safeguarding unit; the Munro Report shifted emphasis away from this structural loss and refocused children's social work departments with appointments of chief social worker for both adults and children at national level. Local authorities were also encouraged to appoint principal social workers who were in touch with front-line practice. Munro also shifted the attack on the much lambasted front-line social worker; she suggested a reduction in the prescription of front-line practice. Munro spoke to social workers involved in bogged-down, cumbersome front-line bureaucratic practice; creating a discourse for social workers where doing the right thing was more important than doing things right was a compelling message and narrative for the much bureaucratically embattled front-line social workers (Bamford, 2015). The Conservative–Liberal coalition government (2010–2015) and successive Conservative government (2015–present) have also revisited the problem family as a concept, in modern format, through the Troubled Families initiative. Funds were released for local authorities of up to £4,000 for each 'troubled family'. The Troubled Families initiative aimed to turn around families by promoting more than 85% attendance at school, a 60% reduction in anti-social behaviour and a 33% reduction in youth offending (Bamford, 2015; DoE, 2011). The Troubled Families initiative has challenged social work to stop colluding with families, and encouraged them to more authoritative and challenging in their dealings with 'troubled families' (Casey, 2013). The themes of individual responsibility, and the transfer of responsibility from the state to the individual, in the form of tough love for troubled families, is consistent with the neoliberal themes of self-care and self-management for complex social problems.

The Conservative–Liberal coalition (2010–2015) and Conservative government (2015–present) have also seen significant change in the regulation of social work and education of social workers. There has been a reduction in commitment to funding and training of social workers in higher education (Hill and Frost, 2018). We have seen a reduced bursary component for students. The College of Social Work has also been scrapped and the professional regulation of social work practice is in the process of moving from the HCPC to a newly created regulatory body, Social Work England, in 2018 (MacNicoll, 2017). From the review of social work education, a new stream of front-line social work training has been created for both adult and children's social work with Think Ahead, Step Up and Frontline becoming established education providers (Donovan, 2017). This emergent commissioned education highlights a neoliberal strategy within higher education to open up the internal market to external forces. Higher education is finding itself in a situation where it has to undergo a competitive tender for services and courses with private organisations, creating an entrepreneurial business culture in a once closed public system. Supporting this process of marketisation is the push of social work training moving towards an ever-increasing specialisation agenda in its general undergraduate and postgraduate provision, with students been streamlined into statutory adult and children's placements, respectively. The focus on statutory social work alone can be considered an intellectually and culturally limiting move; as social work as a professional role and activity is larger than the local government role, much of our rich historical and professional tradition draws heavily from the ethics and practice from our foundations within the voluntary and non-governmental sector. This shift in social work training is also matched by a post-qualification system that is becoming increasingly focused on specialisation that will be delivered by private corporations; KPMG and Deloitte are both large multinational companies and prime movers in post-qualification children's training assessment (DoE, 2015; SfC, 2015). Organisations locally, regionally and nationally have an important role to play in facilitating structural change, as do we through our participation.

Summary

The neoliberal period of social work is our period, and as such it is a moment we are living through and directly experiencing. Neoliberal social work is characterised by a reduced and reformed service context that is moving towards technical and professional specialisation.

Key points to remember

This historical moment and period in the development of social work and social welfare has established some coherent themes that remain embedded within contemporary social work practice.

These themes include:

- The development of a social work practice that has become specialised and focused on the technical point of delivery, with a clear focus on the statutory children's and adult roles.

▶

◀

- The transition, or integration of, adult social work with health care, with a key role for social work in the assessment of eligibility for community care.

- The continued development of a children's social work practice that has seen an increased focus on risk assessment and safeguarding as its primary role and focus.

- An enhancement of social work education and training that has become more comprehensive in its provision, moving to full undergraduate and postgraduate awards.

- The development of post-qualification social work education and training that... seeks to separate and increase specialisation within children's and adult social work practice.

- The creation of national regulators for social work and the professional registration for all social workers in the UK.

Chapter summary

This chapter has explored the core themes relating to the historical development of social work. We have examined:

➤ The role of social work within contemporary society.

➤ The political and economic models of governance that shape our lived experience.

➤ The development of social work within the UK through the key historical moments as defined by political and economic discourse of liberal capitalism.

Before we close this chapter, we hope that in reading it you will have reflected on the commendable and questionable historical development of social work within the UK. It is not our intention to present a 'horrible history' of social work to dishearten or frighten the reader. We are merely trying to situate social work within the historical discourse that has shaped, nurtured and created the contemporary role of social work that you are reading and training for. Social work as a professional activity, role and institution is in part formed by macro social, economic and political forces; as such, we have a position and role to play within this process. This chapter has highlighted that radical social change can contribute in a positive way to our social service and welfare provision; as the future of social work you have a significant role to play in shaping social work; this can be done collectively as citizens at the ballot box and through our professional associations and trade unions. If the history of social work has left any impact on you, it should be that we should be participants and not spectators within society. If we want a better society and improved social welfare we have to take a professional and personal standpoint. To develop this standpoint further, the next chapter will explore the contemporary role of social work, giving you further insight into the interdisciplinary professional world of social work.

2

The contemporary role of social work: Working with communities and complexity

In this chapter we will build on some of the themes in Chapter 1 to explore and locate the contemporary role of social work within the UK and its contemporary situation within diverse agencies and multidisciplinary teams. Through a careful exploration of social work agency and institutional models, the reader will build an awareness of the delivery and practical context of contemporary social work practice against a backdrop of austerity and increasing diversification and marketisation within the health and social care sectors.

Key concepts within this chapter include:

➤ The impact of neoliberal policies on the organisation and delivery of contemporary social work services.

➤ Integration and de-professionalisation within adult social care.

➤ The effects of austerity and targeting of services within children's social care.

➤ Increasing regulation and scrutiny of the social work profession.

The discussion in this chapter is also situated alongside the 'Readiness for Direct Practice Level' of the **Professional Capabilities Framework for Social Work (PCF)** developed by the British Association of Social Workers (BASW).

Through reading Chapter 2 students should be able to:

Contexts and Organisations

➤ Demonstrate awareness of the impact of organisational context on social work practice.

Knowledge

➤ Demonstrate an initial understanding of the legal and policy frameworks and guidance that inform and mandate social work practice.

Building on the PCF we would also like you to familiarise yourself with the **standards of proficiency (SOPs)** for social workers in England (2017) by the **Health and Care Professions Council (HCPC)**. The discussion that develops in this chapter has congruence with the following **HCPC SOPs (13, 13.1 and 13.2)**:

> 13 Understand the key concepts of the knowledge base relevant to their profession.

> 13.1 Understand the roles of other professions, practitioners and organisations in health, social care, justice and in other settings where social work is practised.

> 13.2 Be aware of the different social and organisational contexts and settings within which social work operates.

Introduction: What is social work?

Before we explore some of the ways in which social work is undertaken, we will revisit the perennial question of 'What is social work?', a question asked (arguably) of most applicants to social work courses during the selection process. This must seem rather an odd question and one that is rarely asked of a potential nurse, doctor or teacher. The fact that this question features as part of the selection process for social work students reflects the contested nature of social work as a professional activity. The majority of potential students may suggest that social work is about helping or supporting people, and there are some who struggle to identify the contrasting and conflicting roles of social work, thus highlighting the competing dilemmas of practice that are associated with care and control (see Chapter 1). It is not just students that are invited to reflect on the role of social work; the Scottish Executive undertook a review of the role of social workers in the twenty-first century. It was noted that it was almost impossible 'to determine what the role of the social worker should be' and what knowledge and skills and training they should have (Asquith et al., 2005). Cree (1995: 153), in recognition of competing understandings of social work, suggests that:

> History shows that social work has always been up for grabs; its task and future direction by no means self-evident.

Moriarty and colleagues (2015) discuss some of the reasons as to why social work has proven so difficult to define. They draw a distinction between the broader definitions of social work as an activity – for example, the purpose it has within society (such as, social justice) – and between the narrower definitions which seek to explain what social workers do in terms of their roles and tasks – for example, to carry out assessments or to monitor care plans. The redrafting of the global definition of social work reflects some of the debates regarding the future direction of the profession within an international context. Some of the criticisms have centred on the western bias of how social work was defined, the emphasis on individual rights and the lack of reference to social work theory. Although the global definition of social work is described in the passage that follows, the ways in which this is reflected through the specific roles and tasks that social workers undertake varies across nation states and according to different systems of welfare:

> Social work is a practice-based profession and an academic discipline that promotes social change and development, social cohesion, and the empowerment and liberation of people. Principles of social justice, human rights, collective responsibility and respect for diversities are central to social work. Underpinned by theories of social work, social sciences, humanities and indigenous knowledge, social work engages people and structures to address life challenges and enhance wellbeing.

> (The International Federation of Social Work, July 2014)

This global definition seeks to capture its knowledge, skills and values, though there is a lack of consensus regarding social work's specific tasks and functions. Hence, within the UK we are able to see the influence of neoliberal welfare policies on the development of social care provision with a more individualised approach to welfare. In other countries, such as India, social work has a broader community focus, whereas in continental Europe principles of social pedagogy are reflected within social work practice (for a more detailed discussion of the global context of practice, see Chapter 5).

While commentators may differ in their understanding of the purpose of social work within society, the majority agree that social work cannot be separated from the society in which it is located and that, as a profession, social work has become a highly politicised activity. Cree (2003) contends that it is the combination of competing and contradictory discourses (including political ones) that influence what social workers are expected to do. Within the UK, social work is not an independent profession but can be seen as an extension of the state. In this sense, the activities that social workers undertake are largely controlled by government policy, and there are times when social work can be seen as working in and against the state. This view of social work is held by those who hold

Marxist or Radical perspectives on the role of social work within society. However, one could argue that social work has a history of working in and against the state (London Edinburgh Weekend Return Group, 1980), and regardless of one's position on the role of social work within society, there are many examples in which social workers find themselves critical of government welfare policies and their impact on service users' lives. This can leave social workers in a precarious and contradictory position in which, as agents of the state, they are expected to undertake statutory duties and responsibilities, which can be at odds with their professional value base (Humphries, 2004).

Reflective question: What is social work?

- Consider your decision to become a social worker. Has your understanding of the role of social work changed, and if so in what ways?

The nature of social work and the types of work that social workers undertake has meant that the profession has often found itself at the forefront of political public scrutiny. This can be seen by the way in which the media, the government, the public and the profession itself have responded to high-profile events since the late 1990s, and how these events have influenced and shaped contemporary social work practice. This is particularly true within child protection services, in which media headlines can have a direct impact on government policy and the delivery of services. The issues are discussed later within this chapter, but firstly we will explore the impact of policies of marketisation within the organisation and delivery of services.

Marketisation and diversification within services

The 1960s and 1970s were seen as periods of optimism for state-provided welfare services, as social workers played a key role in addressing the social problems of the day (Rogowski, 2010). However, recent decades have been marked by an unrelenting dismantling in the state provision of welfare. This process, begun under the Thatcher administration of the 1980s, continued under New Labour and accelerated under the coalition and Conservative government regimes since 2010 (Rogowski, 2011). Charitable and third sector organisations have a long history of supporting the state as providers of health and social care services; yet neoliberal economic and welfare policies have resulted in increased marketisation and privatisation of public services. These policies have resulted in a shrinkage in the size of the state, reductions in public expenditure and the promotion of values of consumerism and choice, leading to increased bureaucracy and managerialism and in differentiation and fragmentation within the provision of welfare services. Chandler and colleagues (2015) describe marketisation as a process of introducing a free market economy, as the state becomes increasingly dependent on the private or voluntary sector to provide 'public' services. There is now a blurring of the boundaries between state and non-state provision, as services that had previously been carried out by the state are contracted out to private or voluntary sector providers, resulting in a mixed economy of welfare (Rogowski, 2011).

The changes that have taken place in the provision of welfare services have been transformational, as local authorities now operate within a marketplace in which they are both the purchaser and the provider of services. We have witnessed how public utilities such as gas, electricity, water and rail services have been opened up to the market, and now we have seen welfare services such as prisons, probation, schools and health services privatised (Meek, 2014).

In 2014, the government signalled the intention for local authorities to be able to contract out aspects of children's services to profit-making bodies such as G4S and Serco. This decision faced intense opposition during the consultation process, from organisations such as BASW, the Association of Directors of Children's Services, academics and trade unions (Jones, R 2015). Although organisations such as Barnardo's and the NSPCC provide a wide range of children's services, the contracting out of statutory functions such as child protection investigations may just have been a step too far, and the proposals were finally scrapped. However, there is increasing diversification in the provision of welfare by companies such as G4S who are involved in the tagging and supervision of offenders and in the provision of residential care for children. Virgin Care is involved in children's public health nursing and Serco has positioning itself throughout children's services.

This has resulted in changes not only in the role and responsibilities of social workers, but also in the institutions in which social workers are located. There are over 95,000 registered social workers (HCPC, 2017), with the vast majority working within local authorities; however, there is increasing plurality of contexts in which social workers are employed. Approximately half of registered social workers work in the statutory setting, while about a third work in the voluntary sector. The creation of children's trusts, such as in Doncaster, usually as a result of poor inspection reports, has meant that some social workers are now employed within a quango (quasi-autonomous NGO) who report directly to government. Similarly, social workers may be employed within Cafcass, the Child and Family Court Advisory and Support Service, a non-departmental public body accountable to the Secretary of State for Justice (Sayer, 2008). Although there are still some social workers employed within probation, this is no longer considered a social work activity and its training became separated from social work education in the late 1990s, though youth offending remains a social work role (Bamford, 2015).

There are over 1.5 million people employed within the adult social care, a sector that is characterised by a largely feminised, fragmented and low-paid workforce. The majority of those employed are involved in providing direct care or support, in roles such as care worker, support worker or personal assistant, with the overwhelming majority employed by the private or voluntary sector (SfC, 2017). A significant minority (19%) of the workforce in England are overseas or migrant workers and there are serious concerns regarding the effects the decision to leave the European Union (EU) will have on the social care workforce. This is particularly true in London and south-east England, where the proportion of migrant care workers is between 26% and 51%. It is estimated that over 90,000 workers originate from the EU, and with almost 900 people quitting their jobs every day (Community Care, May 2017) the future stability of the workforce is in a perilous position.

Local authorities are reducing the size of their qualified workforce; some of the reasons cited include service restructure, closure of services, outsourcing of services and budgetary cuts (SfC, 2017). However, it can be argued that all of these reasons can be linked in some way to reductions in local authority income. This leaves the number of professionally qualified social workers in 2016 at around 19,000 (SfC, 2017), with the majority of those social workers being employed in adult social care within local authorities. However, the integration of the health and social care sectors is leading to more social workers being employed within the NHS. Although there has been a slight reduction in social work posts (3%), other regulated professional roles such as nursing have experienced more significant reductions, with a 16% drop in the proportion of qualified nurses in the period 2012–2016. Yet it has been suggested that in order to meet the increase in demand for services as a result of population trends, a 31% increase in jobs in the adult workforce is required by 2030. However, the majority of these are likely to be located within the independent sector as opposed to the statutory sectors of local authorities or the NHS. In order to manage current budgetary pressures, local authorities are rebalancing their workforce through a review of the ratio of qualified to non-qualified roles. However, there are risks associated with not having an appropriately qualified workforce at times of increasing demand for services, which were highlighted in the Francis Report into the failings at Mid Staffordshire NHS Trust (Francis, 2013). Although we have focused our discussion on the size and proportion of the paid workforce, it is important to acknowledge the reliance of the sector on informal care, and it is estimated that there are around 5.5 million carers in the UK and by 2037 this is expected to grow by 40% (Carers UK, 2015).

There are similar and different issues that face the children's workforce, where there have been long-terms concerns regarding staff shortages and turnover rates. Although the number of child and family social workers in England has increased by 4.5% to over 27,000 (from 2015 to 2016), there has also been a slight increase in vacancy rates to 16.7% in England with some large regional variations (DfE, 2017). Within Yorkshire and Humber the vacancy rates equate to around 6.5% full-time equivalent (FTE) social workers, whereas in Outer London the figure is 25.8% (FTE) and 23.2% (FTE) in Inner London. Although there were slightly more social workers starting work than leaving their posts, the turnover of staff within children's social work in England was 15.1% (DfE, 2017). The caseloads of individual social workers remain high and the employment of agency workers to relieve pressure on staff is controversial, as this can lead to a lack of continuity of care for children.

Reflective question: De-professionalisation of the workforce

- To meet budgetary constraints many organisations are reducing the number, type and range of professional staff employed particularly within community and social services.

- What do you think are the risks associated with reducing the size of the qualified workforce of social workers and nurses?

Working with adults

Social workers are uniquely placed to understand and advocate for individuals and families with complex needs – especially where health issues overlap with other life pressures including housing, employment and the desire to be accepted within supportive communities. Social workers are helping to make sure health and care services pursue best outcomes collaboratively – anchoring them to the needs of the people they serve. This is true integration.

(Minister for Community Health and Care David Mowat, 2017)

The changing roles of social workers within adult social care can be traced back to the National Health Service and Community Care Act (NHS and CCA) of 1990, which created the purchaser/provider split within adult social care. Central to its successful implementation was the concept of care management. This required social workers to act as 'care managers' who became responsible for identifying individuals' needs, tailoring services to meet those needs, and monitoring and reviewing the provision of those services. As a result of these changes many social workers found themselves being renamed care managers, which at times has proven controversial as registration requires that the title of social worker is protected by law yet the majority of care managers within the wider social care workforce do not require professional training. However, since the implementation of the 1990 Act, it has often been suggested that the skills of qualified social workers are not necessarily required for the role of a care manager and there are times when this has justified attempts to de-professionalise and reduce the size of the social workforce within adult social care. There has been a tendency to view adult social work as less complex and more straightforward than child and family social work – a form of discrimination that exists within the profession.

However, care management is not just about the practical aspects of contracting and the purchasing of services, but also requires the use of sensitive communication skills that are vital in being able to undertake a holistic assessment of people's complex social care needs. Statham and colleagues (2006) highlight the particular skills of social workers in situations of complexity and uncertainty where there may be tensions or conflicts of interest within an individual family or where there is the need to manage and balance needs, rights and risks. However, the emphasis on the technical skills associated with assessment tools can be seen as at odds with the professionalisation associated with analysis and ethical decision-making (Welbourne, 2011). Although social workers can bring a whole-person approach that focuses on people's strengths or assets to maximise their life chances, this is increasingly performed within budgetary constraints. The Kings Fund (2016) has highlighted how the effects of years upon years of cuts to local authority budgets have left a social care system struggling to meet the needs of the community.

There has been considerable discussion in the media and within public policy discourses concerning the costs associated with caring for a growing elderly population. The rise in demand for services largely due to an ageing population has been a feature of health and social care provision for the last three decades of so. However, real-term cuts in spending, as a result of policies of austerity, have resulted in a fall in spending by local authorities on adult social care, from £18.4 billion in 2009/10 to just under £17 billion in 2015/16 (The Kings Fund, 2016). This represents an 8% cut with around 400,000 fewer people accessing publicly funded social care, with the effect that more people rely on privately funded or family-based practice. Research suggests that access to care services is increasingly associated with what you can afford to pay for, rather than what you need, and this leaves poorer service users reliant on the safety net of limited local authority services, informal or family-based care. Although the Care Act 2014 has created expectations and demands for services, this has not been matched by investment in primary health and community services. There has been much debate as to whether reductions in the funding of social care have resulted in increasing pressure on the NHS, which is reflected every winter in the form of media headlines concerning bed blocking due to delays in people being discharged from hospital into the community. In June 2017 there were 178,400 delayed days; that represents an increase of over 5,000 days on the corresponding month in 2016 (Bate, 2017).

Some of the main reasons for social care delays include patients awaiting care packages in their own home; however, other delays can be attributed to the Health Service itself and that includes waiting for other NHS services. Hospital care is relatively expensive, so it may be more appropriate to meet someone's health and social care needs through discharge to a nursing, residential home or to their own home. The philosophy is to encourage partnership, working between acute trusts and local authority social care departments, and assist discharge planning. There is a responsibility for the trust to advise the local authority if someone may need community care services on discharge in advance of the decision to discharge. The resulting assessment notice should give time for a social worker to undertake an assessment. The Care Act 2014 has now subsumed the Delayed Discharge Act 2003, with the intention of reducing the pressure on acute NHS beds. Previously local authorities could be fined by the health body in relation to the costs associated with delays as a way of incentivising speedier assessments, though not all hospital trusts sought reimbursement for delays but instead preferred to reinvest in better services for integrated working.

The integration of health and social care sectors is seen as vital to improve the quality and cost-effectiveness of care by ensuring that services are well coordinated around needs by being both 'patient-centred' and 'population-oriented' in which the patient or user's perspective is the organising principle of service delivery (Goodwin, 2016). Given austerity measures, government policies can be considered overly optimistic as both health and social sectors have experienced increased pressures and demands on their services. To encourage greater integration of services, the government requires Clinical Commissioning Groups and local authorities to enter into pooled budgetary arrangements and agree an integrated spending plan as part of the Better Care Fund (BCF). In 2016/17 around £5.9 billion was pooled into the BCF but despite improvements in joint working, it was acknowledged that the Fund 'has not achieved the expected value for money, in terms of savings, outcomes for patients or reduced hospital activity' (NAO, 2017b).

Reflective questions: Alzheimer's web of care

- The image below is a graphic illustration of all the professionals involved in Malcom Pointon's care derived from a television documentary by Barbara Pointon, whose husband, Malcolm, lived with Alzheimer's disease for 16 years until his death in 2007.

- Can you identify the numbers of individuals and organisations involved in supporting Malcolm and Barbara?

- What barriers do you think exist in providing integrated care?

Barriers to integrated working:

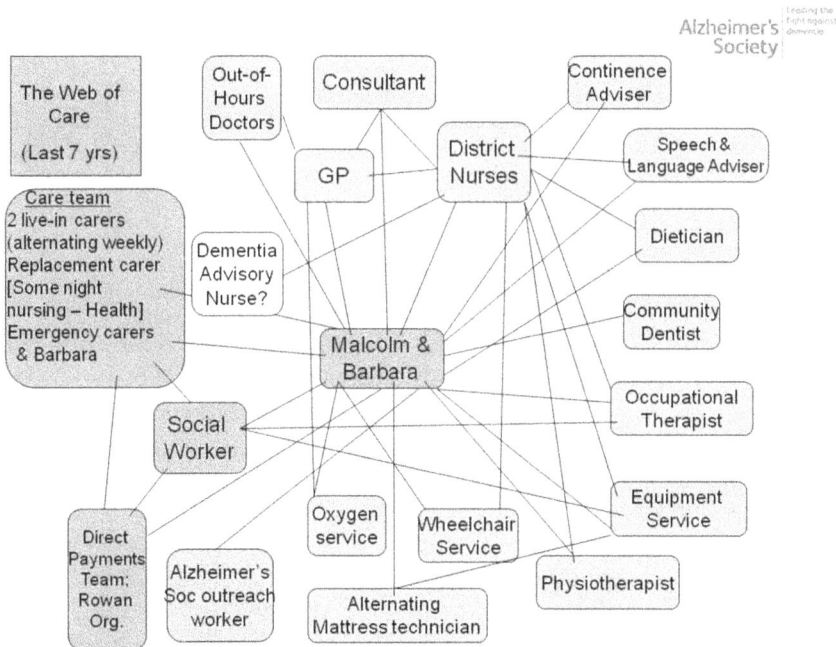

Barriers to integrated care

Some of the barriers to integrated care involve:

- Culture – when integrating different parts of the health system, one barrier is the cultural differences and differences in the management style among professionals, including differences in approaches to managing risk.

- Information – information sharing between organisations and to service users is a barrier to successful integrated care. This also includes poorly connected IT systems.

- Finance – reimbursement is sometimes problematic and can limit the benefits of integrated care because the various components of care are reimbursed separately.

- Accountability and governance – a reluctance to hand someone over to another institution or care setting often arises because of concerns over where accountability lies for their ongoing care. Lack of clarity for overall responsibility should anything go wrong.

- Operating procedures between health and social care – the absence of agreed procedures for the transfer of service users from health to social care can create delays and gaps in the pathway. Related issues include different performance frameworks, finance systems, planning and budgeting, and means testing for social care services.

Sources: *Building Bridges, Breaking Barriers: Integrated Care for Older People*, Care Quality Commission (CQC, 2016); *Health and Social Care Integration*, National Audit Office (NAO, 2017b).

Working with children and families

Anti-welfare culture and targeting of services

There has always been a close relationship between poverty and social work, as we have discussed in our exploration of the origins of social work through the work of the Charity Organisation Society (see Chapter 1). In April 2017 a group of social workers and service users organised a march from Birmingham to Liverpool to campaign against austerity. They visited food banks and projects that were at risk of being cut due to spending restrictions, and the march was one of a number events, supported by BASW, that were intended to highlight the impact of austerity on individuals' lives and on communities. Tunstill and Willow (2017) remind us that there have been occasions when concerns regarding child poverty have influenced the specific role and responsibilities of social workers working with children and their families. They discuss how social workers have sought to prevent children from being brought into the public care system, as result of them being homeless and or in poverty, and explain how the joint campaigning work undertaken by BASW and the Child Poverty Action Group (CPAG) influenced the role of family support and developed what was known as preventative work. The passing of the Children Act 1989(s 17) required local authorities to safeguard and promote the welfare of children in need and to promote their upbringing within their families through the provision of services. Though the meaning of the provision of services is wide-ranging, *it is intended to safeguard and improve* (our emphasis) the health and well-being of children in need. At the time of the implementation of the Children Act, there was much concern regarding the concept of 'need' and how local authorities would define this. There was concern that too wide a definition would broaden the remit for the provision of services and lead to increased expectations. Section 17 did finally identify what constitutes need (see the box 'A child in need'), and although there is no statutory duty to assess under this section, it is implied that at least an initial assessment would be undertaken as set out in the statutory guidance, *Framework for the Assessment of Children in Need and Their Families* (DoH et al., 2000).

A child in need

(a) He is unlikely to achieve or maintain, or to have the opportunity of achieving or maintaining, a reasonable standard of health or development without the provision for him of services by a local authority;

(b) his health or development is likely to be significantly impaired, without the provision for him of such services; or

(c) He is disabled.

Children who are the subject of a child protection plan or who are looked after also fall within the definition of children in need.

Source: Section 17(10) Children Act 1989.

A service in crisis?

Although there was much optimism that surrounded the implementation of the Children Act 1989, it was followed by the global financial crisis of 2007/8, and we have discussed earlier in this chapter the responses of successive governments through policies of austerity. Lavalette (2017: 32) defines austerity as:

> A political and economic project geared towards reducing government public sector social spending and was presented as an inevitable consequence of the 2007/2008 financial crisis.

He challenges ideas about inevitability and instead highlights the conscious choices that governments have taken to undertake cuts to public services as opposed to, for example, raising taxes for the wealthy. Although the cause of the economic crisis was the international banking and financial systems, somewhere along the lines this economic depression has been blamed on an apparently overgenerous system of welfare and public services. Ideologies about welfare and benefits are central to neoliberal policies and an anti-welfare culture has emerged in which welfare recipients are stigmatised as being lazy and scroungers, refuelling a contemporary discourse of 'Benefits Britain'. The following statement made by the former prime minister, David Cameron, reflects a view that is recognisable within sections of the media, politicians and the wider public:

> The benefit system has created a benefit culture. It doesn't just allow people to act irresponsibly, but often actively encourages them to do so.

(Cited in Jenson and Tyler, 2015: 471)

A whole range of social policies have followed, aimed at reducing public expenditure, and many of these have targeted poor and disadvantaged communities through benefit caps and programmes of welfare to work. The Joseph Rowntree Foundation (2017) estimated that there are currently around 3.9 million children living in poverty and that this figure is expected to rise as a result of changes to benefits and tax cuts. Research (e.g. Bywaters et al., 2016b) has identified the likely impact of poverty on the demand for services, yet this coincides with a period of cuts in spending within children's social care. The Children Acts of 1989 and 2004 aim to improve services for children by promoting early help and multi-agency working, and it seems that now, more than ever, it is vital that social work can provide earlier and timely interventions to support families in crisis and improve outcomes for children. However, the number of 'children in need' is rising, and local authorities are struggling to keep up with the rise in demand and are finding it increasingly difficult to fulfil their statutory duties. Children services are receiving more referrals of families in crisis and the NSPCC (2015) estimate that the number of children in the child protection system in the UK has risen by 80% from 2002 to 2014 and that there are more children entering public care. Although children's services in many areas are under intense pressure, policies of early intervention have been promoted to prevent problems escalating.

What's in a name? Early help or early intervention?

The drive towards early intervention, developed under New Labour through the Every Child Matters agenda and progressed under successive governments, and the expectations as to what could be achieved were typified within the Allen Report:

> I recommend that the nation should be aware of the enormous benefits to individuals and society of Early Intervention – a policy approach designed to build the essential social and emotional bedrock in children aged 0–3 and to ensure that children aged 0–18 can become the excellent parents of tomorrow.
>
> (Allen, 2011: xvii)

However, there are differences in how concepts of early intervention and early help are understood. Race and O'Keefe (2017) discuss a difference between prevention, which means predicting and averting at the first signs of problem, and early intervention, which can be understood to mean intervening in a situation as soon as difficulties emerge and identifying those families or communities most at risk of developing problems. The Munro Report emphasised how 'preventative services will do more to reduce abuse and neglect than reactive services' (Munro, 2011a.: 69). Yet more recent child welfare policies have placed greater emphasis on parenting as a social policy in place of professional services. Government policies emphasise supporting children during the early years through parenting programmes and classes, though there is little recognition of the impact poverty and disadvantage can have on parenting.

A tension exists between universal and targeted services and this is reflected through the Troubled Families initiative, which is a targeted intervention for families with multiple problems, including domestic violence, poor school attendance, unemployment and anti-social or criminal behaviour. The first scheme ran from 2012 to 2015 and attracted over £450 million, but there have been mixed reports about the success of this project, as there has been no measurable effect on families' lives in terms of school attendance, employment or behaviour (NIESR, 2016). Race and O'Keefe (2017) question whether the philosophy underpinning 'troubled' equates more to notions of troublesome families – another adage that is used to describe the dangerous or dysfunctional families of the past.

There has also been long-standing debate within children's social work regarding the balance between child protection and family support. Although it has been accepted that there is no distinction between the two, and acknowledged that resources have been narrowly focused on those families in crisis (Frost et al., 2015), there has not been a rebalancing of services to more universal services aimed at prevention; instead, there has been a focus on targeted and reactive services. This can be illustrated by an All-Party Parliamentary Group for Children (2017) report, *No Good Options*, on children's social care, which revealed that for every £1 spent on preventative help – such as respite breaks for disabled children, children's centres or diversionary work that youth offending teams undertake – £4 is spent on reactive child protection work. It noted that although the benefits of early intervention are widely recognised, local authorities opting to deliver early intervention services are often struggling to fund their activities. Resources are targeted towards those children who have already suffered abuse or those in situations of highest risk, as opposed to children in need or in care.

There is inadequate attention afforded to the impact of poverty stress on familial relationships and how this may contribute to family conflict. Rather than early intervention, resources are directed towards late intervention; and research from an early intervention project has found that targeted intervention aimed at supporting parents who are experiencing poverty can improve the outcomes for children (Acquah et al., 2017). Although some of the research is in its early stages, there are some indicators of effective programmes to address interparental conflict to improve child outcomes. In this latest report by Acquah and colleagues, Early Intervention Foundation looked at 13 interventions, which fall into two broad categories: those that focus on addressing problems between parents, which in turn impact on the children in the family; and those which focus on the parent–child relationship, with an additional component to support the parents. Some of the positive outcomes include reduced relationship conflict, reduced depression and anxiety for parents, and improvements in children's behaviours and mental health (Acquah et al., 2017).

The role of neuroscience – a return of biological determinism?

The role of research and its influence on social work practice highlight recent debates concerning the role of biology and, in particular, neuroscience and its influence on the social and psychological development of children. Notions of biological determinism are not new, as Macvarish and colleagues (2014) highlight how links to biology have often been a feature of child welfare policy. They discuss how the political concerns during the late nineteenth century over the quality of parenting, proliferation of the wrong type of people, and child rescuing resonate with contemporary demands for early intervention with so-called troubled families and for government policies to speed up adoption.

The role of biological determinism and medicalisation in social work is seen through the influence of theories of neuroscience within child welfare policy and practice. Neuroscience refers to the study of the brain and nervous system (Royal Society, 2010), and the notion of neuroplasticity is central to the theory and is concerned with how the brain changes physically in response to social conditions. The importance of the child's first three years is based on the theory that most brain development takes place within this period, and by the age of three brain development has reached 90% of its adult size. Concerns about the impact of abuse and neglect for babies and young children on their development have been used to support drives for early help and speedier decision-making. The work of the Childhood Wellbeing Research Centre has influenced practice with the belief that there are sensitive periods within child development. The effect of lack of stimulation or neglect will have a damaging effect on young children under two years of age, resulting in developmental delay and, in particular, the acquisition of language skills, and the ability to play and develop relationships. The notion of critical periods and the impact of neglect on development are said to be irreversible.

There have been calls for the integration of learning from neurobiology in human development and life course modules, child protection, mental health and social work education and training at both initial and post-qualifying levels (Egan et al., 2011). Although neuroscience has gained popularity and has become an important aspect within the education and training of children's social workers, it is not without its critics. Both Bruer and Rutter (cited in Race and O'Keefe, 2017) challenge the evidence base of the theories that were largely based on animal experimentation. They claim that the significance of the first three years and irreversible damage is overstated and oversimplified and argue that the human brain is far more complex and resilient (Race and O'Keefe, 2017). Wastell and White (2012) are also critical of such influences within child protection that have led to a 'now or never' imperative that has resulted in an increase in removals of children from their families.

Lowe and colleagues (2015) discuss how ideas regarding intergenerational disadvantage have been a central feature of British child welfare policy, with the belief that poor families rear poor children which results in a vicious cycle of deprivation and that the role of social work should be to break the cycle of such deprivation. Theories of neuroscience may support a belief that poor families are unable to adequately develop their children and Lowe and colleagues (2015) refer to a number of policy documents that highlight the role of brain development in determining children's outcomes and that emphasise the importance of early intervention. They go on to suggest that this preoccupation with brain development has resulted in the brain as opposed to the child being the primary concern and the target for intervention.

This over-biologisation of child welfare risks reducing children to a 'mindless brain' in which they are perceived as passive recipients of parenting, and undermines the position of children as social actors who can think and make choices. It also minimises the effects of poverty and other forms of economic and social deprivation on the lives of children and their families. This has resulted in earlier, targeted interventions with the risk of permanent removal of children from their families that coincides with policies designed to increase adoptions (Featherstone et al., 2013). An overly deterministic, pessimistic and uncritical acceptance of neuroscience can run the risk of suppressing debate regarding ethical intervention in the lives of children and their families.

Relationship-based practice

Another key influence with children's social work practice concerns ideas about relationship-based practice, although the relationship between social workers and service users has always been central to social work practice. Authors such as Ruch and Trevithick have written extensively on relationship-based practice and note how a re-emphasis on the nature of relationships in social work practice can be partly understood as a response to the overly bureaucratic and reductionist approaches that have emerged within social work over the past 20 years or so.

Though it is recognised that there are differences in how relationship-based practice may be understood theoretically and how it is applied in practice (Hingley-Jones and Ruch, 2016), it is widely accepted that relationship-based practice is drawn from the core principles of a Rogerian person-centred approach. It emphasises the quality of the relationship between the worker and the service user and recognises that the nature of the relationship is shaped by the purpose of the social work intervention. At its core, relationship-based practice highlights the uniqueness of individuals and rejects a one-size-fits-all approach that exists in working with service users.

Driven by procedures or the emphasis on risk and the need to predict the likelihood of future behaviours or actions, social work has been criticised by some commentators for minimising or failing to understand the complexity of individuals, their lives, behaviour and the circumstances that influences their situation (Howe, 1996). Hingley-Jones and Ruch (2016: 237) use the concept of 'relational austerity' to describe neoliberal approaches to welfare that promote increasingly authoritarian and risk-averse practice with families. There remains a challenge in adopting a relationship-based practice that recognises the economic and political context which appears to be 'anti-relational and anxiety ridden' (2016: 238).

Scrutinising and educating the profession

Being anxiety-driven, defensive and risk-averse are characteristics that are associated within a culture of blame that continues to exist within social work, in which the media is said to play a key role. The media has often been significant in the public perception of the social work profession since the death of Maria Colwell in 1973 and subsequent child abuse tragedies to the present day (Jones, 2014). However, it was the tragic murder of three-year-old Peter Connelly (most commonly known as Baby P) by his mother and her boyfriend in 2007 that resulted in an intense and enduring media spotlight, not only for the professionals involved at Haringey council but for the social work profession as whole. The effect of such intense media attention helped to reignite the culture of blame, to reinforce the low status of social work and to ensure a sustained attack through demands for an overhaul in the education, training and regulation of social work.

Parton (2017) argues that the political response to child deaths has been characterised by a lack of attention to seriously address the problem of child abuse, and instead has disproportionally focused on the failures of the child protection system and the behaviour of professionals (predominately social workers) and other agencies. He goes on to contend that such tragedies have often resulted in major policy change, for example Every Child Matters followed the death of Victoria Climbié in 2004. Following the death of Baby P in 2007, the government established the Social Work Reform Board (SWRB), whose role was to improve the public perception of social work through educational and practice reform. Although the reform process took several years, the SWRB has to be commended for its extensive consultation with key stakeholders, as a number of events were held across England and Wales that involved social workers, managers, academics, service users and the wider public. Social work had narrowly become associated with child protection and the SWRB attempted to clarify and redefine the role of social work and provide a public definition (Bamford, 2105). In 2012, the Government created the College of Social Work, as an independent voice of the profession, whose aims were to raise professional standards and act as the interface between the public and the profession.

Although the origins of modern professional social work in the UK date back to the nineteenth century, it was not until 2002 that social work became a regulated profession. The Labour government of the time decided to set up care councils in each country with the effect that England, Wales, Scotland and Northern Ireland all have separate regulatory bodies. The recommendation was that all key social care workers, including social workers and residential care home managers, were required to be registered with a regulator. However, the decision to set up a professional register was controversial and some of the debates surrounding this reflected concerns that registration would result in elitism within the profession, as only certain sections of the workforce would be required to be registered. There was also some doubt as to whether registration would actually have the desired effect of ensuring safe practice and improving public confidence in the profession. Yet despite the initial intentions to register a wider section of the social care workforce, a decision was made that it would only be qualified social workers and student social workers who were required to be registered with the General Social Care Council (GSCC). Regulation meant that only those who had undertaken an approved period of training and who were registered with the GSCC were entitled to call themselves Social Workers in England, as was the same in other part of the UK.

Both the GSCC and the College of Social Work have had relatively short histories, having suffered from political interference. The GSCC survived an arms-length review of its functions, but continued to face further criticisms of its performance and financial management. Following the revelation of a backlog of conduct cases, the Conservative government decided in 2012 to transfer its regulatory functions to the HCPC through the Health and Social Work Professions Order 2001. This shift from a social work-specific regulator to the HCPC, in which social work was now one of 13 professions, was seen as evidence of increasing marginalisation of social work and of a diminishing professional identity within the health and social care sectors (Bamford, 2015).

The creation of the College of Social Work was also not without controversy, as there was already a professional body, the BASW, in existence. BASW had campaigned to be recognised as the official Government-backed professional body, but rather controversially, the Government created a new body, the College of Social Work. The College undertook some significant work and developed the PCF, which at the time of writing provides a competency framework for social work from the beginnings of one's career as a student through to senior leadership. However, the College was under pressure from its inception, as many loyal BASW members refused to join the rival body. After only a few years in operation, and following the election of the Conservative government in 2015, the then Health Minister undertook the contentious decision to shut down the College, citing a lack of funds and sustainability as the prime reason. This was met by condemnation from those within the profession, a view that was also expressed by the Chair of the BASW:

> We can appreciate why many social workers are now doubting the government's commitment to the profession, given that its first action following the election is to close the College of Social Work.

> (Guy Shennan, *The Guardian*, 19 June 2015)

Though the College closed, many of its functions were transferred to other organisations such as BASW. The Government continue to be concerned about the regulation of social work, and despite the fact that the HCPC only took over the regulation of social work in 2012, the present Conservative government passed legislation to transfer its functions to a new social work regulator, provisionally named Social Work England, with an estimated cost of around £25 million. This decision represents a reversal to a profession-specific regulator for social work and appears to be out of step with wider government policy to keep a control on funding and bureaucracy through restricting the number of regulators (Professional Standards Authority, 2017). As in the case of previous regulatory bodies, the functions of Social Work England will include maintaining a register of social workers, undertaking fitness to practise hearings, and setting the standards for initial education and training and professional standards, including SOPs and continuing professional development. However, there are fears that the creation of Social Work England will lead to a decrease in social work's professional autonomy and an increase in governmental control, as the new regulator will be partly funded by the government and will report directly to a minister. It is expected that the Education Secretary will be able to set 'improvement standards' for social workers and introduce assessments for practitioners, and although the new body will have an independent chair and board they will be appointed by ministers and accountable to the Departments for Education and Health.

Under the guise of social work reform, the Government plans for a new system of accreditation for those involved in children's social work practice can be seen as further evidence of increased political scrutiny and interference in the profession. The proposals for a new Approved Child and Family Practitioner status implies that all social workers working with child protection will be required to be further assessed and tested:

> We are committed to building a stronger social work profession, with clear professional standards and the knowledge and skills to protect children and promote their welfare [and] [c]entral to success will be improving the capability and professional confidence of social workers.

(DfE, 2016c)

The Government appears to be determined to proceed quickly with this programme, with the aim of having full accreditation of child and family social workers by 2020; however, there is still much uncertainty and confusion about the scheme. Questions remain as to whether the scheme will be mandatory and if there will be sufficient accredited workers to undertake child protection work. The position of social workers working in the voluntary and private sectors, as well as those who are not undertaking statutory childcare work, is unclear. There are also concerns regarding the relationship of adult and children's workers and services that work across both services, as currently there are no similar proposals for adult workers and the relationships of social workers in England with the other UK jurisdictions are problematic where these arrangements are not in place. These proposals are taking place during a period of increasing vacancies within the children's social work workforce and a rise in the use of agency social workers.

The education of social workers has been highly controversial, and since the introduction of the first school of social work in 1903 there have been debates regarding the content of social work training and its relationship to the wider social sciences and in particular the influences of psychological and sociological theories to inform practice. Since the 1970s there have been a range of qualifications that have been required to become a social worker. However, it was not until 2003/4 that social work became a graduate profession. The introduction of the social work degree was part of a wider government policy objective to modernise social care services and was considered vital in developing a highly skilled and motivated workforce (DoH, 2002). Initial research undertaken in 2008 suggested that the degree was 'fit for purpose' (GSCC, 2008); however, it was the death of Peter Connelly and the publication of the Safeguarding Board Report by Haringey Social Services Department in 2009 that renewed the focus on the skills and competence of social workers. The *Final Report* of the SWRB (DCSF, 2009a) made several recommendations that focused on improving the calibre of social workers, with an emphasis on initial qualifying, support for newly qualified workers and the continuing professional development of more experienced workers.

Following the demise of the GSCC, the approval for delivering the new degree was undertaken by the HCPC, and higher education institutions could seek additional accreditation by the newly formed College of Social Work, which provided an additional quality indicator. The new award emphasised readiness to practise as a key component in the development of the social work student to becoming a newly qualified worker. Yet it was suggested that there was a gap between the aspirations of the PCF and the realities of practice (Higgins and Goodyer, 2015), as many newly qualified workers struggled in negotiating the rhetoric of their qualifying courses and the reality of being in practice (Jack and Donnellan, 2010). The introduction of the Assessed and Supported Year in Employment (ASYE), though not mandatory, sought to bridge the gap between initial training and becoming a social worker. Though it must be said that social work education has often (unfairly) been accused of not fully preparing students for the realities of practice. While the PCF may promote values such as social justice and empowerment, this can be in contradiction with the statutory-based and task-focused realities of contemporary social work practice.

Chapter summary

This chapter has explored the key themes emerging within the contemporary role of social work within the UK, and has situated the role of social work within the communities and agencies it operates within. Key themes that have emerged include:

➢ The impact of social, political and economic policy on the organisation and delivery of social work services.

➢ The de-professionalisation of social work within adult social care sectors.

➢ The impact of austerity within children's social care.

➢ The increasing professional regulation of statutory social work.

Reflecting on this complexity, in order to manage the demands of contemporary practice, newly qualified social workers are advised to adopt an ironic attitude or disposition that will enable them to hold on to the professional values associated with emancipatory practice while adopting a pragmatic and reflective approach to their practice (Higgins and Goodyer, 2015). It is suggested that the use of irony or critical scepticism allows social workers to engage with the complexities associated with being a statutory social worker while remaining committed to the values of the profession (Singh and Cowden, 2009). We have seen how contemporary social work has become narrowly focused on safeguarding duties and in carrying out statutory responsibilities of assessment; but through being reflexive, it is suggested that social workers can remain committed and at the same uncommitted to both the priorities and the challenges of contemporary practice. Yet one could argue that social work has always contained inherent contradictions: of care and control; of being an agent of the state and committed to social reform; and that working with legislation does not necessarily mean that one signs up wholesale to government policy. Since the economic crisis of 2008 there has been greater alignment of social and welfare policies with the financial and economic policies of successive government, and the role of social work has changed in response to those political, economic and ideological circumstances. The adoption of a humane and critical approach to understanding social work is required, while being able to recognise the complexities and limitations of modern social work practice is vital in becoming an effective and resilient practitioner. Building on this humane and critical approach, we will explore models of intervention for social work practice in the next chapter.

3

Preparing for social work practice: Models of intervention for social work practice

In the first two chapters we have seen how the role of social workers has developed over time. This chapter is concerned with how the knowledge and skills that you need as a social worker have also extensively changed over the years as the social, political and economic context within which social work operates has also been subject to almost continuous change. This has meant that, in turn, the models or tools that social workers use in their interventions with service users and families have been subject to evaluation as part of this process. Social workers face considerable challenges at this time and it is more important than ever to have a range of interventions and skills to use within social work practice. The neoliberal context of social work practice, as outlined in Chapter 1, has impacted upon how social work operates within communities and within organisations. The mixed economy of care evident within social work also means that the line between state or statutory social work and functions provided or outsourced to third sector (voluntary) organisations can be blurred and complex. It is therefore important that as social workers you are able to use a range of skills within your work to support you in meeting these challenges. As will be explored, one of the core tensions can be seen between the use of 'technical' or rational skills to complete an assessment or intervention – for example, completing online assessments following certain procedures – and the use of a more evidential approach to inform assessment and care planning. Parker (2017) points out that social workers need to have developed skills to a high standard in order to be effective in their role. In preparing for social work practice, the reflective social worker needs to be able to balance being competent and proficient in their job role with the need for evidence-based and effective practice. This is no easy task, as we explore within this chapter.

The discussion serves only as an introduction to social work models of intervention which support social workers in their role. There are a significant range of approaches, theories and models that social workers can use within their practice. The chapter cannot cover all these areas in detail, but aims to offer some core definitions and differences between models and approaches. We will also look at areas where there is some overlap between concepts and approaches. We will include a broad range of generic approaches within social work practice that are evidence-based, making links to the Knowledge and Skill Statements for Social Work. The chapter will also explore the importance of communication skills and relationship-based practice in social work interventions.

Key concepts within this chapter include:

➢ The similarities and differences between theories and models used within social work practice.

➢ How theory is used and applied within social work interventions.

➢ The core task of assessment within social work practice.

➢ Models and perspectives used within assessment, care planning and evaluation.

➢ Structural factors impacting on assessment and care planning.

➢ Communications skills: written and verbal communication skills used within assessment and care planning.

The discussion in this chapter is situated alongside the 'Readiness for Direct Practice Level' of the **Professional Capabilities Framework for Social Work (PCF)** developed by the British Association of Social Workers (BASW).

Through reading Chapter 3 students should be able to:

Knowledge

➢ Demonstrate an initial understanding of the range of theories and models for social work intervention.

Intervention & Skills

➢ Demonstrate awareness of a range of frameworks to assess and plan intervention.

➢ Demonstrate initial awareness of risk and safeguarding.

Before you read this chapter we would like you to familiarise yourself with the **standards of proficiency (SOPs)** for social workers in England (2017) by the **Health and Care Professions Council (HCPC)**. The discussion that develops in this chapter has congruence with the following **HCPC SOPs (13, 13.4 and 14, 14.4)**:

➢ 13. Be able to understand the key concepts of the knowledge base relevant to their profession.

➢ 13.4. Be able to understand social work theory; social work models and interventions.

➢ 14. Be able to draw on appropriate knowledge and skills to inform practice.

➢ 14.4. Be able to use social work methods, theories and models to identify actions to achieve change and development and improve life opportunities.

What are models of intervention?

A model tends to be a method of social work intervention that follows certain steps or stages. Models of intervention can be informed by particular theories, ideas or perspectives. You may also hear the phrase 'a social work approach or method'. Here, a particular perspective may be advocated in how social workers engage in the social work role and task. The core message for you to reflect on is that social workers use an extensive range of models and approaches in their work that serve as a toolkit. It can be helpful to think of different models as 'tools' which can be used depending on the intervention with service users. When one model or approach does not seem to be working, a different approach can be taken to support positive and effective social work practice. However, social workers need to be skilled in their understanding of theories in order to know when to try different models or approaches and to have confidence in using them. Social workers also need to be able to see the connections between different theories that underpin models of intervention. Humphrey (2011) refers to this as 'tapestries of knowledge' where social workers can learn to differentiate between the value of different approaches.

Why do we use theory?

A useful place to start our discussion is to first understand why we use theories to support knowledge. The following quote provides an explanation:

Theories are particular ways of making sense. They help social workers see regularities and familiar patterns in the muddle of practice. By stepping back and rising above the hubbub, they help us see what's going on.

(Howe, 2008: 2)

Theories also help us to make sense of both individual and structural disadvantage within society (Dunk-West, 2013). Theories that promote change within the personal context are also important to social work practice (Watson and West, 2006: 24–25). For example, theoretical perspectives on empowerment can be used by social workers to support change within people's lives. There is a significant range of theories, methods and tools used within social work practice. It is perhaps for this reason that students and social workers can, at times, find the use of theories difficult within social work practice. What is the relevant theory or approach to use?

Terminology can also be difficult when we discuss social work theories. Social work practitioners and educators will talk about models, theories and approaches and it can be difficult to distinguish between these terms. Payne (cited in Humphrey, 2011) provides a useful discussion on this. Theories are seen as examining in detail the origin of a social issue or phenomenon and examining how this is manifest within individuals and/or society. Much of the basis for theoretical discussion in social work is drawn from psychology or sociology. This is typically informed by research. Theories are often also informed by particular political or social perspectives – for example, feminism or neoliberalism, as discussed in Chapter 1. Models tend to be ways of looking at particular social issues or problems. Often this is about following a particular process or framework to analyse and explore theories. Thompson's PCS model is a good example of this (Figure 3.1). It demonstrates how oppression and discrimination within society can be viewed as occurring at Personal (P), Cultural (C) and Structural (S) levels. For example, derogatory personal comments made by individuals about asylum seekers can reinforce cultural stereotypes of asylum seekers which discriminate against different cultures and races within society. This is then reinforced, for example, in the employment of asylum seekers reflecting differential pay and conditions at a structural level. The model can therefore be seen as a way of explaining and applying sociological theory relating to oppression and discrimination (Llewellyn et al., 2015). It therefore serves as a 'tool' for social workers in their practice.

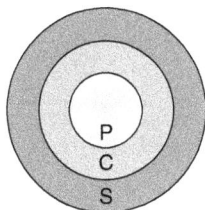

Figure 3.1   Thompson's PCS model: Personal (P), Cultural (C) and Structural (S)

Source: Adapted from Thompson (2003).

Reflective questions

How does Thompson's model make sense to you?

How does it support your approach to theory within your own learning?

Applying theory to practice

Models of intervention can underpin techniques or ways of working used in social work practice that relate to theoretical perspectives. For example, life story work with children who are being adopted or fostered acknowledges the difficulties relating to life course development caused by being brought up outside their birth family. Working with a child to provide them with a record of their birth family through the use of a book of photos and memories is a practice-based task undertaken by social workers. However, it relates to theoretical perspectives relating to life course development. We know that childhood is highly significant to individual development and an understanding of life course development is seen as integral to social work practice (Crawford and Walker, 2017). Life story work provides a way of working which acknowledges the importance of child development and uses this knowledge to underpin practice. It is also an example of the observational skills advocated by the *Knowledge and Skills Statement for working with Children and Families* (DfE, 2015).

This is one example of how knowledge can be applied to social work practice. It is not possible within this chapter to cover all theories, models and approaches in detail but we will look at some of the key theories, models and approaches social workers use in practice and signpost you to relevant theories and further reading. We start firstly with the cornerstone of social work intervention, assessment.

The context of social work assessment and care planning

Skilled assessment is challenged by the current context of social work. Commentators within social work practice have pointed to the increasingly mechanistic and procedural way in which social work assessment is now conducted as a result of the fragmented care and social welfare system within which social work operates (e.g. Postle, 2002; Lymbery, 2006). As previously explored in Chapter 1, neoliberalist policies have led to a mixed economy of care between a reduced public sector and a piecemeal private sector. There is considerable evidence that social workers are increasingly constrained by bureaucratic processes and systems because of a fractured care economy which hampers a skilled approach to assessment and care planning (Lymbery and Postle, 2010). Social workers are needing to balance assessment frameworks and timescales set by government (often relating to the completion of online proformas within set time periods) with an evidential basis to assessment drawn from a range of theories and models of intervention. Parker (2017: 13–14) refers to this debate as the 'art' of completing assessments, in that social workers need a comprehensive range of skills in completing assessments *vis-à-vis* assessment as a 'science', which follows a more technical and rational approach to completing assessments where individuals are assessed against specific criteria, outcomes or frameworks. It is the latter that has predominated in recent years. This approach is also referred to as using 'technical skills' within assessment and other social work care and planning interventions.

There is, however, no doubt that assessment remains fundamental and core to the social work task despite the changing context of social work practice. Quality social work assessment is still seen as being at the heart of the social work task and is emphasised within a range of legal and policy imperatives as well as highlighted within government inquiries into poor social work practice. For example, Lord Laming's report into the death of Victoria Climbié emphasised the need for skilled social work assessment as opposed to a 'tick-box' approach to assessment and other social work interventions (HMSO, 2003). A range of professional social work standards documents have also stressed the place of assessment within social work practice. For example, the 'Knowledge and Skills Statement for Child and Family Social Work' emphasises the centrality of assessment within social work practice (DoE, 2015).

What is assessment?

What is 'good' assessment? This may differ according to professional, organisational or service user perspectives. It will also differ according to individual judgement and decision-making. Later in the chapter we examine how social workers need to build relationships with service users to undertake assessment and care planning tasks. Good relationship building is seen as vital in supporting positive assessment outcomes. This is known as 'relationship-based' assessment and differs from a procedural model of assessment.

As discussed, there are also 'technical' skills relating to the completion of social work assessments. Often these relate to the ability to follow frameworks and procedures relating to organisational functions and procedures. This connects, in turn, with assessment often being a 'legal' function contained within a range of legal and policy imperatives. Additionally, assessment goals and outcomes differ within particular areas of social work practice and in work with service user groups. For example, the assessment of a person under the Mental Health Act 1983 (amended 2007) is very different from completing a person-centred plan with a person with learning disabilities concerning their wish to develop more independent activities. Assessment is therefore a skilled activity needing a range of models, approaches and interventions.

There has also been a recent emphasis on empowering approaches to assessment within social work practice. For example, the Care Act 2014 emphasises a partnership approach to assessment where service users are fully involved and participating in assessment. However, referring to the earlier point about the context of social work practice, completing such assessments can be problematic given constraints on who is eligible for services and difficulty in locating appropriate services within a mixed economy of care. Consequently, social workers can often be seen to be working with the most disadvantaged and vulnerable members of society where self-actualisation approaches are difficult and complex.

Reflective questions

What kinds of assessments might social workers carry out and in relation to what issues or service user groups?

What might get in the way of building relationships with service users in such assessments?

Assessment and the relationship to care planning

There are a number of assessment models that are used as a foundation for assessment skills within social work education and training. Milner and colleagues (2015) suggest this is a staged process involving preparing for assessment and then collecting data or information. This is followed by social workers applying their knowledge and skills to assess the information collected to then decide on the next steps. This will involve looking at the cycle of care planning and intervention.

The Assessment, Planning, Intervention, Review and Evaluate (ASPIRE) model is widely discussed within the literature as a model for looking at both assessment and care planning. Sutton (1999) describes this as a process of carrying out assessments, planning and providing an intervention and then a further process of review and evaluation. Most assessments will involve subsequent planning and actions following an initial visit or even several visits. This may be a question of passing on your assessment to another service or it may be about providing a targeted or longer-term intervention. While the model is cyclical, social work intervention may return to assessment and the process would begin again. For example, in relation to the Care Act 2014, social workers have a legal responsibility to respond to service users' needs and re-evaluate and review care.

Within adult social care, the National Health Service (NHS) and Community Care Act 1990, which has now been superseded by the Care Act 2014, developed the concept of care management. Care management is seen by Brown as the cornerstone of legal provision (Brown, 2006). This connected with a focus on task-centred social work as the antithesis of the psychosocial casework model in many areas of social work. Watson and West (2006) discuss how the radical social work movement saw psychosocial perspectives as ignoring structural issues in society that contributed to difficulties for a range of service users – for example, the impact of poverty on parenting.

It also relates to the pressure to manage resources, and within both adult and children's social work services to the need to close cases due to high demand for services within a climate of austerity. However, there are generally still teams within all areas of social work that focus on longer-term work with service users who have complex issues and support needs. It is still important that a focused model is applied in terms of supporting individuals to maximise quality of life and independence and to decrease dependence.

The role of the 'care manager' has become the role associated with longer-term planning and intervention of work undertaken with service users, particularly within adult social work. The role of the social worker is to lead this process, particularly within the multi-agency context, following a systematic approach to assessment. Care management has been criticised by commentators for its mechanistic nature, with its focus on procedures and administrative requirement (see, e.g., Lymbery, 2005). Returning to a previous point, there is also a perceived emphasis on 'technical' skills in relation to lengthy online assessments and complex processes relating to managing care packages.

However, there are some perceived advantages to the care management model of care planning and delivery. Unlike previous psychosocial casework approaches, focused intervention can prevent cases drifting for a considerable time.

Social work practice in relation to adult social care has become more focused on care management within complex cases only (Parker, 2017). This means that social workers must have the skills to manage complex work. The organisation and delivery of assessment and care planning vary considerably between local authorities. Teams responsible for assessment and care planning are often separated and this means that processes and procedures can shape how intervention is experienced and delivered. How assessment and care planning is experienced relates significantly to the approaches the social worker or care manager take within their practice.

Reflective questions

How are assessment and care planning social work services delivered in your area?

Using models in social work interventions

Models need to be informed by an approach or perspective as to how assessment is conducted. These, in turn, are informed by a range of theories that Milner and colleagues (2015: 62) refer to as the 'theory thicket', which demonstrates the vast range of knowledge and evidence that social workers can and should draw upon in making sense of assessments. A systematic approach to assessment is one such approach where a range of factors are considered when undertaking an assessment. This kind of approach underpins person-centred care practice and has been suggested by the *Knowledge and Skills Statement for Social Work with Adults* (DfE, 2015). A systematic approach is informed by Bronfenbrenner's (1979) ecological theory on where the individual sits at the centre of a complex map of systems (both micro and macro) which needs to inform approaches to how the 'whole' picture is considered within assessment. This idea of the whole picture is known as holism and has heavily influenced what is known as the development of holistic care which is widely referred to within health and social care (Llewellyn et al., 2015). Holistic care has become even more of a contemporary issue as we see a move towards the integration of health and social care teams and services. Using mapping as a tool to show the variety of systems at play can be a useful visual way of examining the whole picture that surrounds a service user and their family. For example, a genogram can show the relationships between family members and can be very useful for complex extended families (Humphrey, 2011). The use of such child observational skills is also recommended in recent guidance (DfE, 2015).

We will explore in Chapter 6 the tensions that exist between task-centred social work practice and psychological perspectives within social work casework. However, social work practice can be seen to be rooted in psychological theories and approaches to support an understanding of human behaviour and life course development. Life course development is part of the assessment and social work standards within the PCF (BASW, 2017). Psychological theories underpinned the casework method that was common in social work practice and is still relevant to the care management process (Horner, 2009).

Psychodynamic approaches based on an understanding of how the past impacts on the present may also be useful within assessment and care planning in terms of making sense of how the current picture for the service user and/or their family is shaped by past events. For example, life course development may help us to understand the current difficulties a person is experiencing in relation to their mental health. Again, this is a significant theoretical area and a range of psychodynamic approaches can be used within assessment. Attachment theory, with its focus on early childhood development, is used widely within children and families social work to examine the impact of early attachments on adult attachments in later life (Howe, 2014). Behavioural perspectives can also be important in supporting both children and adults in terms of understanding behaviour patterns. For example, cognitive behavioural approaches are widely used within mental health social work in understanding the links between how individuals act in response to anxieties or other emotions. Cognitive behavioural approaches can provide a focused method to assessment, particularly in exploring how individuals maintain and manage their emotional well-being.

Theoretical perspectives therefore influence how assessment is conducted. We also need to ensure that time spent conducting an assessment is effective, particularly as time will be constrained and competing demands will be made. Smale and Tuson's model, while somewhat dated, is still widely referred to within the literature and helpfully informs how assessment is approached (e.g. Martin, 2010; Milner et al., 2015). Smale and colleagues (1993) identify a number of differing approaches to conducting social work assessment which are still highly relevant within the contemporary context of social work. These can be broadly summarised as procedural, questioning or exchange models of conducting assessment.

Firstly, a procedural model of conducting assessments could be primarily related to time constraints, the complexity of the situation and the needs of the service user. The assessment may also be about following a specific process or framework in order to meet the objectives and directives of the organisation. The procedural model of assessment is seen as a tick-box approach to assessment, with an emphasis on speed and efficiency in completing the task. Lymbery and Postle (2010), for example, have written about their concerns that this kind of assessment has become more common in adult social care. Assessment relates as much to screening people out as well as in because of resource constraints and the gatekeeping service function of social work assessment.

This, in turn, relates to the questioning model that may be used in assessment and which may not support inclusive communication and may disempower the service user. Here the social worker focuses on obtaining information from service users in order to obtain key facts to support a specific task – for example, an assessment under the Mental Capacity Act 2005. Again, the focus may be on assessing whether a service user is at risk or needs a particular service. The professional is very much in the driving seat as an expert. Questioning and procedural approaches to assessment may often be interwoven and can be seen as the opposite of the exchange model of assessment, as can be seen within the following case study which we will return to later in the chapter.

Case study: Assessment skills

John is a recently qualified social worker. As part of being on the duty desk within an Adult Social Care team he is asked to go out and see Kevin, a 35-year-old man who has multiple sclerosis (MS) and has recently moved to the area. The referral says Kevin can get angry with professionals but does not give any further information and there is no alert on the system with regard to Kevin. John is not very familiar with the assessment form that the local authority uses and takes a copy to use during the meeting with Kevin. ▶

◀

John spends an hour and a half with Kevin going through the form. John has the form in front of him during the entire interview. The assessment visit does not go well. Kevin complains that he has been asked a lot of irrelevant questions and is not clear what will happen next. He becomes angry and says that social workers are 'useless'. John is concerned that he has not completed all the questions on the form and becomes flustered during the visit. The visit does not end well and there are no agreed outcomes, although Kevin says he does not like his carers. When John returns to the office, the duty manager asks John for a summary of the visit and John finds it difficult to provide this.

Reflective questions

What might have affected this assessment?

What kind of assessment model does it appear John has adopted to conduct the assessment?

What might he have done differently?

The challenge for social work is to continue to work with and use the third part of the Smale and Tuson model, the exchange model. Here assessment is concerned with building a partnership with service users where a mutual exchange of communication occurs, allowing both parties to gain information and understanding. Here the service user is the expert. Such an approach is seen as central to partnership working. The focus is on building a productive and useful working relationship (Smale et al., 1993). Milner and colleagues (2015) discuss how the exchange model is the one most aligned with an empowering approach to assessment and to government guidance on effective assessment. The exchange model can also be seen as connecting with relationship-based approaches to assessment and care planning in encouraging service users to 'tell their story'. Relationship-based practice and the requisite communication skills are explored later in the chapter.

Task-centred social work intervention

Relating to how Smale and Tuson's model is used is a task-centred approach to social work assessment and care planning. A task-centred model to practice has become attractive to social work providers because of its focus on delivering specific outcomes to assessment and intervention. There is a significant body of literature on the use of task-centred approaches within social work practice (see, e.g., Doel and Marsh, 1992; Epstein, 1998).

Task-centred practice arose in the 1960s because of a concern that psychosocial approaches traditionally used within casework at the time caused service users to become dependent on long-term support (Reid and Epstein, 1972). Task-centred social work therefore focused on specific goals and outcomes and can be seen to have influenced a range of assessment frameworks subsequently. Assessment frameworks can be seen more recently as becoming focused on problem solving and working in partnerships with service users to set agreed goals or outcomes. A task-centred approach can also then be used in reviewing and evaluating care packages. For example, within assessment and care planning in adult social care it is used for identifying and exploring what particular 'needs' of the service user have changed over a particular time and what can be done to support further care planning.

Finally, more recently a task-centred approach to problem solving with service users has been linked to enabling and empowering approaches to working alongside service users. Again, intervention and care planning are focused but relate to understanding, exploring and identifying how and in what ways service users can take charge of their own lives and support themselves. This can broadly be described as 'person-centred' approaches but also encompasses approaches which relate to looking at service users' strengths (strengths-based or asset-based approaches) or how service users can take charge of their own mental health (recovery approaches). Such approaches encompass the concept of individual resilience where service users are best placed to respond to adverse life events (Anderson, 2013). However, this can be criticised as being part of a neoliberal 'solution' to how individuals need to be responsible for dealing with adverse events rather than the state. Social workers will be assessing and working with individuals who for a variety of reasons may find this difficult or not possible. This is because the issues that they are facing relate to wider societal structural factors such as oppression and discrimination which could be seen as beyond the remit of a problem-solving approach (Anderson, 2013).

Parker (2017) argues that task-centred practice fits the practical and technical skills agenda of the new social work degree in that it focuses on effective problem solving. It can be seen as a bridge between the 'art' and the 'science' of assessment and care planning work. However, task-centred practice can be seen to have its limitations in working with people with long-term and complex issues in their lives where brief intervention is perhaps not always possible.

So, as a social work student at this time, what do you need to think about in relation to assessment and care planning? The answer relates to having a sound understanding of differing theories and models of assessment to use within your practice. Social workers also need to be aware of differences relating to assessment and care planning with a wide range of differing user groups. You will also need to have a range of 'technical' skills. However, this needs to be approached in a critical and reflective manner as we now explore.

The science of assessment and care planning – technical skills

> There is a profound misunderstanding about the role and function of assessment, with an underpinning assumption that appears to characterise it as little more than a shallow tick-box exercise.
>
> (Lymbery and Postle, 2010: 2506)

Social workers are faced with completing long and often complex online assessment forms which follow a linear approach and specific requirements. There is no doubt that the drive for social workers to have good skills in this area has increased. By the end of training and through into the transition into qualified practice, there are expectations that social work students are able to complete complex reports, use a range of assessment proformas and be able to talk comprehensively and clearly about the judgements they have made in relation to assessment and care planning.

Later in the chapter we examine the importance of verbal communication in relationship-based practice. The importance of written communication has also become prominent as part of the development of technical skills within assessment and care planning. However, some social work students report difficulties in this area and in recent years a number of resources have developed to support the complexities of written work within social work practice. Part of completing assessments can be the production of reports or case summaries which are used within care planning and intervention. Such reports need to demonstrate technical skill and be evidence-based. Reports may be used within courts, tribunals or case conferences.

Healy and Mulholland (2012) discuss social workers developing a contextual approach to completing reports. Social workers need to refer to relevant laws and policies to explain the background to their actions. It is also important to be clear as to what is the purpose of a report. Likewise, when writing an assessment or a care plan this approach will ensure that you stay focused and produce a structured report or other document.

Finally, who is your audience? It may be that the communication is for service users, carers and a range of professionals and here you will need to think particularly about accessibility of information and the language used within your report or other written communication.

In undertaking the above task you will also need to draw on a range of information and knowledge in order to ensure your report or other document is evidence-based. This connects with what we have said earlier about having both technical and knowledge-based skills within assessment and care planning. This is also important in terms of keeping case records.

In undertaking social work assessment and intervention it is also important to consider a number of structural and organisational factors which impact upon the role of the social worker and the context within which they operate. Sociological perspectives are useful here.

Power within assessment and care planning

An important issue to consider is the power that social workers have within assessments and subsequent interventions. Smith (2008) points out that social work interventions are likely to have a profound and highly significant impact on people's lives. He discusses how power is invested within social workers by their access to resources, networks and information. The professional language used within social work assessments, meetings and so on can also be seen as a barrier to an effective user-led assessment. This relates to the work of Foucault who argued that the professionalism of knowledge and skills created a power imbalance in the discourse or language that professionals such as social workers use (Foucault, 1979). This can be alienating and disempowering for service users and their families.

This task is made complex by the fact that many service users may wait for assessments or other aspects of intervention and/or may not be seen as eligible for services. Eligibility for assessment or services is also outlined in law and policy across adult and children's services. Social workers in such circumstances can serve as 'gatekeepers' to access to services which creates significant power for individual workers. This function means that social workers are seen as serving as part of the network of structures within which control and power over individuals is exercised (Smith, 2008). This can be illustrated as simply as how information is recorded about service users thus impacting on how and whether they receive a service. Or it may relate to how structural power is exercised in the allocation of resources through the provision of resource allocation panels.

A way of managing this power dynamic is to adopt an approach to assessment where service users' needs are not categorised or specifically defined by use of a tick-box model of assessment. This allows for a more free-flowing style of assessment focusing on service users' experiences (Fook, 2016). It also connects with what we have said about an exchange model of assessment focusing on the relationship with the service user. Such an assessment model would also sit alongside a strengths- or asset-based approach, which we will explore later in the chapter. Power issues can then be explored within a partnership approach with service users and their families. Such a perspective can be applied to complex social work intervention such as risk assessment (Taylor, 2017).

Balancing risk and an empowering approach to intervention

Many commentators have been critical of how risk and risk frameworks have been seen to dominate social work practice. The preoccupation with managing risk not only appears to be disempowering and controlling for service users but can be seen as having de-skilled social workers. Risk and risk management have become an integral part of assessment in contemporary social work (and health and social care) practice. For example, assessing safety in children and families social work is part of risk assessment. Assessing capacity in adult social care is a complex legal intervention involving decision-making frameworks. Taylor (2017) points out that risk assessment has become increasingly complex and relies on a high level of skilled decision-making.

A questioning model of assessment can be seen as the most aligned to risk assessment and management. Dustin (2006) sees risk assessment skills as becoming necessary for social workers as part of the development of community care which challenged 'traditional' social work skills. The care management focus on managing needs and process has placed increased emphasis on managing associated risk.

However, as Llewellyn and colleagues (2015) outline, risk management has become associated with the blame culture that exists within social work practice in response to high-profile inquiries predominantly relating to child protection services where social workers are seen to have failed to address risk factors. This has led to what is known as 'risk-averse' practice where a preoccupation with risk influences judgement and decision-making. Sociological theory is helpful here in looking at attitudes within society relating to risk. Giddens (2009) and Beck (1992) have argued that we live in a risk society where daily judgements are made by all individuals concerning risk taking and risk avoidance. There is a social context to risk in that social disadvantage and social organisation play a role in determining how individuals respond to risk.

This can be illustrated when examining social work practice with disabled people. Brown (2006) discusses the case of Stephen Hoskins, a young man with learning disabilities who was abused and then murdered. Stephen had been excluded from services and was seen as having challenging behaviour. However, a number of commentators have pointed to how risk was assessed in Stephen's case (e.g. Gaylard, 2008) and how professional decision-making was influenced by a risk-averse approach to working with Stephen.

Consequently, social workers and other health and social care professionals have been criticised for focusing on 'negative' risks – for example, risks where the person is seen as a threat to themselves or others – rather than focusing on 'positive' risk which is connected to self-actualisation and promoting independence, empowerment and working with service users' strengths.

While risk assessment and processes can also be seen as clearly defined within law and policy in relation to safeguarding children and adults, social workers need a sophisticated and theoretically based understanding of risk to inform their practice. Again, there is a balance between technical skills and effective evidenced-based practice as a core feature within safeguarding processes. Assessment and risk assessment remain central to the social work job and task, particularly when we consider that because of resource constraints social workers work with some of the most vulnerable and oppressed people in society.

Parker (2017) usefully discusses an ethnographic approach to assessment in that we immerse ourselves in the world of the individual and use skills to draw out the person to talk about their issues and goals. However, immersing ourselves in the world of the service user will have an emotional impact on ourselves and it is important that social workers are supported in managing the complexities of balancing risk and rights within assessment and care planning. Ingram's (2015) work has focused on the importance of social workers examining their own emotions within the practice context to be better able to build and maintain relationships with service users. Ingram argues that both informal and formal support is needed within social work organisations to support how social workers manage their emotions. Attention to this process will support empowering and positive social work practice and emotional resilience, which we explore further in Chapter 6.

Empowering approaches to social work intervention

Earlier in the chapter we talked about power relationships within social work interventions. This section looks at the importance of partnership approaches to assessment and care planning where power is shared and acknowledged. More recently there has been a return to a focus on models of working that focus on an empowering approach to assessment and care planning within social work intervention. A number of terms can be used within different areas of social work practice here but these can broadly be summarised as strengths-based approaches to social work intervention. This section of the chapter explores a range of strengths-based approaches with differing user groups.

For example, a strengths-based approach to social work intervention has been advocated within adult social care in working to support individual well-being and preventing crisis and further issues for service users. The model here focuses on an 'asset-based' approach to social work intervention which focuses on what people want or are able to do rather than focusing on what they are unable to do. These approaches can be seen as offering an **empowering** approach to social work intervention in that they focus on service users' strengths rather than negative risks and weaknesses. Howe (2008) outlines how a strengths-based approach to social work practice arose because of concerns that social workers were overly concerned with service users' difficulties. This can be seen within assessment and risk assessment, but also within a range of interventions with service users. This has been described as a 'deficit' model of service users (Weick et al., 1989) where social workers see service users as victims of their circumstances. A strengths-based approach also connects with a rights-based approach to working with service users that promotes citizenship and inclusion within society. The focus is on actively promoting strengths rather than focusing on risk and concerns.

This debate about social work intervention relates to sociological perspectives on disability which are briefly discussed here. The work of Oliver and colleagues, for example, highlights how social work assessment and care planning define service users' needs within a medicalised framework that focuses on deficits rather than strengths. This is known as the individual model. Rather Oliver and colleagues (2012) suggest a focus on the **social model of disability** which acknowledges and takes account of structural deficits and barriers within society (e.g. employment and social welfare) and supports service users in challenging these barriers. This partnership approach supports service users in obtaining their rights and thus becoming full citizens within society.

The citizenship model presents a challenge to the way in which disabled people and other groups in society are made dependent on social welfare and other services. It argues that citizenship challenges the structural oppression of service users. In this role, social workers are more than gatekeepers to services working in partnership with service users.

An assessment model which works in partnership with service users to maximise personal strengths thus resonates with a social model approach. As Howe states:

> The social worker wants to tease out and recognise what strengths, talents, experience, skills, resources and supports the service user was drawing on to cope with the stress.

> (Howe, 2009: 101)

In terms of applying a social model perspective, a strengths-based approach to practice has strong correlations with this approach. The social model challenges an individual model approach to disability and ill health. Milner and Byrne (2009) discuss how social workers must always have the social model at the forefront of assessment within adult social care. A focus on service users' strengths supports this. Healy offers a number of key practice principles relating to strengths-based approaches:

➤ Adopt an optimistic attitude

➤ Focus primarily on assets

➤ Collaborate with the service user

➤ Work towards the long-term empowerment of service users

➤ Create community – link service users to others to promote self-help communities. (Healy, 2005: 158–164)

At the heart of this process is a willingness to engage in a partnership relationship with the service user. Empowerment as a goal is therefore an important part of social work intervention.

Since the late 1980s, there has also been an increased focus on the ability of service users to find solution to their own problems and the need to support personal resilience. This can be seen in relation to social work practice with service users experiencing mental health difficulties. Strengths-based approaches can be seen to have been shaped by the mental health survivors' movement and the development of the recovery model as a distinct perspective within psychosocial perspectives on mental health. The recovery model focuses on how experiencing mental health problems leads to social inequalities and social exclusion (Tew, 2012). In using the recovery model within risk assessment, for example, the social worker would focus on the individual's ability to manage and cope with their own mental health problems. Risk here would be identified positively with a focus on what strengths or assets the individual has to manage their own recovery. The recovery model emphasises the control mental health service users have in making decisions about their own lives.

Supporting change and recovery is also an important part of social work practice with people who misuse substances. A core practice model here is motivational interviewing which draws on a person-centred and reflective approach to affect change (Forrester and Hutchinson, 2012). By focusing on motivating factors for change, social workers again are looking at strengths and positives. However, as with other strengths-based approaches, the issue can be structural factors, which may be highly significant in encouraging and supporting people who misuse substances to affect change. Similarly, this needs to be considered when working within a staged change model. A significant model here is the one developed by Prochaska and DiClemente (1982) which describes the stages that individuals can go through in affecting change. Social workers need to be intuitive about working with change models where there may be significant structural factors impacting on the ability to empower service users to affect change.

There are also examples of strengths-based approaches in work with children and families. The resilience model is seen as important in work with children and focuses on enabling children to overcome adverse events in childhood by focusing on the support networks around them (see, e.g., Gilligan, 2007). There appears to be some evidence that social workers do not always explain complex issues to children for fear that they may be distressed by the discussion (Gilligan, 2007). Taylor (2017) discusses how working with children around their safety in difficult situations can be seen as creative and empowering, as it is about looking at strengths as well as risks or needs. He discusses the Signs of Safety approach within assessment and risk management which supports working with children around their safety within child protection work.

Solution-focused approaches can be seen as similar to an asset-based approach within adult social care in that it looks for ways in which service users can affect change in their lives. Milner and colleagues (2015) discuss how changes may be small and incremental, but the social worker focuses on how such changes can be maximised within the assessment and care management process. Strengths-based approaches provide a range of models that can be used in differing areas of social work practice. The focus is on empowering service users and affecting change. Under-pinning all this work is the relationship with the service user and/or their family, which is so important for social work practice.

Building relationships with service users

Relationship-based practice is an approach to social work which empha-sises the importance of the helping relationship. This may appear to be self-evident but commentators have discussed the difficulties of building and maintaining relationships with service users when there are difficult or complex issues to address (Howe, 2014) – for example, working along-side parents where there are concerns for the safety of the child. Social work involvement may not be welcomed and how then do social workers build effective relationships?

Hingley-Jones and Ruch (2016) discuss the importance of social workers acknowledging the impact of current austerity policies on vulnerable families and adults who may be at risk. They stress that social workers need to look 'beyond the surface' in identifying what is going on for service users. This may mean coping with hostility from service users. Resistance or non-com-pliance with social work interventions may be due to a number of reasons and social workers need to be reflexive and responsive in such situations.

Relationships need to be built and maintained when working with resistant service users. Gaskell-Mew and Lindsay (2015) suggest several skills that are useful in such situations. They discuss social workers hav-ing an awareness that resistance to social work may have been caused, for example, by a negative previous experience with social work involve-ment, or service users may not see that the way they are leading their lives is problematic. Approaching such conflicts from a relationship-based perspective that focuses on strengths and being self-aware may defuse conflict and resistance.

In such circumstances social workers still need to be able to maintain a confident and authoritative stance. Ruch (2010) discusses the importance of using and applying theoretical frameworks to support practice in dif-ficult situations. This recognises the impact, for example, of austerity and sociopolitical complexities for vulnerable service users which may under-pin what is perceived as risky behaviour. Self-awareness and emotional intelligence are essential. This also includes being aware of individual anxieties which may affect how social workers approach service users who are perceived as hostile or resistant (Hingley-Jones and Ruch, 2016). This is explored further in Chapter 6. Also essential is a range of verbal com-munication skills enabling social workers to deal with complexity.

Developing your communication skills

Chapter 6 discusses how core communication skills are key to the readiness-for-practice 'test' for students prior to undertaking placement. This is generally developed from a counselling skills communication model often involving experiential learning and role play. This learning focuses on the development of core communication skills to support social work practice (Koprowska, 2010). The discussion within this chapter is more concerned with how social workers further develop their communication skills, recognising that social work interventions are shaped by complex and at times conflictual situations. In order to practise using an exchange approach to assessment and care planning, it is vital that social workers develop their communication skills.

Dinham (2006), in his review of communication skills, referred to pedagogical approaches within social work education and training related to core, specific and technical communication skills. Earlier in the chapter we referred to the use of technical skills within assessment and that the ability to communicate clearly and appropriately about assessment frameworks, processes and so on is important. However, social workers will also need to develop negotiation skills and communication skills to deal with complexity, conflict and resistance, as outlined above. As well as working with resistant or hostile service users, social workers can also be involved in breaking bad news and may also be working with service users who are frightened or confused. Some social workers may find these kinds of situation more difficult than working with resistance. Such situations require the use of empathy.

Throughout communication with service users, the development of empathy is critical. Social work training and education focuses on the core communication skill of empathy, but there is a need to develop advanced empathy. This is because we know that the expression of empathy by social workers has significant impact on case outcomes and the health and well-being of service users (Morrison, 2007). Rosenthal (1977) makes a direct link between an individual's ability to identify with other people's emotions having an impact on their own life and work success. A more advanced and sophisticated understanding of empathy therefore needs to be developed. The self-aware social worker can see beyond the surface to what may be affecting or troubling a service user – for example, being aware that anger can be used as a defence when individuals are anxious. This requires a more advanced expression of empathy to support relationship building (Howe, 2014). In conclusion, if we return to our previous case study we can see how relationship-based practice may have helped to change the outcome of John's encounter with Kevin.

Case study

John is a recently qualified social worker. As part of being on the duty desk within an Adult Social Care team he is asked to go out and see Kevin, a 35-year-old man who has multiple sclerosis (MS) and has recently moved to the area. The referral notes John has received says that Kevin can get angry with professionals but contains no further information. As there is no identified risk on the system, John agrees to visit on his own after discussion with his manager.

John spends some time thinking about how to approach the visit and talks to an experienced colleague before leaving the office. Kevin is angry when John arrives as he is not happy with the care agency the local authority have sent and he is also having problems with his benefits. John feels anxious during the first part of the visit but asks Kevin to expand on what has been going on. After a while, Kevin tells John that he has recently separated from his wife and has moved to the area to be nearer to his parents. He is struggling to cope. John agrees to visit Kevin the following week and that he will contact the care agency to discuss Kevin's concerns. He also helps Kevin to make a phone call regarding his benefits. John has to ring the office as the visit has taken longer than intended but the visit ends well. John has also suggested Kevin gets in touch with an old friend who lives nearby and Kevin agrees this would be a good idea.

Reflective questions

How has John approached the visit?

What models of intervention may be helpful in this situation?

Chapter summary

This chapter has explored the core issues relating to the use of models of intervention within social work practice. We have examined:

➤ Core theories within social work interventions which have led to a range of models and approaches for use in social work practice.

➤ Examples relating to intervention with different user groups.

➤ The importance of relationship-based practice.

➤ The need for social workers to develop advanced communication skills in dealing with complexity, conflict and resistance in the context of financial austerity.

In reading this chapter we hope that you have gathered that there is not one overarching model, approach or theory that can solve or address all the socially complex issues we face within practice. To work effectively we need to be flexible and adaptable and draw upon an eclectic range of theories, models, approaches and interventions to inform our practice. Within the next chapter we will be exploring diversity within the communities we serve. A further challenge is adopting these generic skills, model approaches and theories to work with specific individuals or groups within our diverse communities such as asylum seekers and marginalised social groups.

4

Working with diversity: Understanding and locating individuals and communities

Social workers have always worked with a diverse range of people from a wide range of ages and backgrounds and with differing levels of needs, so it would be fair to say that working with diversity is a natural and fundamental part of social work practice. However, diversity is often viewed as a negative and problematic concept, one that poses challenges for practitioners and users of services alike in that social work has often been criticised for failing to recognise the diverse needs of communities through providing a one-size-fits-all or mono cultural service. However, changes in global patterns of migration mean that social workers find themselves working with increasingly diverse populations. Though anti-oppressive perspectives have enabled social workers to develop an understanding of diversity and the negative effects of difference in terms of discrimination and marginalisation, Parrott (2014) suggests that social workers are ill-prepared to deal with the effects of an increasingly diverse client population within a globalised world. As communities within the UK are becoming increasingly more diverse, there is a need to reframe how diversity and difference are understood within society and social work practice more specifically.

Key concepts within this chapter include:

➤ The exploration and location of diversity in social work.

➤ The disproportionality within welfare services.

➤ Social class and intersectionality.

➤ Diversity and super diversity in the UK.

➤ Approaches to working with diversity – cultural competence.

➤ Critical thinking in diversity – understanding the 'other' and critical race theory.

The discussion in this chapter is also situated alongside the 'Readiness for Direct Practice Level' of the **Professional Capabilities Framework for Social Work (PCF)** developed by the British Association of Social Workers (BASW).

Through reading Chapter 4 students should be able to:

Diversity

➢ Recognise the importance of diversity in human identity and experience, and the application of anti-discriminatory and anti-oppressive principles in social work practice.

Rights and Justice

➢ Understand the principles of rights, justice and economic well-being, and their significance for social work practice.

Before you read this chapter we would like you to familiarise yourself with the **standards of proficiency (SOPs)** for social workers in England (2017) by the **Health and Care Professions Council (HCPC)**. The discussion that develops in this chapter has congruence with the following **HCPC SOPs (5, 5.1, 5.2, 5.3, 5.4, 13.3, 13.4)**:

➢ 5 Be aware of the impact of culture, equality and diversity on practice.

➢ 5.1 Be able to reflect on and take account of the impact of inequality, disadvantage and discrimination on those who use social work services and their communities.

➢ 5.2 Be able to understand the need to adapt practice to respond appropriately to different groups and individuals.

➢ 5.3 Be aware of the impact of their own values on practice with different groups of service users and carers.

➢ 5.4 Be able to understand the impact of different cultures and communities and how this affects the role of the social worker in supporting service users and carers.

➢ 13.3 Be aware of changes in demography and culture and their impact on social work.

➢ 13.4 Be able to understand in relation to social work practice: the impact of injustice, social inequalities, policies and other issues which affect the demand for social work services.

Locating diversity in social work

Diversity discourses within social work have traditionally been understood to describe increased racial, cultural and religious heterogeneity within society and how those differences are manifested within the needs of particular users of services. This relates to ideas about equality and ensuring that users of services are treated fairly and receive equal opportunity and access to services. Such concepts of multiculturalism have extended beyond race and ethnicity to recognise wider differences such as class, gender, sexual orientation, age and disability, which we will later describe as diversity factors. Understanding diversity within social work has centred upon the importance of recognising and valuing difference, a core tenet of social work values. Traditional values in social work emphasise respecting people irrespective of their background, avoidance of discrimination and being non-judgemental (see Banks, 2012). It is the ethical duty of social workers to promote social justice and this responsibility has been translated into international (IFSW, 2014) and national standards or codes of practice, and the importance of equality and diversity are reflected by the professional and regulatory requirements for social workers. Professional and regulatory bodies such as the BASW (2017) and the HCPC (2017) emphasise the importance of working with diverse communities through their regulations and standards. The current professional regulator of social workers, the HCPC, requires that social workers 'understand the impact of different cultures and communities and how this affects the role of the social worker in supporting service users and carers' (HCPC, 2017: 8). The Knowledge and Skills Statements for adults and children requires that social workers can explain the impact of poverty, inequality and diversity in social work and how they relate to child welfare, family functioning and to people's health and well-being (DfE, 2017; DoH, 2017).

Disproportionality in welfare services: Focus on race

Though social workers are required to recognise the effects of difference, the failure of social work to respond to the needs of diverse groups has been well documented. The concept of '**disproportionality**' has traditionally been used to refer to the disproportionate representation of Black, Asian and Minority Ethnic (BAME) communities within criminal justice, mental health, education and child protection systems. It refers to the ratio between the percentage of persons in a particular ethnic group at a particular decision point or experiencing an event (entry into care, or school exclusions), compared to the percentage of the same ethnic group in the overall population. Either being under- or over-represented within a particular service or in having a particular experience is considered 'out of proportion', though within social work racial disproportionality is often considered; yet disproportionality could also be experienced in terms of gender, social class, family structure and so on.

In their analysis of child protection systems, Katz and Connolly (2017) discuss a number of assumptions that are associated with the notion of disproportionality. Firstly, it is assumed that racial or ethnic groups should have similar rates of involvement within child protection systems and that this should be proportionate to their ratio within the general population. That means that if the population of children from Asian backgrounds in a city is 6%, one could expect that the proportion of children on child protection plans from an Asian background would also be around 6%. It is also assumed that over-representation in child protection is damaging for children and that over-representation within the system is an indication of racism within social work and wider society (Katz and Connolly, 2017). Research has highlighted that Black and mixed race children are disproportionately more likely to appear within the looked-after and children in need populations, whereas Asian children are disproportionately less likely to be on child protection registers or plans (Barn et al., 1997; Owen and Statham, 2009; Sinclair et al., 2007). One could argue that under-representation may be equally as concerning as over-representation, as this can indicate a lack of recognition and neglect of the needs of children from a particular background, which can leave them vulnerable and at risk. Some of most high-profile child deaths have concerned children of minority ethnic backgrounds who are less likely to be referred to therapeutic services such as child and adolescent mental health (Brandon et al., 2008; Edbrooke-Childs et al., 2016).

Most of the research regarding disproportionality has been conducted within the USA and while there are some differences between the respective welfare systems and the nature of Black and minority ethnic communities, research indicates that those groups tend to be over-represented in the more controlling aspects of welfare and under-represented in the more supportive and therapeutic services (Dominelli, 2008). Butt (2006) suggests that inadequate responses to racial and ethnic diversity in social care are due to a range of complex and interrelated factors. These include a lack of knowledge among ethnic minorities of the availability of services; a lack of choice in appropriate and quality services; and a lack of workers with effective experience, communication and skills needed to work with diverse communities; as well as direct and institutional racism. It would be reasonable to say that children from minority ethnic backgrounds are also likely to be over-represented within deprived and disadvantaged communities and that poverty and disadvantage are widely accepted as known risk factors that are associated with abuse and neglect (Bywaters et al., 2016). However, it is the concerns regarding racism within child protection and other aspects of welfare, such as mental health services and the criminal justice system, that are highlighted in debates concerning disproportionality. It is suggested that successfully promoting diversity and meeting the needs of minority service users not only requires avoiding perpetuating those behaviours, but also involves developing conscious strategies to overcome their effects of racism and other forms of inequality (Butt, 2006). The response to this by social work is summarised by Bywaters and colleagues (2016: 11):

> When such high proportions of black and Asian children are living in the most disadvantaged neighbourhoods, questions are raised about the nature of society and the role that social workers can play in reducing or reinforcing social inequalities.

Uncomfortable truths: Social class and diversity

The relationship between social work and social class, in particular how social workers predominantly engage with communities from lower socioeconomic backgrounds, has been recognised by a number of commentators (Llewellyn et al., 2015; Parrott, 2014). The research of Bebbington and Miles (1989) in the 1980s was highly influential in identifying how poverty was a major determinant of children coming into public care. Almost 30 years later Bywaters and colleagues (2016) highlighted the strong correlation between deprivation and the risk of children being looked after or placed on the child protection register, and question the effectiveness of how social work services recognise and consider the impact of poverty on families and their children. The research highlights that:

> Children in the most deprived 10% of neighbourhoods were over ten times more likely to be LAC [looked-after children] than those in the least deprived. In the most deprived neighbourhoods, roughly 1 child in 60 was 'in care'; in the least deprived only 1 child in 660. On average each 10% increase in deprivation brought a 30% increase in LAC rates.

(CWIP, 2017)

Bywaters and colleagues (2016) argue that despite the obvious impact of poverty on the lives of families with whom they work, they found that social work assessments and care plans gave little weight to the material conditions in which families lived. They identified that social workers saw that addressing poverty was not part of their intervention with families but the work of other agencies. Contemporary social work practice is considered to have become professionally preoccupied with the management of risk and the allocation of resources to mitigate or manage risk. Risk management often focuses on domestic violence, drug dependency, physical harm and neglect as key indicators of social work intervention. The role of poverty within risk management is more imbedded; it serves to underpin many of the risks we work with and inequality becomes an uncomfortable and unresolvable risk for the narrowly defined contemporary role of social work. The concept of structural poverty and social class has become so integral to social work that we often fail to recognise or act on poverty in an adequate manner. It must be recognised that structural poverty and socioeconomic inequality are a normalised experience within late modern society. This normalisation, combined with the refocus of social work from welfare provision to safeguarding and risk management, has been explored in earlier chapters and it is recognised that poverty and social class are, and must remain, paramount in social work. It is the greatest uncomfortable social truth that we work with and a pervasive factor that compounds risk and acts as a catalyst for most forms of social crises we work with. However, given the very politic of the socioeconomic framework we live and work within, social workers can feel that addressing poverty is too great a burden for individual casework, and in all honesty it is. The scale of the problem embodied in poverty, social class and inequality has been accentuated by the impact of the recent recession and the austerity discourse of governments (see Chapters 2 and 5 for more details). Austerity practices from central government in the UK have seen a retreat from and reduction of broad welfare services. Despite the challenges, as social workers, we must work as advocates and gatekeepers to broaden welfare services, and act collectively as professionals within our networks to lobby at a local, national and regional level to address poverty and social inequality. It can be posited that social class interconnects and intersects all aspects of diversity within social work; poverty and inequality can be considered both an alpha and an omega in social work – they are the first, last and always of our community-based practice. Having established the relevance of diversity within social work and the significance of social workers in recognising the differential experiences of those who use the services and the impact of inequality and disadvantage on their lives, we will turn our attention to exploring how diversity is understood within social work and within the broader social sciences.

Understanding diversity

There are many definitions of diversity, and in its literal sense diversity means difference, though, as we have suggested, within communities there are many factors that make people different. Differences between people could be physical, cultural, political and religious, extending beyond race and culture to include identity factors pertaining to gender, sexuality, social class and (dis)ability. Diversity is multidimensional and shapes human experience, and can be considered as critical to the formation of identity. Diversity can also imply a concern with valuing peoples' differences – but what does 'valuing' difference mean? Clements (2008) suggests that it is partly about avoiding the creation of a 'monoculture' in which one size 'fits all'.

Equality and diversity are often used together, particularly within the context of policies; however, it is worth differentiating between the two terms. Thompson (2009) identifies the legal context in which equality is framed with an emphasis on equal opportunity, access to services and avoidance of discrimination. The tendency to focus on making people aware of their legal obligations in this area tends to overlook the positive aspects of recognising and embracing difference because of the emphasis on legislative compliance. Diversity, on the other hand, not only focuses on the importance of legislation but looks more broadly at how valuing diversity will bring benefits to the workforces, service users and society as a whole. As Thompson (2009) emphasises, a diversity approach will seek to address any forms of unfair discrimination and will not simply emphasise compliance with the law as being a *measure of this*.

Gardenswartz and Rowe's (1994) model for understanding diversity (see Figure 4.1) provides an accessible model to understand the multifaceted nature of diversity. Reflected pictorially as a 'diversity wheel' it describes four layers of experiences within diversity to reflect the complexity of diversity within individuals and organisations. The first layer, *Personality*, refers to the traits and stable characteristics of an individual that are viewed as determining particular consistencies in the manner in which that person behaves in any given situation and over time (see Washington, 2008). The next layer, *Internal Dimension*, refers to the characteristics that are assigned at birth, such as age, race, ethnicity, gender and physical ability. These characteristics are often the source

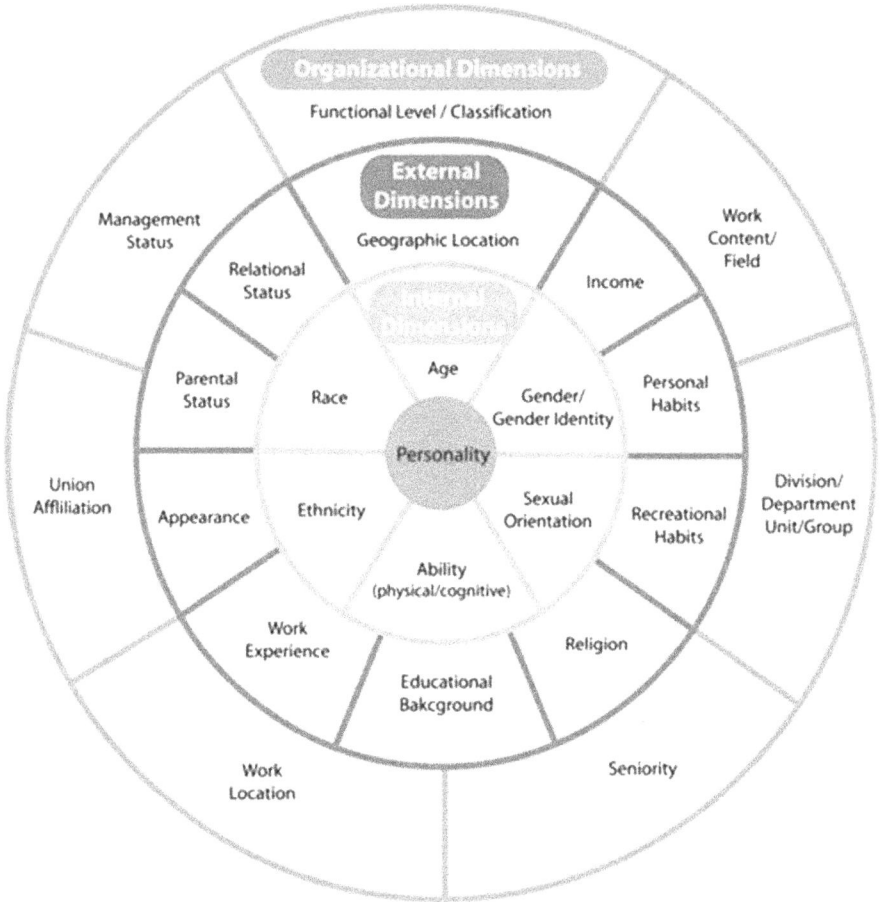

Figure 4.1   Diversity wheel

of disadvantage and discrimination. The *External* dimension represents those characteristics which are considered to contain some element of choice – for example, personal habits, religion, educational background, work experience, appearance, status, marital status, geographic location and income. The fourth, *Organizational*, is the outermost layer and describes the traits that are influenced by the organisation in which one works – for example, management status, union affiliation, work location, seniority and department. The level of influence is limited because control rests with the organisation in which a person works, though people in professional or managerial jobs are more likely to feel that they can influence local decisions than people from routine occupations.

> ### Case study: Diversity and intersectionality
>
> Let's consider the situation of Alicia, a 23-year-old newly qualified social worker (NQSW) working in an integrated team within adult social care within a rural town. From a Christian background, Alicia was born in Birmingham, and her parents originated from Zimbabwe. She is the first member of her family to go to university. Most of Alicia's service users are older and were born locally. Drawing on the notion of a diversity wheel, consider aspects of difference and diversity. Alicia's situation highlights the multifaceted nature of diversity within social work and enables us to consider the concept of intersectionality.

Intersectionality is a useful concept for social work, as many communities and people who use services are often affected by various forms of marginalisation and inequality. It helps to identify the multifaceted way in which difference is experienced. Intersectionality has traditionally referred to the ways in which race and class interact to shape Black women's experiences (Crenshaw, 1989). It has since been extended to include the complex processes in which the power relations associated with various aspects of social identity, including social class, sexuality and ability intersect to shape people's experiences. So, in the case of Alicia, it could be suggested that factors relating to gender, race, age, class, educational status and so on intersect to shape her experiences. The effects and impact of difference may change throughout Alicia's life – for example, if she has children, gains promotion or loses her job as a professional social worker. Though intersectionality seeks to focus on the relationships between factors and mutually constructed processes that create difference, Vertovec (2007) offers an additional concept of 'super diversity' to describe processes of differentiation as a result of processes associated by the effects of global migration and immigration status.

Diversity and super diversity in the UK

The effects of a global economic crisis, the impact of global inequality, war and political conflicts have resulted in substantial changes in patterns of migration as populations flee from war-torn areas such as Syria and Afghanistan. People also flee from political conflict and oppression from countries including Nigeria and Pakistan; or cross borders to find work or other opportunities from Eastern Europe, in search of a better life. The political and economic processes are complex, but their effects are simple as populations go on the move to find safety and security or a better life for themselves and their families. There has been an increase in both political and popular discourses concerning the population changes that have taken place within the UK and Europe since 2015. This has mostly centred on migrants and those people seeking asylum. Rather than valuing diversity, the rhetoric often is negative (and at times racist), focusing on the problems associated with migration, such as the lack of integration and pressure on public services. However, there is no doubt that some communities have experienced significant changes in their ethnic composition, as population predicators suggest that by 2051 the ethnic minority share of the population will increase from 8% (2001) to 20% (Rees et al., 2012). The increase in speed and scale of patterns of migration in the UK and Europe can mean that cities are no longer dominated by a couple of ethnic minority groups but there instead exists a significant diversification and heterogeneity amongst ethnic groups whereby it is not uncommon for some schools to have over 50 different languages spoken (CSE, 2017). The northern English city of Leeds reflects some of the population changes that have taken place within the UK since 2010. Figure 4.2 illustrates the range of languages spoken. Leeds's traditional immigrant and ethnic minority population has conventionally been characterised by large Irish, African-Caribbean and South Asian communities whose citizens originated from the former colonial territories or Commonwealth countries. Contemporary Leeds is now one of the most ethnically diverse cities outside of London, with over 140 ethnic groups, representing 19% of the population reporting to come from a BAME group (Census, 2011), compared with 11% since 2001. Within Leeds, the largest ethnic category is 'mixed race', and it has experienced a doubling in the population of those born outside of the UK. This extension of European citizenship led to both temporary and more permanent increases in populations from Eastern European backgrounds, though it is unclear how the decision to leave the European Union (EU) will affect current immigration and economic policies.

Before we move on to consider the notion of super diversity, it is worth reflecting on how the communities with which you are familiar may have become more diverse.

Reflective question: Community and ethnic diversity

Select a community with which you are familiar.

- Has the ethnic diversity of the community changed?
- Can you identify the nature of those changes in the migrant population within the past five to ten years?

▶

- From where have those communities originated, and how does this compare to patterns of migration 50 years ago?
- Consider the reasons for migration?
- What are the discourses concerning migration within the community?
- How have local services responded to such changes?

Ten most spoken non-English languages in Leeds

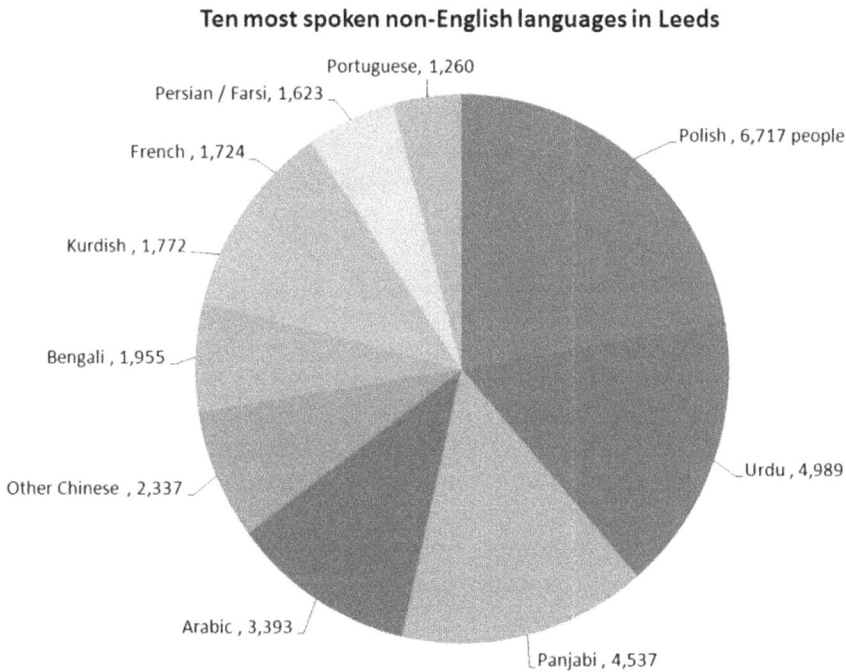

Portuguese, 1,260
Persian / Farsi, 1,623
French, 1,724
Kurdish, 1,772
Bengali, 1,955
Other Chinese, 2,337
Arabic, 3,393
Panjabi, 4,537
Polish, 6,717 people
Urdu, 4,989

Figure 4.2 Languages spoken in Leeds, UK

(Clarity Social Enterprises, 2017)

Vertovec (2007) introduced the concept of super diversity to refer to increased levels of diversity or the 'diversification of diversity' across Western Europe. He uses it to describe the changing patterns of global migration since the 1990s that have resulted in complex migrant populations that incorporate different nationalities, religious and linguistic backgrounds, migration channels and immigrant status, which may affect an individual's rights and entitlements. The different categories of migrant reflect an individual's pattern of migration that in turn dictates their ascription of rights and entitlements to public services. Vertovec (2007) describes a complex array of migrant statuses and their respective legal rights and access to public services that could include, for example, a worker from Romania through the extension of the EU treaty, or a student from Australia through a study visa, or an asylum seeker from Afghanistan. The concept of super diversity not only recognises these differences in diversity as created through ethnicity and migrant status, but also highlights the need for policymakers and practitioners to recognise and respond to the conditions created by these changing patterns of migration. Therefore, while members of a particular community may share the same nationality or ethnicity, they may hold different rights to public resources depending on their immigration status. Vertovec (2007) goes on to discuss how persons of a shared Somali background may share the same ethnicity though one could have British citizenship whereas another could be described as an asylum seeker, or be granted refugee status with leave to remain, whereas someone else could be in the UK illegally. An approach to working with diversity that focuses simply on ethnicity or country of origin would fail to recognise the complexity that a super diversity lens enables.

However, Boccagni (2015) discusses how the concept of diversity can be challenging for social work, as policymakers and service providers struggle to respond to the challenges presented by notions of diversity itself, without the additional consideration of being 'super'. It is within the context of asylum that social workers often struggle with the ethical issues of the effects of super diversity and the case study about Kabir highlights the situation faced by many unaccompanied asylum seekers, the complexities of service users lives and the challenges posed to social workers in responding to their needs.

Case study: Kabir

Kabir has fled from Iran where he had lived with his mother after his father had been killed and his brother imprisoned for opposing the political regime. He arrived in the UK aged 15 having travelled here in a lorry. The police discovered him and asked the local authority to come into the police station and assess his age. The social worker who saw Kabir believed him to be over 18 and he was kept in a police cell for four days before being transferred to an Immigration Removal Centre. This experience was very difficult for Kabir; for two days he was unable to communicate with anyone as there was no-one from his country to help him and he had only been in the country a few days so could speak no English at all. He was there nearly four weeks before someone alerted the Refugee Council. As soon

▶

as he met Kabir, the Refugee Council Adviser was very concerned that the social worker had been mistaken and wrote to the local authority to ask them to reconsider their decision. They agreed to conduct a further assessment and Kabir was assessed to be only 16 years old, which led to his release into the care of the local authority. However, Kabir still suffers from mental health difficulties as a result of his detention in the police station and in the removal centre. The psychiatrist who assessed him stated that the six weeks he was locked up, when he felt abandoned and terrified about his future, were the cause of his current disorder, particularly because he was not able to mix with anyone of his own age. We hope that with the right care Kabir will make a good recovery from his experiences, but we will have to wait and see.

Source: J. Dennis (2012), *Not a Minor Offence: Unaccompanied Children Locked Up as Part of the Asylum System*, Refugee Council.

Approaches to working with diversity

Cultural competence

Working with diversity has traditionally been located within the context of cultural competence with the intention of providing culturally sensitive or competent practice to meet the needs of ethnic minority communities and service users. However, culture is a problematic and contested term, and is often open to interpretation. To many people, culture implies a shared ethnicity, language, religion, beliefs or the shared values, norms and behaviours that are associated with a particular group. Yet cultures are not fixed but fluid and change as individuals and communities change over time. Culture extends beyond ethnicity to include wider forms of difference, and distinctive cultures exist in relation to particular groups – for example, religious groups, sexual orientation, geographical groups, political groups – though cultural competence is often framed within the context of ethnicity.

Cultural competence is an approach to working with difference that originated in the USA within social work education; in the UK it has been more widely used in nursing, though it has become increasingly popular within social work in recent years (Furness, 2005; Laird, 2008). Cultural competence arose from a perception that inadequate cultural knowledge and understanding among professionals is one of the main reasons for social care agencies' failure in providing appropriate services and interventions with ethnic minority communities. Walker's (2005: 57) definition of cultural competence in the context of working with children and families refers to it as 'a set of knowledge-based and interpersonal skills that allows individuals to understand, appreciate and work with people/ families of cultures other than their own'.

There are, however, different models of cultural competence, though they usually involve aspects of self-awareness, knowledge and skills (Weaver, 1999). Cultural competence tends to focus on the Eurocentric bias that exists within social work education theory and practice, and typically involves four levels:

➤ 'Cultural knowledge' means that you know about some of the cultural characteristics, history, values, beliefs and behaviours of another ethnic or cultural group.

➤ 'Cultural awareness' is the next stage of understanding other groups; being open to the idea of changing cultural attitudes.

➤ 'Cultural sensitivity' is knowing that differences exist between cultures, but not assigning values to the differences (better or worse, right or wrong).

➤ Being culturally competent brings these concepts together for operational effectiveness.

(Community Tool Box, 2017)

In this way, *cultural competence* can be seen to develop over time to bring together those previous stages at an individual worker level, but this can also occur at an organisational level (see the section 'Critiques of cultural competence' below). For individual workers, Tedam (2013) discusses how cultural competent practice enables social workers to work effectively across a range of differences (not just ethnicity) promoting reflective practice, assisting improved decision-making and resulting in better outcomes for service users. She refers to the use of a 'cultural web' or culturagram (see Congress, 2015) as a tool for social workers in working with families from different cultural backgrounds (Figure 4.3).

In recognising the extension of cultural competence beyond ethnic diversity, Jack and Gill (2013) explore the application of a cultural competence model to working with poverty with children and families. To address the avoidance and ambivalence that exist within social work in relation to addressing poverty, they propose a four-stage approach that involves recognising individual differences in the experiences of poverty; understanding the links between poverty, family functioning and individual behaviour; developing the capacity to talk about poverty issues with families; and developing the anti-poverty potential of social work

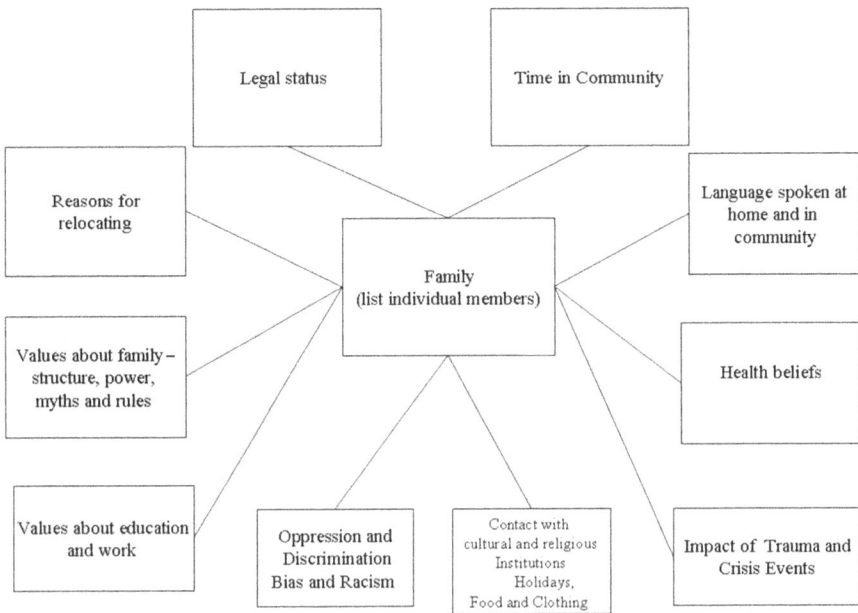

```
        Legal status              Time in Community

Reasons for                                    Language spoken at
relocating                                     home and in
                                               community
                    Family
                    (list individual members)

Values about family –
structure, power,                              Health beliefs
myths and rules


Values about education   Oppression and   Contact with         Impact of Trauma and
and work                 Discrimination   cultural and religious   Crisis Events
                         Bias and Racism  Institutions
                                          Holidays,
                                          Food and Clothing
```

Figure 4.3 Culturagram

services. They argue that the adoption of such an approach would seek to challenge poverty within families as opposed to practising in a way that reinforces such patterns of disadvantage (Jack and Gill, 2013). With regard to disability, Dupre (2012) argues that despite recognition of the importance of cultural and social diversity in social work education and practice, there is a lack of contemporary social work literature related to disability culture. She argues for a critical understanding of disability culture that is informed by the voices of disabled people.

Critiques of cultural competence

Criticisms of cultural competence approaches focus on the emphasis on the worker's individual attitudes and beliefs and an apparent lack of attention to institutional racism and other forms of oppression that occur on global and structural levels. Within Thompson's (2016) Personal, Cultural and Structural (PCS) model, cultural competence is located at the personal and cultural levels – for example, the individual and agency practise within social work and fail to address oppression that takes place on an institutionalised and systematic basis. Yan and Wong (2005) challenge the simplistic assumption of self-awareness within the models of cultural competence in that they imply that social workers are able to control and put aside their own cultural influences to become almost culture-neutral and impartial in their interactions with service users from different cultural backgrounds. Das and Anand (2016) also discuss the ambiguity within cultural competence and its confusion with associated concepts such as multiculturalism, cultural awareness/sensitivity and anti-oppressive practice that may have contradictory assumptions and agendas. It is suggested that contemporary social work practice has too readily been willing to reduce issues of human complexity to technocratic competency-based approaches (Williams and Graham, 2016), with a list of dos and don'ts based on stereotypical assumptions of culture and difference (Das and Anand, 2016).

To counter the criticisms of the lack of a structural focus, there has been some discussion of ideas of developing culturally competent or culturally responsive organisation. McPhatter (2004) describes a dynamic and protracted process for organisations in becoming more culturally competent that requires strategic leadership and genuine commitment from senior management to all levels of staff through the pursuing of a range of identifiable and measurable outcomes. These may include the development of a strategic plan for becoming culturally competent supported by a values or mission statement and backed by economic and human resources, training, community engagement and the employment of a workforce that reflects the community or service user population. There have been different approaches to make social work practice more reflective of the diversity that exists within the populations through attention to staff recruitment. The use of Section 11 of the 1966 Local Government Act was a highly controversial way of recruiting social workers in the 1980s and 1990s. While increasing participation in the social work profession is a desirable aim in itself, it should not be assumed as a prerequisite for culturally competent practice, and attempts to recruit a more culturally diverse workforce have not necessarily resulted in a fairer and more equitable service. The Laming Report (2003) concerning the death of Victoria Climbié highlights how social workers erroneously based the assessment of Victoria's subordination to a sign of culturally appropriate deference as opposed to a sign of fear and abuse.

Ratna Dutt, Director of the Race Equality Unit, highlighted that:

> There is some evidence to suggest that one of the consequences of an exclusive focus on 'culture' in work with black children and families, is that it leaves black and minority ethnic children in potentially dangerous situations, because the assessment has failed to address a child's fundamental care and protection needs.

(Dutt, 2003: 345)

Gelman (2004) suggests pursuing a 'racial match' between practitioners and service users may not be desirable, as a worker's ability to understand someone's situation need not solely rely on cultural factors. Our understanding of intersectionality or super diversity would suggest that the challenge for social work lies in developing an understanding of the intersection of other factors associated with poverty; legal status, sexuality or ability may be of equal significance at an individual and organisational level (Boccagni, 2015).

Critical approaches to working with diversity: Constructing difference

Ploesser and Mecheril (2012) explore some of the dominant discourses within social work regarding difference within social work practice. These have included a neglect of difference, and we have discussed some criticisms of social work that are based on a belief that everyone is equal, which fails to recognise difference, as well as colour-blind approaches, which fail to recognise ethnicity. The role of power, values and attitudes is important as these have the potential to disadvantage or negatively affect individuals or groups who, as a consequence of their differentiation, may experience discrimination, marginalisation and alienation as well as privilege, power and status. Such approaches tend to ignore the privileges and power relations linked to categories of difference, such as race or ethnicity, and thus negate social injustice on structural and institutional levels (see Dominelli, 2008; Laird, 2008). As we have discussed such criticisms have led to the belief that the recognition of difference is not only significant but also unavoidable; however, one could argue that in merely recognising difference, differences are reproduced and that social work creates and reinforces difference through the effect of targeting services at particular communities. Recipients of social work services are often stigmatised, particularly in the statutory services of child protection and mental health. Long-standing beliefs around the deserving and underserving create stigma and blame and differentiates between those who use services and those who do not. The label of client, service user, looked-after child, troubled family or person with complex needs provides an added layer of difference – one that has been created through professional assessments and intervention. The recognition of difference can lead to the reinforcement of stereotypes of what it means to be defined as a user of services. In addition, Fook (2016) discusses how we construct differences in terms of binary opposites and in this sense difference is defined not only as oppositional but also as mutually exclusive, having no sameness or lacking commonality. Continuing with the example of users of social work, being a service user is considered as being different to being a professional or a social worker. The difference constructed may imply that a social worker possesses power and authority, is knowledgeable and objective, whereas a service user lacks power and control, has limited knowledge and understanding and is manipulative or uncooperative. Differences are determined by dominant discourses within social work and society more widely and lead to the creation of hierarchies. The differences constructed are binary, oppositional and are constructed as fixed or essentialist (Fook, 2016).

Difference and the 'other'

The concept of other is implicit when we consider difference. In constructing difference there is a tendency to define one category in terms of the other and in doing so construct the other. This concept of the 'other', or processes of 'othering', is useful in understanding how social identities are constructed. Identities pertaining to race and gender, for example, are considered to be natural or innate; however, sociologists have explored how these are socially constructed. Othering is a process that identifies those that are thought to be different from oneself or the mainstream. In identifying the self as the norm, the individual or group is casted as the 'other'. It is a relational concept in which the 'other' is identified in relation to the perceived norm. Powerful groups are able to define and divide populations into us and them, those who belong and those who don't, not like us or just like us; through this creation of hierarchy, powerful groups seek to justify and reinforce patterns of domination and subordination. As Bauman (1991: 8) states:

> Woman is the other of man, animal is the other of human, stranger is the other of native, abnormality the other of norm, deviation the other of law-abiding, illness the other of health, insanity the other of reason, lay public the other of the expert, foreigner the other of state subject, enemy the other of friend.

Masocha (2015) examines discourses within the UK and Australia that construct asylum seekers as 'others' in which exclusionary and negative processes attribute negative characteristics and perceive asylum seekers as a 'subversive, dangerous and an illegitimate social group' (2015: 569). We can also see how political and media narratives concerning global terror and radicalisation have constructed Muslims or Islam as the 'other' (Silva, 2017).

One of the fundamental challenges in recognising diversity within social work is to do so in ways that acknowledge how difference is socially constructed, that challenge patterns of domination and oppression while not reinforcing and essentialising false categories of social identity. Ploesser and Mecheril (2011) adopt a deconstructive approach to difference in which they recognise not only the identification and recognition of difference, but also the problematic effects that accompany the recognition and representation of differences in arguing for new political approaches to difference.

Critical Race Theory

Critical Race Theory (CRT) seeks to recognises the problematic ways in which racial categories are ascribed to individuals and groups, and how processes of racialisation intersect with other forms of oppression to create patterns of domination and subordination (Delgado and Stefanic, 2001). CRT is a theoretical framework that originated in the USA in the 1970s as a response to discourses concerning Critical Legal Studies and the alleged objectivity of the US legal system. It has since transcended the social sciences and has been successfully applied as a theoretical framework to understanding race and racialised discourses within areas such as sport (Hylton, 2009) and education (Gillborn, 2008). Within social work, a CRT framework has been developed to inform social work pedagogy in the USA (Abrams and Moio, 2009; Constance-Huggins, 2013) and there is emerging literature in the UK (Crofts, 2013; Sargant, 2014). Unlike other anti-discriminatory perspectives, CRT highlights the centrality of racism in shaping patterns of domination and oppression in countries such as the USA and the UK. Some of the main features of a CRT framework include:

- A belief that racism is so endemic and pervasive within society that it is almost viewed as a normal part of everyday life. However, as race is socially constructed, racism is constantly changing.

- Its aim to extend beyond providing theoretical framework and retain a strong commitment to political activism, as its overall objective is the eradication of racism and the elimination of all forms of oppression.

- A critique of liberalism which challenges dominant liberal approaches, including neutrality, objectivity, meritocracy and universality.

▶

◀

- The notion of interest convergence – where racism as extreme white privilege operates to change policy law in the short term to preserve long-term interests of whiteness – promoting white self-interest, a concession.

- Concepts of 'whiteness' and white privilege that are not about attacking white people, but are instead about developing an understanding of the construction of whiteness and the power and privilege associated with that category.

- Storytelling and counter storytelling – constructing narratives of black experiences – of how inequality manifests itself, challenges a historicism and the importance of experiential knowledge.

- The recognition of intersectionality – which recognises debates around essentialism and anti-essentialism – and group identification.

Critical Race Theory, social work and adoption

CRT can be used to understand race within adoption social work. Sargant (2015) draws on a CRT lens to challenge notions of race neutrality and objectivity within the political narratives concerning transracial adoption practice and changes to adoption legislation. Since the 1980s good practice within adoption has considered that BAME children should, where possible, be placed in adoptive families that reflect their racial backgrounds, commonly known as ethnically matched or same-race placements. This practice was endorsed by legislation that stated 'in placing the child for adoption, the adoption agency must give due consideration to the child's religious persuasion, racial origin and cultural and linguistic background' (Adoption and Children Act, 2002, Section 1(5)). However, growing concerns about the effects of delays in matching led to the repeal of Section 1(5) with the introduction of the Children and Families Act 2014, with the effect of removing any reference to race and religion from adoption legislation. However, the experiences of Black children within adoption is more nuanced with differential experiences for children of mixed race, African/Caribbean and Asian backgrounds, and the Ofsted (2012) *Right on Time* report identified the court system as being largely responsible for delays within the process of adoption, as opposed to social workers seeking the perfect match.

We have discussed earlier how social workers are required to respond to the specific needs of an increasingly diverse population; however, changes in adoption legislation gives a contradictory message as to how far social workers should recognise the racial, religious and cultural backgrounds of children. A CRT perspective would suggest that this is not a legislative mistake but a deliberate neoliberal and ideological attack on so-called political correctness within social work (Kirton, 2016; Sargant, 2015). This reversal to colour-blind approaches with adoption is hidden under the guise of neutrality and objectivity of adoption legislation, but instead allows racism to operate unchallenged. Neville (2000) purports that if race is not seen racism is more difficult to challenge, and colour-blindness not only makes racism invisible, but also suggests that race does not matter and denies how racism contributes to system of inequality and oppression.

Other forms of critical thinking

Other critical approaches have developed as a way of understanding difference and oppression. Critical theories originate from a Marxist tradition from within the Frankfurt School of sociology, and unlike traditional theories that seek to explain and understand society, their emphasis is on developing a critique of society with a view to changing and eradicating disadvantage and oppression.

➢ **Queer Theory**, which has been largely absent from anti-oppressive perspectives within social work, emerged in the 1990s out of feminist studies (see Butler, 1990). It is based on the notion that sexuality is socially constructed and is a rejection of sexual normalcy, in particular the so-called heterosexual norm; it seeks to challenge the categorisations of gender and sexuality as fixed identities and distinguishes between what a subject does (role-taking) and what a subject is (the self). This challenges the idea of individuals as 'sexed-subjects' within a single restrictive orientation and recognises the intersectionality of other forms of identity, for example Black Queer Theory.

➢ **Critical Gender Theory** is based on the distinction between sex and gender, with sex referring to biological attributes and gender referring to socially constructed attributes and practices that are associated with a particular sex. It views gender oppression as endemic within society and provides a challenge to the hegemonic norms associated with gender to provide a counter-narrative. Like Queer Theory and other critical approaches, Critical Gender Theory regards identity as being **performative** (what we do) rather than **essential** (who we are). This view is recognised by the term 'doing gender', which discusses the ways in which gender is performed throughout everyday interactions.

➢ **Critical Disability Theory** is an emerging theoretical framework for the study and analysis of disability issues. It draws on a social model of disability in recognising that disability is socially constructed and that disability is not the inevitable consequence of impairment, but rather of complex socially constructed processes through the interrelationship between impairment, individual response to impairment, the social environment and disadvantage. A social environment that fails to meet the needs of people who do not match a society's expectation of 'normalcy' causes the experiences of people. Critical Disability Theory is intentionally political in that its objective is to support the transformation of society so that disabled people in all their diversity are equal participants and fully integrated into their communities. It provides a conceptual framework to understand the relationship between impairment, disability and society, and to inject disability interests into all policy arenas in promoting the voices of disabled people to contest mainstream conceptions of disability and to provide a counter-narrative to the negative constructions of disability and ability within society.

➢ **Critical Whiteness Theory** is another emerging US theory, which provides an analysis of the normalisation of whiteness within society, the effect of which establishes cultures and structures in which whiteness becomes invisible and masks sources of inequality based on racial categorisations and maintains white privilege in which people categorised as White are the beneficiaries of racial privilege. The intention of this approach is to make whiteness visible and understand how it permeates society to maintain power and inequality. Whiteness is not just about skin colour, and is not about an attack on white people, but about the recognition of a socially constructed category linked with power and privilege (for an introduction to critical whiteness studies, see Nayak, 2007).

Chapter summary

This chapter has explored the core themes relating to the diversity of the communities that social work serves and in this chapter we have examined:

➢ The concept of disproportionality within welfare services.

➢ The impact of social class, poverty and social inequality on social work practice.

➤ The context of diversity and super diversity in the UK.

➤ Different approaches to working with diversity, including cultural competence.

➤ The importance of critical thinking in diversity and critical theory.

In summary, we would like to leave you with a reflective piece of critical analysis: Lee and Greene (2008) suggest that the teaching of diversity within social work education is impacted by the lack of readiness of social work students to engage in challenging discussions about race and other forms of discrimination. There is a resistance to exploring white privilege among student groups, and social work educators may not feel competent to deal with the challenges and potential pitfalls. The context of contemporary higher education with large student groups may not create a conducive environment in which personal challenge and critical reflection can effectively take place. Rajan-Rankin's (2015) research regarding the perception of race and identity within social work education describes situations of tension and discomfort in which she describes a 'silent-scream' as white students squirmed in their seats, with feelings of being pinned down when race was discussed within the classroom. For Black students she identified experiences of colourism that reflected preferences for a light skin among Black and white communities and experiences of racism while undertaking social work training (usually within practice placements). She suggests that a challenge for social work is developing critical practice in which race and other forms of oppression are explored reflexively; yet within a climate of a fear of being accused of being a racist or unprofessional, that can leave some students paralysed to express their views, creating a conspiracy of silence (Rajan-Rankin, 2015). In discussing some of the ways in which social work theory has sought to understand and operationalise ways of working with diversity, this chapter has highlighted the complex nature of difference and its relationship to forms of inequality and disadvantage. Building on this critical context the next chapter will draw on some of the themes highlighted within the diversity discussion and explore them within a global context, connecting macro global theory to micro social work practice.

5

Global social work: Locating and understanding the impact of globalisation on social work

Within this chapter, we will explore the dynamic and compelling narrative of global social work. Before we move forward in presenting and locating the emerging discussion points within the chapter, we would like the reader to explore and position themselves intellectually; to do this, we would like the reader to reflect on the quote below:

> The World is becoming increasingly complex as the spread of hitherto unknown diseases, disasters both (hu)man-made and natural, poverty, and migratory movements of people pose new challenges for social workers.

> (Dominelli, 2010: 1)

Drawing on the global themes and issues raised by Dominelli in the quote above, this chapter will expand and develop the following key discussion areas.

Key concepts in this chapter include:

➢ The context and role of international social work.

➢ Global social work and civil society organisations.

➢ Globalisation and social work: understanding the macro to micro relationship.

➢ Global capitalism: social work in the age of austerity.

➢ The global movement of people: disaster, conflict, migration and social work.

The discussion in this chapter is also situated alongside the 'Readiness for Direct Practice Level' of the **Professional Capabilities Framework for**

Social Work (PCF) developed by the British Association of Social Workers (BASW).

Through reading Chapter 5 students should be able to:

Contexts and Organisations

➤ Demonstrate awareness of the impact of organisational context on social work practice.

Knowledge

➤ Demonstrate an initial understanding of the legal and policy frameworks and guidance that inform and mandate social work practice.

Rights and Justice

➤ Understand the principles of rights, justice and economic well-being, and their significance for social work practice.

Building on the PCF we would also like you to familiarise yourself with the **standards of proficiency (SOPs)** for social workers in England (2017) by the **Health and Care Professions Council (HCPC)**. The discussion that develops in this chapter has congruence with the following **HCPC SOPs (13.2 and 13.4)**:

➤ 13.2 Be aware of the different social and organisational contexts and settings within which social work operates.

➤ 13.4 Be able to understand in relation to social work practice: the impact of injustice, social inequalities, policies and other issues which affect the demand for social work services.

The context and role of international social work

As social work students, practitioners and educators we often start from a very localised or micro position of viewing social work as an activity that is located within our local community and delivered at a regional level through local government. We often embark on a social work course with the desire to work within the local social work department. Social work is often conceptualised as a moral and practical activity that is operationalised within the community, with individuals who require support or assistance to improve their social, material and welfare conditions (Jordan, 1984). Building on the position of a localised 'micro' perspective of social work practice, it is important to recognise that social work as a professional activity has developed in part as a response to macro social, economic and political forces (as discussed in Chapter 1). This chapter will develop a narrative that highlights the interconnection between **macro** global forces and **micro** social work practice.

Connecting the macro to the micro: Interconnected social work practice

The concept of the **macro**, or a larger global context, connecting to the **micro**, or small localised social work practice context, is essential to understanding contemporary social work practice. We live in a global community that has seen the world become more interconnected; this process of globalisation is formed, or constructed, in part from multiple macro social, political, economic and technological forces that intersect and act out on individuals' lives across the globe (Burawoy et al., 2010). Social work and social work practitioners experience globalisation in multiple moments of our lived experience; we live and act within a global framework. The fluid nature of global capital and international finance resonates across our lived experience. The impact of austerity measures on social work organisation, planning and delivery and the subsequent pay freeze for public sector workers after the financial crash or 'great recession' of 2008 are a visible reminder of the power of global capital to shape our economic and social experience. Social workers experience the process of migration or the movement of population in a direct way through the service users we work with. Working as a social worker you may never leave the locality social work team, but you will encounter individuals from multiple countries with complex social needs; often the local authority social worker will work directly with adults, children (often unaccompanied) and families who have migrated to the UK as a result of conflict, persecution or ecological disaster. While globalisation and our experience of it has many facets, the primary driver can be located within the social, political and economic force of liberal capitalism and its associated contemporary neoliberal mode of global, political and economic operation. Liberal capitalism can be viewed as the dominant and ascendant political and economic order: it has no significant challengers, and remains the dominant mode of local, national and international government and economics (see Chapter 1 for a concise definition of liberal capitalism). Building on Chapter 1, we will now explore and locate the key features of neoliberalism, so that we can situate and position global social work.

Neoliberalism

Neoliberalism continues the traditions of classic liberalism in its commitment to individual property rights, to the rule of law and to private enterprise. Neoliberalism has (and continues to) moved the political and economic model from the practices of embedded liberalism, essentially breaking down and reforming the social-democratic post-war consensus. This new and dynamic model operates on free market principles – with the ambition of removing all barriers to private enterprise. The freeing up of the market under neoliberalism was advanced through the dissolution of internal markets. In reality, this involved the removal of publicly owned services through the sale of national assets in the form of public utilities and manufacturing to private business. Neoliberalism has also promoted liberal and agile working practices through the removal of barriers to labour protection, and has promoted the removal of barriers, tariffs and protectionist practices that hinder free trade on a global scale.

Reflective questions

After reading the brief description of neoliberalism:

- Do you think neoliberalism is a good way of managing and ordering society?
- What social tensions can you see arising between the processes of free market ideology and public service provision?
- How do you think social work and welfare services will continue to develop under a neoliberal policy format?

The global **macro** economic and political forces of neoliberalism have resulted in the construction of open borders, free trade and the deregulation of international financial markets (Harvey, 2007). This has had a **micro** impact of creating vast wealth for technological, political and social elites, while simultaneously creating housing and employment insecurity for working people and public social services (Harvey, 2007). As a result, poverty and inequality have increased significantly, since the late 1970s, placing greater need on structural welfare and social services. This increased need has been combined with deregulation and privatisation of essential public services, which is a core requirement of political and economic neoliberal practices. As Neil Thompson posits in his recent work *Social Problems and Social Justice*, these social crises or

Social problems are not just isolated issues or concerns – they are parts of a broader nexus of social processes, institutions and structures.

(Thompson, 2017: 8)

Building on this narrative of global interconnectivity within this chapter, we will locate international social work and global social work practice within the twin narratives of **social order** and **social justice** (see Chapter 1). To understand the macro context we must position the role that international social work plays in responding to, managing and improving the social and material conditions of the populations it serves within a global context. International social work practice has a dual role to play in highlighting global issues and promoting **social justice** within a global arena. However, international social work also plays a significant role in promoting **social order** or maintaining the status quo of political and economic relationships through the provision of direct relief to those who experience inequality, natural disaster and manmade crises. This tension is a continuous theme that needs to be acknowledged.

Thinking global, acting local: The fluid role of social work

Within a global context, the role of social work has developed and evolved to meet the local, regional and national welfare priorities of governments, charities, religious institutions and political organisations in providing welfare services to citizens. The structural forces that have shaped social work may be located in wider social, political and economic forces; however, the professional context remains very much localised. The professional title of social worker is a relatively recent phenomenon and one that is deeply rooted in the post-World War II construction of welfare services within western liberal democracies. However, it must be argued and maintained that social work has wider vocational and professional roots. Globally, social support professionals have been in operation in religious organisations, philanthropic societies and self-help groups prior to the state maintaining a comprehensive social welfare programme (see Chapter 1). We must also recognise that globally, and locally, social work is congruent with wider vocational groupings, and can be placed within a much larger interconnected family of social and community-based helping professions. Members of this diverse professional family, while vociferous in maintaining their unique identity, have commonalities and coherency in their social focus in working with individuals and communities in social crises (see Figure 5.1).

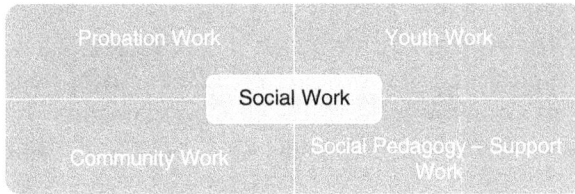

Figure 5.1 The social work family

One profession, many names: Learning from European social pedagogy

Even within countries where there is a coherent social work role, there are often multiple professional titles that work within a social work context (Figure 5.2). Despite the multiple titles, requirements and expressions of difference, the one binding commonality is our commitment to practice within the terrain of the social.

Social work within Europe is contingent on the social policy and legislation of the nation state that it resides within; as such, social work has evolved to suit the needs of the communities and state it serves. We have many names but one primary function, that of care and support of others in a time of social crises. One role that is worth exploring from a UK context is the role of the social pedagogue. The social pedagogue as a role has much to offer contemporary UK social work; in this globalised and professionalised world of statutory responsibilities, social work has become limited in how it engages, works with and supports others. It is time to remember our rich global traditions and roots – to support a new and engaged contemporary local practice. The social pedagogue role within continental Europe has a rich vocational and academic tradition; within the UK, the social pedagogy role often falls within the social support professions, and it is often marginalised

Figure 5.2 The multiple titles of international social work

by the higher status of social work as a statutory profession (Hill and Laredo, 2017). In writing this text, we the authors believe that this division is unhelpful, and the notions of status and professional activity create barriers to genuine learning and best practice. The role of a social pedagogue offers an interesting and refreshing insight into the direction and evolution of international social work practices (Petrie et al., 2008).

Head, heart and hand

Central to the social pedagogue approach are the following principles:

- A grounded education of the **head** that promotes cognitive learning and problem solving.

- An awareness of a person's emotional and spiritual development, locating their **heart** and allowing them space and time to develop as a whole person.

- Direct support and guidance to build practical skills of the **hand**, from independent living and self-care techniques to managing daily activities.

Sources: Cameron, 2005; Boddy et al., 2001.

Within UK social work practice there have been calls for a return to a connected, and grounded, way of working with individuals and families. Social pedagogy offers social work in the UK a chance to engage with a tactile and relationship-based approach with service users (Ferguson, 2011).

Global social work and civil society organisations

Social work within a global context has developed at an international level across multiple organisations and platforms.

The three global social work platforms shown in Figure 5.3 work at a regional, national and international level, with each nation state having a national platform that feeds into the international organisation, using the micro to macro framework of knowledge exchange and practice transfer. In the UK the BASW acts as a conduit for the International Federation of Social Workers (IFSW). Despite multiple social work or social professional roles, different regional and national social work requirements and multiple professional tasks, the key global platforms have attempted to

Figure 5.3 Global social work platforms

define social work. The global definition of social work that follows was approved by the IFSW General Meeting and the International Association of Schools of Social Work (IASSW) General Assembly in July 2014:

> Social work is a practice-based profession and an academic discipline that promotes social change and development, social cohesion, and the empowerment and liberation of people. Principles of social justice, human rights, collective responsibility and respect for diversities are central to social work. Underpinned by theories of social work, social sciences, humanities and indigenous knowledge, social work engages people and structures to address life challenges and enhance wellbeing.
>
> (IFSW and IASSW, 2014)

Social work beyond borders: A short history of global social work platforms

To understand how we arrived at a global definition of social work, it is necessary to explore the development of international and global social work platforms. The desire to promote social order and stability through the management of the multiple social crises that arise from rapid social change can be considered a cornerstone and catalyst for the development of local and global social work practice. The vast social upheaval of the late nineteenth century and early twentieth century had seen the movement of populations across Europe from rural agrarian communities to urban environments (see Chapter 1). The rapid social change undermined traditional community welfare structures, placing people in new economic and social relationships in an industrial environment that was prone to social and economic crises due to the 'boom and bust' cyclical nature of capitalism. Global social work as a profession can be observed as developing, in part, as a response to the global forces of industrialisation and urbanisation. The First International Social Work Conference was held in Paris, France, in June 1928:

It was part of the larger International Social Welfare fortnight, which included meetings of the International Congress on Voluntary and Statutory Assistance, the International Conference of Social Work, the International Housing and Town planning Congress and the International Exhibition and Social progress.

(Kuilema, 2015: 3)

By the early twentieth century, the processes of global industrialisation, urbanisation and economic inequality had unified local and national social work, welfare and housing agencies to form an international conference to discuss the planning, provision and promotion of welfare practices. The conference platform highlighted the interconnected position of social work and its complex relationship with housing and wider social welfare and health organisations. The First International Social Work Conference developed a nuanced understanding of the multidisciplinary nature of social work. The conference attendees included urban planners, trade union officials, midwives, medical doctors, child welfare workers, academics, public health workers, government officials, prison officers, rabbis and priests (Strauss, 1929). Then, as now, social work can be situated as a multidisciplinary activity that intersects multiple agencies and organisations. The conference also acknowledged that through its multidisciplinary nature, there was a need for coherent education and training to support practitioners and volunteers working in the newly emerging social work arena. This process of professionalisation has become a cornerstone of social work education, training and practice (Eilers, 2003; Kniephoff-Knebel and Seibel, 2008). The conference also established the position that social work transcended nation states – that international and national social work had commonalities that required an international platform to share experiences and best practice. This foundation of international dissemination and coordination of collaboration remains a solid cornerstone of international social work practice and education. The first conference set a marker for development and a precedent for established international relations with social work (Alden, 1929).

With a clear marker set for international collaboration and practice a Second International Conference on Social Work was called to renew and explore international collaborations. During the Second International Conference on Social Work, held in Frankfurt in 1932, a more formalised social work formation was created at an international level. This included the provisional statutes of the International Permanent Secretariat of Social Workers (IPSSW), which were agreed by eight founding members: Belgium, Czechoslovakia, France, Germany, Great Britain, Sweden, Switzerland and the USA. The IPSSW was initially based in Berlin (IFSW, 2017c). The historical context to the Second International

Conference on Social Work is important. Post-World War I (1914–1918) Europe had transitioned into the Great Depression (1929–1941). The fault lines of western liberal capitalism, in the form of political and economic conflict, were laid bare. Global conflict, both political and economic, had highlighted the failings of the values of liberalism, those of self-help, hard work and individualism, to provide economic and social security. Within this economic context, the social work international formation has met regularly since and has developed into the International Federation of Social Workers (IFSW, 2017c). It was the Fifth International Conference on Social Work, held in post-World War II Paris in 1950, that saw the development of an agreement to form the IFSW. This was further developed in Munich in 1956, with the establishment of the permanent secretariat of the IFSW which was established with offices in New York, in close proximity to the United Nations (UN). The post-World War II world of clearly defined superpowers in the Capitalist West and Communist East heralded a new era of liberal global interventionism. Social work within this period can be observed as a rapidly expanding global political and social actor, with a newly emerging mission and role in international development. The contemporary IFSW describes its role and mission as:

> A global organisation striving for social justice, human rights and social development through the promotion of social work, best practice models and the facilitation of international cooperation.

(IFSW, 2017a)

The opening statement of the global social work platform highlights a social justice-driven foundation, highlighting congruency with western liberal values of freedom, justice and individualism. The IFSW, developing a deeper global role, saw the introduction of the *Journal of International Social Work* and an increased role within the UN, when in 1959 it was granted consultative status with the UN Economic and Social council (ECOSOC). The 1960s saw the international scope of the IFSW develop through its training and education role with the UN. The 1970s and 1980s saw an increased political role for the IFSW, with its suspension of an IFSW platform member in South Africa for its involvement with apartheid (IFSW, 2017c). During this period, the IFSW also developed a global definition for social work as a professional role; and it was given 'peace messenger' status by the UN, in recognition for its global development activities (IFSW, 2017b).

Within late modern society, the IFSW has continued to develop the range and scope of social work as a global actor through partnership work with the IASSW. This partnership has seen the development of a global training manual, *Social Work and Rights of the Child* (IFSW, 2002). The IASSW, as an organisation, developed in parallel to the IFSW from the First International Social Work Conference held in Paris in 1928. The IASSW is an umbrella organisation that covers all the schools of social work and supports international educational, research, scholarship, cooperation and good practice in social work education. The combination of the IFSW and IASSW highlights an increased and pragmatic response to global social change through cooperation. This mutual aid and cooperation has continued with IFSW and IASSW having a Global Definition of Social Work adopted at the UN level in 2001 (IASSW and IFSW, 2017a), and the publication of both the *Statement of Ethics in Social Work* (IFSW, 2017b) and the *Global Standards for the Education and Training of the Social Work Profession* (IFSW and IASSW, 2004). This global programme and coherent message for international social work has also seen an increased role for the IFSW with the World Health Organization (WHO) recognising the IFSW through consultative status. This international platform continues with the development of the Global Agenda for Social Work (IASSW and IFSW, 2012). A new partner has joined the platform of the IFSW and IASSW: the International Council for Social Welfare (ICSW). The Global Agenda for Social Work focuses on macro themes of the dignity and worth of the person; environmental sustainability; well-being and sustainable human relationships; and social work education (IASSW and IFSW, 2012). Building on this collective discourse the Global Agenda for Social Work highlights the important and intrinsic link between the role of social work in maintaining **social order** within the development framework of western liberal capitalism and the promotion of **social justice** for those communities that are often left behind by the global forces unleashed by capitalism. A key highlight from the global development of international social work is a multi-professional and multi-agency approach to practice; to situate and explore global social work coherently, it is necessary to locate it, within the organisations it operates within.

Global social work and civil society organisations

The role of international non-governmental organisations (NGOs) or civil society organisations (CSO) deserves exploring, as they are often responsible for the delivery of structural global social work interventions. Many major CSO have formed international networks such as the Conference of Non-Governmental Organisations (CoNGO). This loose federation allows greater interaction with global institutions such as the UN and its associated agencies including UNICEF and UNDP. CSOs are a loose flex- ible definition and social work platforms previously discussed such as the IFSW and IASSW fall under the CSO category. However, for the con- text of this discussion, we will focus on international organisations that operate within disaster areas or provide a humanitarian or social relief function. There are far too many CSOs to name; however, the most vis- ible social work organisations include the International Federation of the Red Cross and Red Crescent Societies, Help the Aged International, World Vision, Oxfam and Cafod. These CSOs are major actors and have operational bases in both the Global North and the Global South. It must be noted that many CSOs originate within societies located within the Global North; critics have highlighted that they are a soft extension of the political and economic power, acting as a **social order** role, for the Global North and can often undermine the activities of local NGOs and governments within the Global South (Mohanty, 1992). Often CSOs have more money and resources than local and regional government, resulting in a conflictual relationship; they have been called the 'lords of poverty' through using aid as an enterprise business (Hancock, 1991). The criti- cism has a historical, political and economic context. Many nations within the Global South have been historical colonies of the Global North. The countries of the Global North, such as the UK and other West- ern European nations (and later the USA), developed through the coloni- sation of the Global South; this mercantile imperialism saw the extension of power not only through force of arms and acquisition of land and resources, but also through the intervention of western religious, phil- anthropic and charitable organisations. Many of the global CSOs have their routes and history within the early colonial expansion period due to their religious foundations and geographic-political location in the Global North. Colonisation was a multifaceted process, with social organisations playing a central role, alongside political and economic actors – such as governments and private industry. Given this historical context, interven- tionism within the Global South must be reflected on critically and expe- rienced through the process of colonisation. We must also recognise that many of the resources for industrial advances and western civilisation are obtained from the Global South. The asset-stripping of resources by the Global North and return of limited economic support in unequal interna- tional financial support/debt and humanitarian intervention is a legacy that continues to this day. Social work at a local, national and global level can be viewed as a social order safety measure for capitalism. Where unequal, social and political relationships develop, institutions and pro- fessions develop in part as a response and as a measure to maintain social order. Unequal economic and social development requires management and intervention on both a micro and a macro level. As Dominelli (2010) highlights, complex global power relationships are all matters that social workers must face when working within local and international organisations. Quite simply, within social work we are either part of the solution or part of the problem (Thompson, 1992). We cannot often choose or define our practice; however, we can recognise power relationships, and in doing so seek to minimise the harm and work in ways that do not replicate them in our daily micro practice. Building on this analysis of power relationships, our next macro to micro analysis of power and social work will explore global capitalism.

Case study

Social work has different priorities within the communities it serves; these priorities are usually determined by the geopolitical and economic context of the countries within which social work CSOs operate. Social work in the Global North differs from that of the Global South; we have much to learn from the different social, political and economic contexts of global social work practice.

Read the following descriptions and answer the reflective questions.

Waterdeep Town

Waterdeep is a large city; it has up to a million residents within the metropolitan area. The town was a former manufacturing centre for textiles. Within the last 20 years, the heavy industry has closed down. There has been a consistent local recession since this period with jobs not replaced in the same numbers, and the industry that has relocated does not offer the same pay and conditions. Many residents are unemployed and the older population has complex health problems related to industrial diseases. The residents have national health care, education, local social care, criminal justice services and access to basic welfare benefits. Recent changes to the welfare benefits system have led to people becoming sanctioned or removed from benefits due to new administrative requirements. Owing to the recession, traditional welfare services have cut service provision. The town has a high birth rate and a big youth population. Crime and anti-social behaviour are on the rise; this is in part related to illegal substance use supply and consumption. Recently new immigrants have arrived and there is competition for social housing services.

Cimmerian City

Cimmerian City is a newly emerged city, situated within a large rural area, with access to the coast and natural resources. It has a population of 1 million with

▶

◀

over half of the citizens migrating within the last five years (from rural areas). Global corporations have opened up factories, a port and mining operations in rural areas. The population is primarily young, and there is a high birth rate per person. Basic services such as utilities are struggling to keep up with the newly emerging suburbs and shanty towns at the edge of the city. The city also has limited public services such as criminal justice, education and health care. Some, mainly working-class, areas have a high infant mortality rate, and do not have access to water or electricity. Educational access is a limited resource. There is no national welfare support system. Employment is available but conditions are precarious and conditions are harsh.

Reflective questions

Reflecting on the descriptions of Waterdeep City and Cimmerian City:

- Where would you position both of the towns in a geopolitical context? Do you think they are situated in the Global North or Global South?

- What would be the social work priorities in those areas? Can you list them in a hierarchy of needs?

- How should social work be delivered in both these areas? Should it be through local agencies or global social work CSOs?

Global capitalism: Social work in the age of austerity

One of the primary premises of this chapter is to explore the implicit link between macro forces on a global scale and micro social work practice. Global and international social work practice is not just contained within the macro international platforms and global civic society organisations; it is also the micro activity of the social work practitioner, coming to terms with the impact of global forces on the communities and individuals we serve. Without a coherent and critical understanding of the society we live and work within, we are reduced to reacting to social crises through a narrow individualised framework. This contemporary tendency of global macro political, social and economic forces to shift the burden of care from the collective state to an individual citizen can be considered one of the greatest threats to the social foundations of society. The burden of individual responsibility for the provision of all social and health-related needs is too great to bear for any one family or individual (Bauman, 2009).

Reflective questions

Reflecting on your personal, social, educational and health development from the moment of your birth:

- How many institutions have contributed to your personal, social, health and educational development?

- How many people from these institutions have had a positive impact on your life?

- Would you be able to afford these services if you had to pay for them directly at the point of access?

The welfare state or the 'social work state' is one visible example of the interconnected nature of human existence (Bauman, 2009). The provision of collective welfare and care services as a political and social construct is a visible reminder that working as a collective, and as a societal group, to socially and materially reproduce for ourselves, is one of the greatest achievements of our civilisation. Quite simply, isolated and on our own we cannot achieve or deliver the social and material conditions we need to thrive and exist as an individual within a larger community. Since the Great Recession and financial crash of 2008 we have seen a shift in the macro discourse emanating from global social, political and economic institutions. This can be observed as a visible speeding up of the free market individualisation discourse that seeks to isolate and divide our public and social-democratic–social work structures; this critical narrative will be further explored in the discussion later in the chapter. The movement of global capital and the experience of global and local austerity after the Great Recession have had a profound impact on global and local social work. This book is not advocating a revolutionary political position. We are proposing that social work and social workers seek to counter the worst excesses of the dominant social, political and economic forces that shape our services, practice and helping relationships. The majority of students entering the social work profession seek to do so from the position that they would like to help and care for others. I believe a truly radical position, for social work, is to start from the perspective of a critical examination of the social, political and economic context that places individuals, communities and services in the position of been unable to care for themselves or others. The **Great Recession** (2007–2008) has seen an increase in poverty and inequality within the UK and the reduction of the human and social services that seek to alleviate and manage social and economic inequality (IFS, 2017). However, we must acknowledge that the Great Recession is merely a 'lens' or 'focus' for a greater examination of the much broader position of global capital, and its role in the process of globalisation, that has taken place within the neoliberal period and which has dominated our social, political and economic lived experience from the late 1970s onwards. This position of the Great Recession as a catalyst and context for broader understanding of neoliberal forces is important to the discussion moving forward within this chapter.

The Great Recession: Global capital, austerity and local social work

The Great Recession of 2007–2008 has had a truly profound impact on the structure of society on a global and local scale. Understanding the operational context of capital is of central importance within a global and local social work context. The service users social work operates with and supports often comprise the most vulnerable sections of society (Ferguson and Woodward, 2009). The users or recipients of social work services are often located within the 'working class', 'blue collar' or 'underclass' section of society, depending on which term of reference you prefer (Skeggs, 2004; Van Horn and Schaffner, 2003; Wright, 1994). I personally prefer the term working class, and find the use of underclass both divisive and derogatory; the 'othering' of working-class communities though language is an act of symbolic violence, and can be considered a tool that political and social elites nurture to foster division and reinforce the contemporary political and economic order (McKenzie, 2015). In locating and exploring the position of our service users, it must be acknowledged that our service users are often found within the most precarious section of the working class; they are often underemployed or unemployed as a result of global free market reforms around labour flexibility (Standing, 2011). Owing to our service users' precarious position, they are often the first to experience the impact of economic recession. The effects of global recession are often multifaceted, with our service users often being the first to lose their employment (as they are often underemployed or on flexible employment contracts), while simultaneously experiencing a reduction in service provision for the broader collectivised welfare services that they often rely on (Seymour, 2014). Before we move forward with the discussion, we should explore the context and meaning of recession within an economic and social context.

What is a recession?

Recession is a term used to describe a reduced period of economic activity; in an academic context, recession is a contraction phase of a business cycle with two or more consecutive quarters of gross domestic product (GDP) contraction. GDP is the measure of all final goods and services produced. It is often used to determine economic performance within a whole country or region. The Great Recession only met the criteria for a global recession under International Monetary Fund guidelines, highlighting a reduction in global GDP, for the single calendar year in 2009.

The Great Recession can be positioned as having its roots within the process of globalisation and the political and economic practices of neoliberalism. One of the primary driving factors that caused the Great Recession can be found within the deregulation of international and local financial practices. This 'freeing' up of the market created and facilitated a situation whereby protective regulatory factors were removed. (Smith and Craft, 2011). Many of the original local and global protections such as the Glass-Steagall Act in the USA had been put in place due to the last international financial crash in 1929 (Nersisyan, 2015). The economic zeitgeist of global neoliberalism prior to the Great Recession was premised on the deregulation of international finance (global capital), and the continued development of housing as a commodity; this was further supported by accessible credit-debt for citizens, who had seen a reduction in their income through wage stagnation–depreciation (Harvey, 2017; Hetzel, 2012). The Great Recession was facilitated and nurtured though the opening up of home ownership to many individuals on low incomes, and in many cases those on social welfare and low incomes, particularly within the USA and the UK (Harvey, 2017). The promotion of cheap credit and financial loans to low-income families formed part of the process of financial deregulation; those who could not afford to own homes suddenly had access to the credit needed to buy them. The privatisation of housing and the move towards owner-occupiers rather than affordable social housing saw a rush of people wanting to leave the rental market. With house prices increasing and wages remaining stagnant, if not losing value in real terms, families and individuals were forced into ever-increasing borrowing arrangements. These financial loans were then repackaged and sold on to other financial organisations: this process was called securitisation (Hetzel, 2012). Mortgage-based securities became a high-risk high dividend investment. All of this was possible only through the calculated economic and political position of neoliberalism in freeing up the global markets (Farlow, 2013). Housing and material security for families and individuals can be considered as one of the basic premises of all good social work and welfare provision. As the economic cycle shifted, to a downturn, people began defaulting on their mortgage repayments. The packaging of the mortgage-based securities as safe regulated investments, when in fact they were high risk, caused a collapse within the global banking and financial sector (Farlow, 2013). The entire world looked on in shock; the leading financial experts in the UK and globally gathered; nobody, apart from a few lone voices, had seen this crash coming. The shock and horror at the crash was played out across global platforms; the Queen of England penned a letter to leading experts at the London School of Economics, asking how the crash could not have been foreseen (Harvey, 2017). The experts of global finance reported that they did not foresee the structural risk inherent within the system. This is an uncomfortable answer for those who have experienced the direct importation of neoliberal practices within social work practice: one of the primary values diffused within practice is the systematic assessment of risk. Social workers are constantly asked to assess risk to the individual, community and organisation. The assessment of risk is common across all the specialisations and technical practice areas of social work. It resonates as both perverse and dubious that government would seek to use neoliberal models of risk to regulate all aspects of social life under safeguarding of children and adults within social work, but fails to regulate and safeguard a macroeconomic system that is the primary means for all individuals to socially and materially support themselves within society.

Capitalism in its neoliberal global format can be observed as either failing or acting out a standard economic pattern, that of the boom and bust cycle of capital (Flaschel and Greiner, 2012). The removal of safeguards and free market policies had created a situation whereby the global banking sector was in a state of terminal collapse. A cynical and detached observer may position that the crisis, if not orchestrated, was, at the very least, used as an opportunity to further the process of neoliberal globalisation. The mantra of free market neoliberalism had placed a sacrosanct faith in the provision of the market; the prime message of capitalism is that the success or failure of business is decided by the market. However, in the case of the Great Recession the doctrine of free market ideology was reversed, and national governments stepped in to bail out a range of financial institutions who were deemed too big to fail (Michie, 2015). The incumbent Labour government in the UK bailed out the financial and banking sector to the tune of an overall package of £500 billion (Swaine, 2008). This practice was also mirrored in the USA, with government intervention to buy up toxic mortgage securities. What we have observed within the process of the Great Recession is the socialisation of private financial debts on a macro and micro scale.

Within Europe, the great recession played out within vulnerable European countries in the Mediterranean and Celtic fringe. Many EU countries moved the recession into a sovereign debt crisis, seeking to deliver relief through the intervention of taxpayer funds from national economies. Greece experienced acute problems as it faced large-scale public debts. The European intervention included a bailout of several key countries headed by 'the troika', which included the European Commission, the European Central Bank and the International Monetary Fund. The rescue packages all contained a premise that national economies and economic structures would be reformed on free market and neoliberal principles; the premise of which was a redefinition of the relationship between public ownership and private enterprise having access to untapped public markets (Clark et al., 2015). Many European countries, most notably Greece, Ireland and Spain, embarked on 'austerity' budgets to counter deficits relative to GDP. This reduction in spending to improve long-term economic performance is a contested field, with key critics such as Krugman (2008) highlighting that austerity does not support pragmatic growth in real terms. However, reflecting on this position, austerity must be viewed through economic ideology; austerity is about redefining the relationship between the state, the individual and the community. Austerity 'programmes' have primarily reduced public welfare, social services and education and welfare institutions within the UK and Europe (Jordan and Drakeford, 2012). The crisis post Great Recession continues to be used as an opportunity to redefine the post-war consensus within Europe, removing the social welfare safeguards put in place by the embedded liberal model of government, and further freeing up possible untapped markets to private enterprise. The resolution for the crisis has quite simply been a further prescription of globalisation, neoliberalism and further entrenched business practices.

The transfer of privately accumulated debt, as well as mismanagement within the global financial sector, leading up to the 'Great Recession' can be viewed as one of the greatest sleight of hands by the political and business elites in modern history. We have seen a socialism or collective rescue from above for capitalism, in the form of direct state intervention that runs contradictory to the free market economics of contemporary neoliberalism and globalisation (Toarna and Cojanu, 2015). The socialisation and collectivisation of private finance has been named 'Capitalist Socialism' by Slavoj Zizek (2009). The narrative of 'too big to fail', and that 'we must do something', was a prominent discourse of the period (Zizek, 2009). The 'shock' of the crisis was another dominant theme; a discourse was created that the financial collapse was an event beyond the control of government, which not even the greatest political and economic thinkers of our time could have predicted. Zizek (2009: 9) challenges this 'we couldn't have predicted it' discourse:

> The only truly surprising thing about the 2008 financial meltdown is how easily the idea was accepted that its happening was an unpredictable surprise which hit the markets out of the blue. Recall the demonstrations which throughout the first decade of the new millennium, regularly accompanied meetings of the IMF and World Bank: the protesters' complaints took in not only the usual anti-globalizing motifs (the growing exploitation of Third World countries, and so forth), but also how the banks were creating the illusion of growth by playing with fictional money, and how this would all end in a crash.

The global forces of neoliberal capitalism have, within all its forms and cycles, periods of economic expansion and contraction. A detached observer may reason that this boom and bust cycle is a natural consequence, due to the arrangement of political and economic social relationships. However, the presentation of crises and the need to intervene have demonstrated that political and business elites have used these crises as an opportunity. It may even be argued that the rapid expansion of liberal capitalism is positioned on the exploitation of crises in the form of a kind of shock therapy (Klein, 2008). After the shock of economic and financial collapse, it can be observed that the chaos and confusion lead to a situation in which government and political and business elites have deuced that the solution would be to further entrench and expand the free market principles that led to the global recession. This business-as-usual model promotes a culture of disaster capitalism, further locking in the global social, political and economic macro force of neoliberalism (Klein, 2008). It also should be acknowledged that social work as a professional activity has developed in part as a response to the cyclical nature of capitalism. Social work has acted and operated as both a buffer and a safeguard against some of the worst excesses and economic shocks that capitalism has forced working-class communities to endure (see Chapter 1). The development of welfare safeguards, personal social services and wider education, housing and health care services all seek to mitigate the worst impact of unemployment and exclusion from the labour market. The removal of social work and social welfare safeguards poses a threat not only to our professional role and institutions, but to the marginalised communities we serve.

The global movement of capital: Social work and austerity in the UK

The impact of the global recession, while technically short-lived in economic and academic terms, has had a far-reaching impact on the political, economic and social landscape. The austerity discourse that began with political and economic response has continued to shape local government and non-statutory social work agencies long after the period of economic instability. The Great Recession and the austerity period that followed should be explored and located within a greater economic, political and social narrative. Since the inception of the welfare state and the development of embedded liberalism (see Chapter 1) within the UK post-war consensus, we have seen political and economic elites attempt to reshape and reform the system from above and below. It should also be acknowledged that social work has also been a promoter as well as a critic of this social reform at key moments. Social work and community social care have often been championed and promoted as a cheaper and more flexible alternative to residential care within institutions, as well as a more ethical and socially better way of managing child and adult social care provision (Jones, 1983). One of these key themes, or moments, that we will explore through the lens of the Great Recession is the process of deinstitutionalisation and free market reforms to health and social care within adult and children's services. This process began during the post-war period and has continued under every successive government administration since. The political administration may be considered a side show – the key word within this context is administration. Government, within the neoliberal period, should be viewed as the 'administrators' and organisers of the economic macro force of global capitalism. The Great Recession was another opportunity to further deepen these reforms; once again, disaster capitalism can be seen as making every crisis an opportunity for further growth. The last 40 years or so of policy and legislation developed within health and social care can be viewed within this context. Below are three major policy–legislative frameworks that have had a significant impact on the delivery of social work and social care pre and post Great Recession.

- The National Health Service and Community Care (Act NHS and CCA) 1990.

- The Health and Social Care Act 2012.

- The Care Act 2014.

The freeing up of the market within social work cannot be examined from the position of social work agencies alone. The multidisciplinary and collaborative nature of social work sees its professionals and services dispersed across wider health and social care institutions. It must be recognised that market reforms have become part of the economic doctrine of neoliberalism and cultural zeitgeist of consumer experience, which extends beyond the period of the Great Recession. The Great Recession was merely another opportunity to promote the new economic order through a crisis. As students, practitioners and academics of social work, we must be careful not to romanticise the vast public service institutions that formed historical service provision. The provision of public services by the state (as explored in Chapter 1) has not been without controversy: vulnerable children and adults have been confined, abused, neglected and denied a voice within multiple historical institutions. The dominance of state provision led to a lack of choice, control and personal autonomy. In acknowledging this conflictual foundation, we can see how the promotion of market-based reforms has had both a popular resonance and commonalities with the ethical dimensions of professional social work. Gilbert and Powell (2012) highlight that contemporary market reforms under the neoliberal framework of policy and economic arrangement are broadly congruent with the desires of service user movements, feminist social work and wider disability advocacy movements; given this conflation of economic practices and social movements, we can see a compelling narrative within the reshaping and reordering of public services.

The most visible aspects of contemporary market reforms within health and social care have come in the form of a dual transfer of responsibility for service funding and provision from the state to the individual, combined with the private sector becoming the major provider of adult care services. The Great Recession has been used as a mechanism to further implement and deepen market reforms. One of the primary drivers of this transfer of responsibility from the state to the individual–private sector – or liberation, as the policy narrative positions – is contained within the Health and Social Care Act 2012 and its associated supporting policy documentation. This process was described as the 'liberating' and freeing up of services through the commissioning of broader health and social care services within a competitive tendering model. One of the most compelling features of neoliberalism and its associated economic and social change has been to draw on a powerful and compelling narrative that conflates business practice and economic change with the philosophy of individualism, choice, control and autonomy. This careful positioning has allowed the most drastic cuts to services and welfare provision to be positioned as radical and desirable change. Who does not want choice, personal freedom or control over their care and service provision? One of the major reforms within contemporary health and social care has come in the form of personalisation. The introduction of personalisation as a concept with social care services has been a central driving force within adult social care (DoH, 2010a). Personalisation has been implemented in the main using direct payments and personal budgets; money and resources have been transferred from local government to individual service users (Leece, 2012). Through this process, local government social work services have become a facilitator of advice and information, in the provision of a menu of options within health and social care. This process has not been done within a context of expansion and investment from central government. This transfer of responsibility from the state to the individual, with the private sector and social enterprise as broker and provider, has been implemented in a time of economic austerity. In this context, personalisation can be viewed as a means for reducing costs for the state and promoting individual responsibility within a competitive free market environment. Personalisation, while offering choice, also positions the service user as a broker of informal care, and with the added responsibility of becoming an employer.

The implementation of personalisation has been positioned alongside the increased and deepening role for the private sector in providing solutions to adult social care provision. It must be recognised that private health and social care have become part of the overarching framework of neoliberalism since the late 1970s; the opening up of public sector services as new markets is a core requirement of political and economic neoliberal practices. The Great Recession has merely been its latest conduit or form of shock therapy to remove the last vestiges of the post-war welfare state. This gradual privatisation of public resources has had two very public crisis points during the years after the Great Recession that are worthy of exploration: that of Southern Cross, and the Mid Staffordshire NHS Trust. These crises in the free market have exposed the fragility of the public sector and private sector relationship, and they have highlighted the overarching themes that underpinned the foundations of the Great Recession: deregulation and asset-stripping for profit. The Southern Cross debacle has its roots in the NHS and CCA 1990. Initially care home provision was transferred out to multiple small unit providers under the direction of local governments who had to commission 90% of all social care services.

> Between 1980 and 2001 we see a transition from public to private sector in care. From 1980 to 2001, private care accounted for 18 to 85% of all residential care. This was further entrenched in 2005 with 90% of care being in private organisations.

> (Johnson et al., 2005: 236)

This process of marketisation in adult social care, while initially pro-ducing growth in small to medium business, has seen the introduction of large multinational private equity organisations buying up smaller units. In 2004 the US-based company Blackstone acquired the New Zealand-based company Southern Cross Healthcare for £162 million pounds. Southern Cross had only been in the hands of another private equity company West Private Equity (Jordan and Drakeford, 2012). This global movement of private finance then capitalised on the market, with Blackstone selling the freeholds or property rights of the care homes to free up further investment. This led to Blackstone essentially stripping assets and then creating more capital to buy more care organisations; this process has been highlighted as a business cartel approach to adult residential care (Scourfield, 2007). Blackstone, through Southern Cross, then acquired Surrey-based NHP in a deal worth £564 million (Jordan and Drakeford, 2012). This rapid high-risk turnover of care homes for profit and gambling with the property as capital represented a high-stakes game. It almost mirrors the high-stakes game that was played with mort-gages and private equity that led to the Great Recession. Residential care, from the perspective of a multinational corporation, is an asset; it can be considered as merely another high-risk profit game that comes with the added benefits of state guarantee for payment and services. This guar-antee came in to effect in the years following the Great Recession; the Qatari Investment Authority then bought Southern Cross and sold off its physical estates or free holds creating a large profit (Jordan and Drakeford, 2012). Public perception of care costs going directly to care provision is a misconception; this process of privatisation essentially allows private organisations to move large amounts of public money and transfer it overseas, all within a legal framework – in this example through complex tax avoidance schemes, using off-shore companies and tax havens. By 2011 the removal of key assets, or tax avoidance methods, combined with austerity economics had created a complex and terminal situation where Southern Cross collapsed. The government and taxpayers were left with the cost of deferring a £20 million tax bill. The 'rescue' of the care home service was built on precarious grounds with Four Seasons Healthcare taking over. Four Seasons themselves were found to also have a complex trading history as a private organisation. A group of lenders exchanged £1.5 billion owed to them by the group in exchange for shares. This put Four Seasons in the unique position of being 40% owned by the Royal Bank of Scotland, which at the time was 80% owned by the public purse as a result of the financial rescue package put in place by the Great Reces-sion (Jordan and Drakeford, 2012). What can be observed in this process is the opportunism of private interests; the only income within care is the money from the public purse or private individuals for care services provided. If you take away structural facilities such as buildings and allow profit to be extracted, this will undermine the integrity of the organisation, as it has a fixed income. This profit extraction and collapse were foreseeable as a financial outcome. What we can observe in this process is a privatisation of profit and a socialisation of public risk. There are no clear lessons to be drawn from this, other than systemic change in the form of a return of care services to public ownership. The freeing up of the social work–social care market has supported a further integration of high-stakes, casino-style financial gambling with vulnerable populations; the end of the public sector monopoly within care can be observed as creating a situation where the most vulnerable sections of our society are held hostage to profit and returns on investments. The example of Southern Cross is not unique; it represents a pathology in profit-motivated behaviour; it is the essence of disaster capitalism. The £378 million's worth of debt, which the new provider is left with, will continue to be paid from the payments received for direct care services (Jordan and Drakeford, 2012). The real victims and losers within this will be service users and employees who will bear the burden of cost-efficiency savings to transfer debts to private investors. Dealing with the liberation of social care and social work has led to some difficult questions; in response to this the UK government set up the Dilnot Commission (2011) in the aftermath of the economic collapse of adult care. The Dilnot Commission recommended a National Care Service (NCS) with a range of measures to improve fairer access to care services, including raising the means-tested support and extended care to those who had invested large sums of personal finance into their own care packages (Jordan and Drakeford, 2012). Austerity can now be seen as an ideological position; quite simply, it has been used as a tool to promote neoliberal ideology through the reduction of spending, the retrenchment of services from public to private, and the transfer of power to the individual from the state.

This dual relationship of transfer power to private enterprise and individual consumers or service users can be considered as symbiotic in the development of late modern social work service provision (Parton and Williams, 2017). Using a similar model of crisis intervention, we have also seen a bold move from control of local government children's services to children's trusts. The legislative framework was essential in providing the operational context; the Health and Social Care Act 2012 and Children's Act 2004 are key driving factors behind Children's Trusts. However, it was the crisis or failure of local government children's services in Doncaster in England that provided the impetus. Children's services had been centrally managed by government since 2009, after seven children died in the borough through abuse or neglect within a five-year period. The Doncaster Children's Trust was set up as a response in 2014 and has involved the outsourcing of statutory children's and young people's service to the trust. The Children's Trust represents a break with the provision of social work services from local government and marks a watershed in how we conceptualise and locate children's social work services. It is a clear break in the embedded liberal model of Seebohm, which had been in place within the UK since the post-war settlement (see Chapter 1). The formation of the trust has not been a panacea for social problems; while revolutionary in its transition, reports from Ofsted have highlighted key developmental needs in the Trusts Children's Services (Stevenson, 2015). The repackaging of the service structure, while dynamic, has not necessarily changed the social landscape in which children's services operate. The main message that can be drawn from the experience is that change, while welcomed, requires a broader structural context. The introduction of market reforms and the transfer of social work service provision into private and social enterprise can only have a limited impact on what are essentially complex social problems with causation in wider social, welfare, economic and political structures. While the Children's Trust model operates at an intersection between public and private, it clearly marks the possible transition from social enterprise to free market corporate intervention. The changing of corporate imagery and leadership can only have a limited impact on deeper social complexity; however, what we are really observing is an ideological shift of marketisation, and the separation of the state from publicly controlled service provision as a long-term goal. Moving on from the movement of global capital, we will explore another important facet of globalisation, the movement or migration of people.

The global movement of people: Disaster, conflict, migration and social work

One of the defining themes of human existence can be observed through the migration of populations across the globe. Migration and movement can be considered a defining feature of humanities evolution, settlement and expansion across the globe. Since the dawn of humanity, people have moved to obtain resources, secure shelter and generally improve their social and material conditions. Migration can also be observed as a response to conflict and disasters (both natural and human-based), as displaced populations seek shelter and safety within new geographic areas. Migration and social work have a strong interconnected foundation. Historically, the global development of social work as an institution and professional activity has been defined by the migration of populations from rural agrarian settlement to the cities – during the period of urbanisation and industrialisation within the Global North (explored in Chapter 1). It is also of note that our way of living, by that I mean the social and economic conditions created by industrial civilisation, under western liberal capitalism (in its multiple economic and political expressions) requires the constant movement of populations to produce, consume and sustain western industrial civilisation. The migration of people can be considered a built-in requirement of western industrial capitalism; people as a 'resource' are the building blocks of capitalism – we are both the producers and the consumers. With this in mind, let's consider the reflective questions exercise.

Reflective questions

Reflecting on your own personal circumstances:

• What is the longest distance you have travelled for work or education?

• Did this movement require you to move location or even countries?

• Think about your parents and grandparents; have they always lived in the same place?

• Did they ever move for work or educational purposes?

With the settlement of populations into defined nation states, we have seen a rapid growth in social and material advancements. One of the most dynamic features of western civilisation under liberal capitalism has been the organisation and production of resources into scientific advances, goods and services and improved living conditions. Unfortunately, those same material conditions and scientific improvements are not shared equally. Social and material expansion has historically been, and continues to be, located within a competitive hierarchical social and economic environment that has produced a complex set of unequal global relationships, with nation states located in the Global North maintaining economic and political dominance. Historically, the UK, as an example, has rapidly expanded through economic intervention in the form of trade and exchange. Economic exchange has also been supported through the use of direct military intervention and direct settlement or colonisation of the Global South. The UK has been much reduced as a global empire and international actor since the end of World War II through the process of decolonisation. However, other western nations within the Global North have continued to develop the economic model and established dominance as the central players within global trade. The USA has become one of the global centres of economic and political power. However, this primacy has been redefined by emerging (and re-emerging) contemporary superpowers in the form of Russia and China. Political and economic power, and its location in geopolitical terms, is integral to the process of migration. This is important for several reasons. Nation states and larger political unions (such as the European Union or African Union) compete for access to resources. This competition for key economic control in the form of central banking and the acquisition of key resources such as oil and valuable minerals often form part of the rationale for manufactured disasters in the form of planned conflict or war. Direct military intervention, and the resulting destruction and collapse of nation states, creates a political and economic vacuum; population movement in the form of refugees is often a direct consequence of military intervention. Another major component of migration can be observed in the form of natural disaster and environmental catastrophe. Earthquakes, famines and floods all displace settled populations and require population movement as an interim factor in disaster management. It must also be recognised that environmental disasters are being exacerbated by the impact and advances of industrial civilisation. The consumption and production of resources in the form of fossil fuels are having a profound impact on our environment, changing the way we experience weather patterns and affecting the settlement of human populations.

Within the UK, migration and migrants are placed within a complex economic, political and social relationship. As a former colonial superpower, we have settled migrant populations within our large cities. The development of the UK as a global power has required the importation and exportation of migrant labour to settle colonies, and provide human resources for the rapidly developing economic power base of the UK. Migrants have formed an essential component of our workforce. Migration has been a contentious issue within our society in the UK, both as a historical narrative with the importation of labour from the British Empire and more recently with the movement of economic migrants deriving from the UK's membership of the European Union. Migrants bring vast economic benefits to employers and government. Tensions have often arisen over the competition for social and economic resources between populations already resident within communities and new arrivals. The arrival of migrant labour often undercuts the employment economic conditions of established populations, allowing employers to play off economically and socially vulnerable populations against one another. Individuals and communities are often placed in a competitive framework for welfare resources such as housing, health care and education.

Placed alongside competition for limited resources migrant communities often bring a range of customs and practices with them from their home countries that are alien and different from the contemporary culturally accepted norms. These differences are often highlighted by political parties within and outside government to promote conflict and create instability. The creation and positioning of migration as a conflict for resident populations often acts as a diversion to the primary cause of conflict in society; the real centre of conflict within society can be observed as residing within the unequal social and economic distribution of resources, and forced competition for social and material resources. If working populations are focused on ethnic, religious and cultural difference, that is underpinned by competition for employment; they have little time to focus on the system of inequality that places them in these conflictual relationships.

Social work and migration: Refugees and asylum seekers

Within social work practice the global is the local; social works' most local–global connection is often through local contact with migrants seeking support and advice within the communities we serve; often the statutory social work role is limited in its contact with migrants due to limitations of silo-based service provision. However, non-statutory or third sector social work in the form of NGOs often provide broad welfare support and advocacy to migrants seeking advice and support. The UN Refugee Agency (UNHCR) report *Global Trends* (2015) highlighted that by the year-end in 2015, 65.3 million people were forcibly displaced as a result of persecution, conflict, violence or human rights violations. This number of people displaced has not been seen since the end of World War II, within Europe, and is the largest displacement of people globally for over 20 years. Of the 65.3 million, 21.3 million persons were refugees, 40.8 million were internally displaced persons and 3.2 million were asylum seekers. It is estimated that about half of all the refugees were children. Despite the political rhetoric emanating from the media and politicians within Europe, 86% of the refugees seeking shelter were hosted within developing regions in the Global South. At the end of 2015, within Europe, the largest number of refugees resided within Turkey (2.5 million), Germany (316,100), the Russian Federation (314,500), France (273, 100) and Italy (118,000) (UNHCR, 2015).

Given the volume of migrants, the process of migration and resettlement of displaced populations has become a highly contentious political issue. In responding to the claims of migrants we have seen the development of a politically motivated moral framework that places emphasis on the principles of eligibility for asylum, creating a contemporary social work 'deserving' and 'undeserving' context for migrants (see Chapter 1). This concept is a familiar foundation for social work students and practitioners. Concepts of deserving and undeserving poor formed the cornerstone of historical welfare within the UK (see Chapter 1). The contemporary migrant is positioned as underserving if they are an economic or social migrant seeking a better life, or deserving if they are an asylum seeker or refugee fleeing oppression, conflict or disaster. The 1951 UN Convention Relating to the Status of Refugees describes a refugee as:

> A person who owing to a well-founded fear of being persecuted for reasons of race, religion, nationality, membership of a particular social group or political opinion, is outside the country of his nationality and is unable or, owing to such fear, is unwilling to avail himself of the protection of that country; or who, not having a nationality and being outside the country of his former habitual residence as a result of such events, is unable or, owing to such fear, is unwilling to return to it.

Asylum seekers have been placed under intense media and government scrutiny with resultant stigmatisation and marginalisation within society. Individuals and families have been subject to a malign campaign of vilification as economic migrants who attempt entry to secure welfare benefit payments. Given the complexity of migration – which includes genuine refugees and bona fide economic migrants through the UK's historic membership of the European Union, which is currently under review after the triggering of Article 50 of the Lisbon Treaty due to the controversial EU referendum and Brexit process – we have seen highly emotive media and political campaigns based around migration. This anti-migrant rhetoric from the political establishment sits alongside an economic model of neoliberalism that supports structural unemployment, precarious casual jobs and a reduced welfare state. This political and economic context has created a toxic mix, where the people, both refugee and economic migrant, have been, and continue to be, placed at the centre of a controversial discourse that seeks to locate societal and economic ills in individuals and families seeking support, shelter, and social and material advancement. The discourse surrounding the migrant in all its forms is a contemporary shield for structural social and economic change. This social and economic change, in the form of neoliberal economic and political practices, has seen a diminished share of collective wealth, through redistributive methods, for working-class people within the UK. The migrant has become an easy narrative, or quick fix, for a political and economic elite looking for a narrative that avoids substantial critical analysis. In reality, the UK has experienced a limited increase in asylum seekers; we have taken far less than our European neighbours have during the recent crises. Most migrants or asylum seekers do not come to seek benefits, but to find secure employment. Those asylum seekers involved in the asylum process receive less in the way of benefits and income than UK residents. The marginalisation and exclusion of asylum seekers is built on a carefully layered myth that acts as a political smokescreen and vehicle for government to provide a causation for welfare and social decline on a section of the population that has few resources to defend our articulate for itself.

The experience of adult migrants is subject to a complex legal framework that requires a decision to be made by government as to the status of individuals seeking asylum within the UK (Refugee Council, 2017a). The key international guidance and policy directing this process comprises the following components:

➢ The 1951 Geneva Convention Relating to the Status of Refugees.

➢ The 1950 European Convention on Human Rights (ECHR).

➢ The European Union Asylum Qualification Directive (EUAQD).

➢ The Immigration and Asylum Act 1999.

➢ The Nationality, Immigration and Asylum Act 2002.

Within all of these legislative and policy-based directives the onus is placed on the asylum seeker to demonstrate that they are a refugee because they are at risk from persecution on grounds of race, religion, political grouping or membership of a social group. They must also be unable or unwilling to get support from their own authorities. Under the ECHR position, asylum seekers must demonstrate that they will be subject to torture or degrading treatment under Article 3, or that their private and family life is compromised under Article 8. The Nationality, Immigration and Asylum Act 2002 provides the UK context for compliance with international legislation and the process of settlement or removal from the UK. Before an individual is assessed as a refugee, they are an asylum seeker. The process is often lengthy and the leave to remain within the UK is not guaranteed. Within the UK, the Home Office, through the UK Border Agency, has the final say on the decision for asylum. In 2007, the Home Office developed a faster system for approving asylum claims, the New Asylum Model (NAM). This process is composed of the following components:

➢ Screening interview.

➢ First reporting event.

➢ Substantive interview (Home Office, 2007).

The process can take several weeks and may involve follow-up interviews. The welfare support provided for asylum seekers under Section 4 of the

Immigration and Asylum Act 1999 is limited. They receive an allowance that is lower than the current payments of welfare benefits and they are provided with a card that allows them to obtain food from supporting scheme supermarkets; accommodation is also provided from a preferred list of contactors. To be an asylum seeker in the UK is to experience total control by the state. If the claim is successful, they obtain refugee status under the Geneva Convention for five years. If the decision is based on humanitarian issues, this decision is also subject to five years and will be placed under review. If they cannot return after five years, they can apply for Indefinite Leave to Remain (ILR). If the asylum claim is refused, asylum seekers can appeal to an independent review by an immigration judge not employed by the Home Office. However, individuals making this application are not always entitled to public funding (they must have a 50% success rate). We have also developed a system within the UK where failed asylum seekers who pose a risk or may abscond are detained. Detention is also extended to those who are to be removed. The detention of asylum seekers is a highly controversial issue. The detention centres (now renamed removal centres) have come under fierce attacks from critics, who highlight the degrading conditions asylum seekers are held in; despite criticism:

> The UK's immigration detention facilities are among the largest in Europe: between 2,000 and 3,500 migrants are detained at any given time. (TMO, 2017)

These removal centres are run by a mix of public and private sector organisations, including Her Majesty's Prison Service, SERCO and G4S Group. Critics have highlighted abuse issues between staff and inmates as well as high rates of suicide and self-harm (Cohen, 2008). There have also been deaths during forced removals during the boarding of flights (No Deportations, 2017). To be an asylum seeker in the UK is to be totally marginalised. The entire process is a carefully constructed system of total control both in detention and within the community, which can be observed as safeguarding and confining individuals, not only to set geographic locations, but also to regulate how they eat and what services can be obtained. The community-based process resembles a highly managed open prison system with limited rewards and multiple sanctions. The role of social work is limited within this process as adult asylum seekers are placed within a Home Office context. However, asylum seekers with care needs will be assessed by local authority social service departments for relevant support. Social works primary role resides with working with unaccompanied child asylum seekers. Historically children and young people have been detained as individuals or with family members. Fortunately, the detention of young people has gone under review and has been withdrawn. The current figures highlight that:

> Over 1,000 children were detained for the purpose of immigration control in 2009, and this number was reduced to just under 130 in 2011. It rose to 242 in 2012, before falling to 71 in 2016.

(TMO, 2017)

With this in mind, the next section will look at the experience of the child asylum seeker.

Child asylum seekers: Unaccompanied and alone

One of the primary interventions with social workers and migrants resides within the assessment, support and care of children arriving in the UK alone. The acceptance of children claiming asylum has become a visible political and social issue given the scale of the crises. Lord Alfred Dubs, himself a child refugee, tabled an amendment to the Immigration Act 2016. This amendment aimed to mandate the Secretary of State to prioritise the support of unaccompanied refugee children from Europe. However, the Dubs amendment has received significant political setbacks and only 350 children have been located through this process. It was hoped that up to 3,000 children would benefit. The government has cited increased fiscal pressure on local authorities, who do not have the capacity or resources to facilitate the resettlement. As with adult migration processes economic austerity is used as both a division and a deflection from responding to and managing social complexity and human crises. It is estimated by the UNHCR that the total number of unaccompanied children who applied for asylum worldwide numbers at around 98,400 (UNHCR, 2015); 350 children represents a minority of the global displacement. Recent figures by the Refugee Council (2017a) highlight:

> In 2016, 3175 separated children claimed asylum in the UK. These children arrive in the UK seeking safety from countries where the state cannot protect their rights as children. This may be due to conflict, political instability or other reasons for which the child is persecuted in their country of origin.

Children arriving at UK borders alone face significant challenges and can bring with them a complex history. The experiences of unaccompanied children are diverse; they have often fled conflict, disaster and experienced trauma and distress (Kohli, 2006). Unaccompanied children can also be trafficked by criminal networks who are attempting to use them as a commodity for domestic or sexual services. The vulnerability of a young person or child alone in a foreign country represents a unique social problem, one which requires professional planning, ethical consideration and a comprehensive resettlement package. Social workers have a pivotal role in the support for unaccompanied minors and have a duty to provide direct support and services to them if they are unaccompanied.

As we have alluded to at the beginning of the chapter, the needs of individual children in times of crisis are being placed as secondary to the organisational needs of national and local government. The austerity economic narrative since the Great Recession has seen an ideological dismantling of the public sector through reduced financing, marketisation and underfunding of much-needed front-line services; it is estimated that up to £11.3 billion will be cut from local government budgets by 2015/16 (Unison, 2017). Austerity economics has become a fig leaf for neoliberal marketisation and economic and political conservatism; running parallel to imposed austerity the conservative government has developed a tax concession of up to £5 billion a year for top-rate taxpayers and up to £5 billion a year for company shareholders (Unison, 2017). Within the austerity discourse, we are observing a class war in the reduction of state spending, in its welfare provision and in its function to support socially marginalised groups. Child refugees are another group that are finding themselves trapped within a political and economic conflict. The easiest way for government to save costs is to reduce entry and impose eligibility criteria for those seeking support. There has been an increasing tension within contemporary local authority social work budgets to manage economic targets; this has led to organisational needs taking priority, in some cases, over service user need.

Consider this...

To understand this context better, let us look at the figures:

70,440 children were in the care of local authorities on 31st March 2016.

(DfE, 2016b)

The most recent data from the National Audit Office highlights that it costs £29,000–£33,000 on average to place a child in foster care; for a child in residential care, it costs between £131,000 and £135,000 (NAO, 2017a). The cost of maintaining the 3,175 children accepted in the UK comes out at £104,775,000 at the foster care rate and £428,625,000 at the residential care rate (NAO, 2017a).

Given this context, we can begin to discern where pressure is coming from to manage, ration and allocate resources. In this austerity environment, social work is coming under pressure to manage financial resources. Once again the tension between providing social justice through meeting the needs of children who are alone and vulnerable within a foreign country is being balanced by the social order role of managing and maintaining the status quo of financial and statutory obligations. The assessment of unaccompanied minors has become a controversial issue within contemporary social work. Home Office statistics highlight that, between January 2006 and June 2016, 45% of the 11,847 applicants whose age was disputed were not children (Home Office, 2017). David Davies, the Welsh MP for Monmouth, was also criticised for sensationalism, asking for dental record checks for unaccompanied children attempting to enter the UK. Despite this emotive economic, political and social context, the assessment of age remains a last resort for social work professionals. Guidance highlights that it is recommended that social workers should not undertake age assessment as routine if they believe they are assessing a child.

> Age assessments should only be carried out where there is significant reason to doubt that the claimant is a child. Age assessments should not be a routine part of a local authority's assessment of unaccompanied or trafficked children.

> (ACDS, 2015)

Age assessments have become a key feature of the asylum and detention of children and young people. The Home Office often does not refer individuals it defines as adults who claim to be children or young people who are held in immigration removal centres. These individuals are often referred via third sector or NGOs such as the Refugee Council to advocate for comprehensive assessment. Social work has a key role to play in providing a social perspective outside the criminal justice Home Office model and medical and psychological models of practice and assessment. To provide extensive and comprehensive assessment, social workers need to have a solid understanding of global issues and cultural diversity. Individual research must be undertaken on a case-by-case basis. Within any age assessment, if it is needed, the welfare and needs of the child are paramount. Social workers are ideally placed to work with and assess the age of children due to the professional proximity and relationship-based nature of the work we undertake with children and young people. We assess not from a medical or psychological perspective, but instead provide a contextualised social assessment based on the lived experience of the child or young person. This social perspective is of direct importance when assessing the age of children and young people who come from diverse cultures with challenging social contexts. Detailed guidance on completing age assessments can be found within the **ACDS (2015),** *Age Assessment Guidance.* Children and young people who are applying for asylum present a particular challenge for social workers.

Firstly, vulnerability must be recognised and social workers should be aware of any extra complexity including the possibility of children and young people who:

Are trafficked, either for sexual or domestic services. These children and young people may be handled by a criminal organisation who provide a cover narrative and background. Those children identified as been at risk from trafficking require a robust safety plan and intervention under Section 47 (Children Act 1989). This should include safe and secure accommodation; research highlights that many of these children disappear within 48 hours.

Have additional vulnerabilities, including additional physical or mental health needs. Children and young people may have learning disabilities or be experiencing complex mental health issues derived from their experiences in their home country or journey. Special attention must be paid to identifying physical and mental health complexity, as these issues can impact on communication and functioning within the age assessment process. Children and young people who have experienced, or witnessed, torture, sexual assault and death require time and space to communicate their history and needs.

In providing age assessment and understanding social complexity, the following global factors should be taken into consideration at the local level. Chronological age and the transition to adulthood is a western concept; maturity and adult responsibility come to children at different times within different cultures. Social role expectations will vary. Many children and young people who are seeking asylum will have had different developmental experiences and may have being carers, and worked or participated in adult activities beyond education. This diverse experience will have had an impact on social presentation and communication. Children who have had challenging life experiences can appear physically and emotionally more developed. Assessing age from the position and context of childhood experiences in the Global North can be a confusing and unhelpful contextual foundation. The assessment of age in a global context requires a sociopolitical awareness of the world around you. Social workers need to understand and research the social, political and economic complexity that brings any global child into their local practice. Assessments need to be well balanced and based on the position of the child or young person; each child assessment will be unique and offers an opportunity to develop and build an ongoing therapeutic relationship.

Chapter summary

This chapter has explored the core themes relating to the historical development of global social work. We have examined:

➤ The context and role of international social work and its associated global social work and civil society organisations.

➤ The concept of globalisation and its macro economic, political and social framework and how this impacts on the micro practice of social work in the UK, with reference to global finance–austerity and migration–refugees.

We hope that by reading this chapter you have gained a sense of perspective, and can locate global social work as a locally based practice, particularly one that can be found within your local social work area office. Part of the social construction of late modern society has been to create a mystical barrier in relation to global social forces, particularly political and economic ones that shape our lived experience. The perception that the world is just too big and too complex to understand can be considered both a myth and an obfuscation by political and economic power networks. We would like you to understand that complexity can be grounded and located through any point of contact, particularly within social work. Through the grounding of complex social forces we can seek to challenge the power networks that seek to isolate us as professionals, and reorientate our practice to one that is informed by social justice. Building on this grounding of local practice, the next chapter will explore your preparation for practice, with particular reference to your professional placements.

6

Preparing for practice: From first placement to final placement

In this chapter we will explore the essential and central role of social work placements within the social work education process. Many students coming onto pre-qualifying social work programmes approach social work placements with both trepidation and excitement. Indeed, it has been indicated that social work students value their placements above other aspects of their social work training (Shardlow and Doel, 1996). Students see their practice learning as essential to their development and to the transition into employment and being employable (Tham and Lynch, 2014). Some commentators have argued that learning on placement has a greater impact than classroom teaching (Bellinger, 2010). This chapter explores the connections between learning at university and learning in practice. It adopts a linear approach to this process from prior to entering social work training to the transition into qualified practice and employment. The changes within social education and training at the current time can be seen to increase the pressure on social work students to be 'prepared' for the challenges of placements and practice learning, and the chapter aims to see this as a 'journey' from when you are thinking about embarking on social work training through to your placements and supporting you in the transition into qualified practice. Each stage requires you to reflect on and re-evaluate your skills and learning. Firstly, we examine the context within which practice learning currently occurs.

Key concepts within this chapter include:

➢ Changes to how practice placements are being delivered within social work education and training.

➢ Steps you need to take prior to your first placement to enhance your learning and experience.

➢ Readiness for practice process, including values and ethical issues.

➤ Progressing from Placement 1 to Placement 2 and developing your practice knowledge base.

➤ Managing the transition into qualified practice, and maintaining resilience and career progression.

The discussion in this chapter is also situated alongside the 'Readiness for Direct Practice Level' of the **Professional Capabilities Framework for Social Work (PCF)** developed by the British Association of Social Workers (BASW).

Through reading Chapter 6 students should be able to:

Professionalism

➤ Describe the mutual roles and responsibilities in supervision.

➤ Describe the importance of professional behaviour.

➤ Describe the importance of personal and professional boundaries.

➤ Demonstrate the ability to learn, using a range of approaches.

➤ Describe the importance of emotional resilience in social work.

Professional Leadership

➤ Demonstrate awareness of the importance of professional leadership in social work.

Building on the PCF we would also like you to familiarise yourself with the **standards of proficiency (SOPs)** for social workers in England (2017) by the **Health and Care Professions Council (HCPC)**. The discussion that develops in this chapter has congruence with the following **HCPC SOPs (1, 1.1 and 1.2; 2, 2.1 and 2.2; 12 and 12.1; and 15)**:

➤ 1 Be able to practise safely and effectively within their scope of practice.

➤ 1.1 Know the limits of their practice and when to seek advice or refer to another professional.

➤ 1.2 Recognise the need to manage their own workload and resources effectively and be able to practise accordingly.

➤ 2 Be able to practise within the legal and ethical boundaries of their profession.

➤ 2.1 Understand current legislation applicable to social work with adults, children, young people and families.

> 12 Be able to assure the quality of their practice.

> 12.1 Be able to use supervision to support and enhance the quality of their social work practice.

> 15 Understand the need to establish and maintain a safe practice environment.

The context of practice learning and education

The importance of quality social work placements has been stressed by successive governments, social work education providers and local authorities. In recent years, the publication of two reviews of social work education in quick succession caused the issue to be re-examined again (Croisdale-Appelby, 2014; Narey, 2014). The reviews occurred due to concerns about the quality of social work practice following child protection enquiries. Following the reviews, the government developed the Social Work Teaching Partnerships, which are working to develop closer relationships between employers and local authorities concerning social work education, but which are also working on placement provision (DfE, 2016d). The key issue, for this chapter, is the work of the Teaching Partnerships to develop two 'statutory' placements. The definition of statutory placements is further discussed in guidance relating to Teaching Partnerships but broadly means two placements that undertake statutory duties relating to law and policy and which take place predominantly in local authority settings (DfE, 2016d). This is a significant change from previous placement provision in that it removes first placements that have traditionally taken place in the third sector and have been seen as valuable experience for social work students (Humphrey, 2011). However, social work education providers do normally ask for social care experience and/or volunteering experience as part of developing personal and professional skills for social work practice, which we explore later in the chapter.

While the evaluation of the pilot Social Work Teaching Partnerships sites stated it was too early to see the overall impact of the initiative on students, there was support for having two statutory placements within the initial evaluation (DfE, 2016d). There has been a subsequent expansion of the initiative. There is some evidence, then, that the Social Work Teaching Partnerships initiative can be seen as addressing the dissonance between academic and practice learning that has been highlighted in the literature (Domakin, 2014). For example, the evaluation discusses the positives of practitioners being more involved in teaching and in developing quality placements. However, there is also a concern that the placement focus on statutory duties and tasks may mean students are not as aware of the third sector as previous students.

Additionally, there are two 'fast-track' schemes into social work which operate separately from other social work education programmes. These are Step Up to Social Work (DfE, 2014) and Frontline (www.thefrontline. org.uk). Together with Social Work Teaching Partnerships, these programmes have caused considerable change to the direction of social work education and training and to the provision of practice placements. The exact nature of these arrangements will depend on the area that you live in, but it is important to be aware of how social work education is organised in your area.

Discussion points

- What do you see as the value of two 'statutory' placements?
- What might be the challenges of preparing for this?
- What is practice learning?

Practice learning is the term given to how students learn on placement and how they apply theories and model of intervention that they have learnt from their academic studies. Students are supported in placement by practice educators (mentors) that provide support, guidance and assessment through the placement process. The core issue here is how students *apply* their learning from the university or academic setting to the work they undertake in practice with service users, families and, frequently, an extensive range of professionals. Domakin (2014) argues that how students make sense of what they have learnt at university, and how this is then synthesised with learning from practice, is essential to personal and professional development. She also discusses how practice educators and academics would benefit from having further engagement about how practice learning is taught and links with university curricula. The Teaching Partnerships initiative provides opportunities to develop this and to support students further with practice learning.

The background to this, from some commentators, has been about social work students being seen as not developing critical social work skills that are used within practice learning and employment. This has also arisen from the tension which has been seen between how social work education programmes train social workers and the political, economic and social context within which social work operates (Crisp and

Hosken, 2016). Much of the debate focuses on what social workers need to be 'competent' in when they qualify. However, views about what competency is can be seen to differ between social workers, educators, service providers and employers. Notions of competency may focus on the application and learning of skills in a mechanistic way, with a focus on acquiring 'technical' skills – for example, the ability to complete an assessment form (Wilson and Kelly, 2010). It may also relate to university teaching being seen as not sufficiently up to date with current issues in practice therefore meaning students are not 'competent' for practice (Clapton et al., 2008). Additionally, students may see theory learnt at university as not relevant to practice and that the focus needs to be on the helping relationship in practice (Parker, 2010).

Many social work commentators continue to argue for a more reflective model of learning based on the individual student experience. Academic commentators would also argue that social workers need to be trained within ideas of social pedagogue, as discussed in Chapters 1 and 5. While it can be argued that the 'signature pedagogy' within social work is practice learning, it is important that practice placements offer opportunities to work within local communities engaging with a range of individuals and groups. Here you need to be aware of the needs of marginalised groups, as well as contemporary issues relating to social welfare provision, and to work with and be challenged by ethical issues relating to social justice and social inequalities. Knowledge of these issues is developed through practice learning opportunities.

Reflective questions

- What kinds of communities have you worked within (in terms of social care)?

- What did you learn from this experience?

- What kinds of issues or social problems can exist within communities?

Developing practice knowledge

You may be reading this book as part of preparing for applying to a social work degree. One of the requirements tends to be about obtaining relevant social care experience. This is important not only in developing your confidence, but also in developing understanding of how community services and the voluntary sector relate to social work. Humphrey

(2011) makes the point that voluntary agencies are quite different from statutory agencies in several ways. They tend to be more independent from government, as they are part of what is called the third sector. They also tend to focus on particular issues or concerns for service users in obtaining or finding appropriate services or resources. However, in recent years, local authorities have contracted out services to the third sector, meaning that some larger organisations can be seen as taking on more statutory functions (e.g. in relation to substance misuse or work with young carers). However, it is important that students develop their knowledge of a range of third sector services, as this will support learning in your placements. Many of the support services that social workers work with will be provided by the voluntary sector, or what is known as the third sector.

While practice placements provide valuable learning opportunities around these areas, the more relevant work experience the better. It may be that this has been obtained with work experience as a support worker or carer within a range of settings. However, many universities now suggest that students undertake some relevant volunteering prior to placement as part of their skills development. This will give you an added understanding and awareness of the context of social work from differing perspectives – for example, of the impact of addiction on parenting or how domestic violence affects children. Organisations such as the Kings Fund (2013) have also talked about the value of volunteers to health and social care services, although this can be viewed critically in terms of alleviating the pressures on state services. Research also shows that volunteering has a positive impact on the individual undertaking it in terms of the personal skills gained (Paylor, 2011). It can also support an understanding and knowledge of professionalism and professional practice.

Another way that you may develop your practice knowledge base is to undertake shadowing a qualified social worker for a number of days. Parker (2010) outlines how this process can be managed and arranged by social work education providers. It is also helpful if you draw up a list of questions or issues to discuss prior to your shadowing opportunity. The aim is that you know something of the role of a social worker and the environment that they work in preferably prior to starting your first placement. Edmondson (2014) discusses the importance of observing other social workers' practice and reflecting on the issues raised by observation. This can later support your own practice in similar situations. Developing your practice knowledge is also important as part of the Readiness for Practice process undertaken prior to the first placement.

Reflective questions

- What has motivated you to start a social work course?
- Where do you see your strengths and weaknesses lying in relation to academic and practice learning?
- How do you justify your view?
- What would be your action plan for development?

Preparing for practice

Prior to starting placement, it is important that you are ready to engage and work with service users, carers and families. As Parker (2010) states, it is also important that social work students have had an opportunity to explore ethical dilemmas and issues. Tompsett and colleagues (2017) discuss how social work students are now being assessed more rigorously than previously, before embarking on their first practice placement. As well as being assessed against certain indicators for placement, students are also assessed against a number of capabilities for being ready to practice (BASW, 2017). These indicators stress that students need to demonstrate core communication skills and an ability to build relationships with service users. Students also need to be able to respond to feedback and show a comprehensive awareness of the PCF.

The way in which this process is assessed is generally known as preparation for practice, or readiness for practice. It generally involves examining students' competencies or capabilities, although specifically what this means depends on current assessment frameworks and perspectives on what constitutes being ready for practice placement (O'Connor et al., 2009). Many social work education programmes use role play and experiential learning to practise communication skills and relationship-building with service users and carers and assess readiness for practice. This is done through practising communication skills in relation to developed or 'real-life' scenarios which may be common within social work practice. Social work commentators have highlighted the benefits of involving service users and carers in this learning, particular in relation to realism. A higher degree of deeper learning can be seen in service users working with students around role play situations which reflect real-life experiences (Moss et al., 2007). Hitchin (2016) discusses research, highlighting the benefits for both service users and students in involving service users in the assessment of readiness for practice. Certainly, the more experiential learning through role play achieves deep learning for students, the more students will be ready for practice challenges.

Role play may be something that some students find difficult and anxiety-provoking; however, it can help students understand and identify ways in which they communicate and interact with others. Bolger (2014) discusses the benefits of students observing themselves through videoing role plays and discussing the development of their communication skills. Role play is also useful in enabling students to explore their own identity, feelings and values, thus preparing students for ethical dilemmas and conflicts which are common within social work practice.

Developing ethical understanding

As you develop your social work knowledge base and prepare for practice, it is important to have an understanding of where social work has come from to understand better some of the current dilemmas in practice. Chapter 1 discusses historical perspectives relating to social work practice today and how social work values have been rooted in supporting the disadvantaged and marginalised. Chapter 2 outlines the kinds of areas in which social workers practise and the communities they work with. This chapter outlines the ethical issues in preparing to practise with service users and within local communities. The development of such practice understanding and what Humphrey calls 'practice wisdom' (Humphrey, 2011: 92) should also increase your understanding of what being a social work professional is all about. But what does professionalism mean? One way of understanding this is to explore how you would react personally and professionally to the ethical dilemmas and issues which social workers may face in practice.

This involves students embarking on a significant exploration of personal and professional identity and values (O Connor et al., 2009). A key part of developing professional behaviour is in developing the means to manage professional life as separate from personal life. This involves understanding the similarities and the differences between your personal and professional values. This is important as professional duties, for example, may conflict with your personal values – for example, in having to recommend how resources are allocated to service users or in following specific agency procedures. Values and ethics are integral across social work programmes. You will be working with a wide range of service user groups, differing communities and also dealing with a range of topical and often controversial issues, particularly concerning the economic, social and political context within which you are practising – for example, public perceptions of families or people who are unemployed and reliant on social welfare services. Conducting yourself in a professional manner while also competently and skilfully assessing and supporting service users can be seen as a complex activity and is a task you need to prepare for.

Reflective questions

- What are the current political, social and economic issues within your local community?

- How do you feel personally about these issues?

- Do you think your views and feelings may cause you difficulty or tension if you were a social worker in your community?

Values and ethics are part of professional standards within social work training and regulation. Beckett and colleagues (2017) outline how professional values within social work are part of a professional ethos concerning supporting social justice and human rights. They also discuss how, for many social workers, professional values may be linked to personal values about supporting others within society which has motivated the individual to train to be a social worker. Your social work training will support you in looking at the ethical issues involved in balancing your personal and professional values through case discussion, and encourage you as a student to tell your own story about what is important to you in terms of values and ethics (Woods, 2015). It is also important that you use placement experiences to discuss and explore issues relating to values and ethics. Before we explore this in more detail, we examine what values and ethical frameworks mean in the context of social work practice.

What do 'values' and 'ethics' mean in relation to social work practice?

Many social work commentators stress the crucial nature of values in making ethical decisions within social work practice (e.g. Valutis et al., 2012). Values can be seen as relating to what we feel we and others ought to do and how people behave within society, forming our own moral code (Parrott, 2010). However, how we view morality can be seen within how we view dilemmas and decisions that we make in life (ethics). An understanding of values and ethics draws on a range of philosophical and political thought which we summarise here. Pasini (2016) discusses how a number of ethical perspectives have influenced how values and ethics have been taught within social work programmes. Broadly speaking, perspectives relate to approaches based on principles or from situations that social workers face in their practice which cause ethical dilemmas to occur. So, before and during placements, your tutors and practice educators will be encouraging you to reflect on and deconstruct incidents within your practice to examine the values issues and ethical dilemmas.

Principled or rights-based approaches include perspectives based on individual rights and are also seen as important for ethical decision-making within social work practice – for example, rights linked to the Human Rights Act 1998. Rights-based approaches also consider rights within the context of social justice and citizenship for individuals and communities who have been marginalised. Groups within society who have been seen as oppressed and/or discriminated against are seen as particularly important for the focus of social work practice (Parrott, 2010). This in itself may produce ethical dilemmas for social workers in terms of the context within which they are operating – for example, in working with asylum seekers who are subject to immigration law regarding legal status and access to services.

Principle-based approaches also tend to be based on 'classical' philosophical approaches. For example, deontological approaches draw on the work of Kant around actions being based on what is considered right, which draws on the idea of moral duty. Deontological approaches concern doing something because it is 'right to do so' (Pasini, 2016). This comes from the principles of Kant that every person should be treated with respect (Parrott, 2010). Decision-making within social work should therefore include moral reasoning concerning actions to be taken (Valutis et al., 2012). Deontological perspectives can be seen to have influenced a duty of care within health and social care services, and also to have influenced codes of conduct and ethics which govern professional organisations. Some commentators argue that social work needs to return to its 'roots' in caring for others in society because such an approach lies at the heart of social work practice (Bisman, 2004). Such an ethical approach would underpin a duty of care to others and to local communities that social workers work within. This may also involve challenging social injustices through highlighting issues such as poverty or poor housing within their work (Bisman, 2004).

Social workers work within organisational procedures and processes governing access to services and how resources are distributed. How do social workers make ethical decisions in such a context? Utilitarian principles can be useful here. Utilitarianism is based on the ideas of Bentham and Mill concerning whether actions taken achieve overall more 'good' than injury or harm to others (for a useful discussion about these principles, see Beckett et al., 2017: 23–27). Beckett and colleagues (2017) discuss how social work decision-making necessarily includes a utilitarian element – for example, in balancing the needs of the child with a parent or in allocating resources to a number of people rather than one person. A utilitarian approach can support decision-making in considering different actions and different outcomes. However, in its purest form, utilitarianism can be criticised, as achieving the 'greatest good' may have significant implications for individuals or communities within this process. Additionally, organisations may use such a principle to decide who is most in need or benefit from services limited by resources. This returns us to the discussion in Chapter 1 about who may be most deserving in terms of a need of a particular intervention or service.

How social workers listen to and respond to the 'story' of the service user is influenced by what action should be taken which should consider a principled stance relating to ethical decision-making. Additionally, this may be the first time that a person has revealed a difficult situation or dilemma to you and a duty of care to the individual should apply. Although as a social worker you may be making a difficult decision (e.g. the removal of a child from his or her parents), hearing and understanding the service user's perspective is important. Social workers will also be facing ethical conflicts and dilemmas within their organisations concerning access to support, resources and the decision-making of other professionals within the health and social care system. Building a professional identity based on an understanding of self with an opportunity to explore ethical dilemmas in practice is part of training. Pasini (2016) talks about 'situated' perspectives concerning understanding values and ethics within social work practice. Here social workers are learning from ethical dilemmas resulting from situations in practice. Practice placements allow students to incrementally develop awareness of practice situations that cause moral dilemmas about managing complex situations with services users, families, procedures and organisations and the interplay between these factors. A further factor to be considered is how professional regulations relate to values and ethical decision-making.

Reflective questions

- Reflect on a personal dilemma you have faced in your personal life. What helped you to make a decision regarding this dilemma?

- Think about a situation from volunteering or practice placement where you were concerned about an ethical dilemma. What helped you to make a decision regarding this dilemma?

Making sense of professional regulation

Following a code of ethics has become standard for contemporary professionals, and it is important that social workers adhere to these professional standards (Banks, 2004). This is because codes of ethics should serve to regulate professional behaviour and conduct. Codes of ethics also define professional accountability which can be seen as serving 'rules' to which social workers adhere to (Parrott, 2010). Social workers, on qualifying, are registered with the HCPC. Social workers who are seen as breaching or not meeting these standards may be suspended and/or removed from professional registration. The HCPC Code of Ethics can be turned to in supporting professional decision-making – for example, in how personal and professional boundaries apply to the role of the social worker or in how professional power may be misused (HCPC, 2016). As such codes of ethics are also there to protect service users from being mistreated by professionals (Parrott, 2010). The BASW also provides a code of ethics for social workers and there are also international codes of ethics for social work practice (Valutis et al., 2012). It is important to familiarise yourself with your obligations in relation to professional codes and be aware of how these impact on your social work employer or education provider.

Banks (2009) has warned against social workers becoming preoccupied with codes of ethics as a way of deciding accountability rather than being able to critically reflect on ethical decisions. Additionally, it is important to consider how ethical social work practice is shaped by the social, political and economic context within which social work operates. Political decisions made by government nationally will shape the context of local social work practice. For example, there has been a recent debate about the care 'cap' which is set to determine what older people pay towards their own care. Such decisions then shape the care or support offered to service users.

Balancing personal and professional values

In conclusion to this section of the chapter, connecting perspectives on values and ethics with the duties and accountability of the social worker is a complex task. The debate in the literature about ethics and values within social work will also connect and resonate with your own personal values. Your personal values will be shaped by your own background and will relate to a wide range of factors – for example, your religious beliefs may be of importance in assessing what is perceived as religious or spiritual needs in others. There is also a need to be aware of how religious beliefs shape such issues as dietary requirements or living environment (Beckett et al., 2017). Or you may have particular spiritual beliefs which affect how you view, for example, working with people who are dying. More recently, there has been a recognition that spirituality is an area which needs further research and understanding within social work practice (Furness and Gilligan, 2010). The key point is that social workers need to develop self-awareness concerning the connections between the personal and the professional. In terms of practice learning, this is also important in terms of reflective practice and how you are assessed regarding personal and professional development.

Reflective questions

• What are your personal values shaped by?

• Do you think issues such as religion, culture or political values shape your views on the above question?

• How do these views relate to your approach to social work practice?

Assessing practice

As explored in the introduction to this text, social workers are assessed against national standards for their training in relation to the PCF and the SOPs (BASW, 2017; HCPC, 2016). Additionally, social workers are also assessed against the Knowledge and Skills Statements (KSS) (DoH, 2015; DfE, 2015) which have been published in recent years. At the time of writing, the primary focus of assessment in relation to practice learning in social work is the PCF with the nine domains of the framework forming the basis for assessing student 'capability'. The PCF is also important as it supports assessment and development beyond practice placement and into qualified practice. (Jones, S 2015) discusses the importance of students immersing themselves in understanding how the PCF domains relate to practice learning and assessment.

How are you assessed as capable? It is worth noting here that there have been changes from using 'competency' as a basis for practice assessment to 'capability'. Edmondson discusses how the term capable is often used to describe how able someone is to complete a task or activity (Edmondson, 2014). He also points out that the term has been criticised as being too task-focused rather than looking holistically at students' learning as a whole. The core issue is that students are being assessed as to their effectiveness within the practice learning environment. Students are assessed formally through the production of a midway report and a final report. Students are, however, assessed throughout placement by a range of informal and formal mechanisms which we explore shortly. Parker also makes the point that students need to assess themselves throughout placement, measuring progress against the assessment standards (Parker, 2006).

The following is a summary of the types of evidence that may be used within your placement experiences to assess your practice progress:

➢ Observations will be carried out of your practice. These are normally carried out by your practice educator and provide valuable evidence of how your social work skills have developed (Lomax et al., 2010).

➢ Regular reflections will be required by your practice educator throughout your placement. Reflection on practice to support development is essential.

➢ Supervision needs to occur regularly, and supervision records maintained (see section below on supervision).

➢ Feedback from colleagues and service users will be vital to chart your progression from the start to the end of the placement. This may be verbal or written feedback.

➢ Reports from your practice educator at midway and end points of the placement will show your development needs either for Placement 2 or to support the transition into qualified practice (depending on the placement).

➢ Demonstrating your progress in relation to the PCF domains and other national standards through the submission of a portfolio (which is often now an e-portfolio) is a useful way of collecting evidence about your progress (Lomax et al., 2010).

You will also normally be required to produce academic work which demonstrates how you have applied theory to practice. One of the most common ways of doing this is by providing reflective case studies. Edmondson (2014: 108–112) provides some useful guidance on how to select a case from practice to write about and how to structure and develop your case study.

Managing your placement journey

As there are key commonalities in both practice placements, we explore some of the core themes relating to managing your placement journey, as well as how you navigate between placements. While there have been some changes to social work education since 2012, students are still required to complete 70 days at Placement One and 100 days at Placement Two. In addition, there are 30 skill development days which will be incorporated into your social work education programme and will focus on skills that support your learning and development through the placement journey. For example, your social work programme may include work on advanced communication skills which are developed alongside both placements. Having completed your preparation for practice you will embark on your first placement. Several texts provide useful summaries of what you need to consider in preparing for both your first and second placement (see, e.g., Jones, S 2015 and Edmondson, 2014).

At the time of writing, there are changes occurring to the types of placements that students are going to be undertaking. This is likely to mean that students will probably have two statutory placements as part of the Teaching Partnerships initiative discussed earlier. This may well increase the pressure that students feel under in practice, particularly with the first placement. It is particularly important that students manage their opening weeks in placement and are open about any difficulties that they might have. Edmondson (2014) talks about students feeling overwhelmed by anxiety on placement and this may cause withdrawal, avoidance of certain tasks, or irritability or anger with other people. Being aware of sources of support on placement is essential to your progression.

Reflection and personal accountability

First and foremost, relating to your practice learning, the more you put into your placement, the more you will gain in terms of your personal and professional development. Shardlow (2012) stresses the importance of reflection on your personal values and linking this with the professional tasks that you undertake on placement. Reflection is seen as a significant task within social work education and training and you should be familiar with a number of reflective models to support this process (e.g. Gibbs, 1998; Kolb, 1984). Reflective models offer a staged approach to an event or learning experience and how we learn and develop from that experience. It is important to explore the reflective model that supports your development in practice.

The practice educator role

The role of the practice educator has changed to some extent in terms of how educators are assessed and trained, with the introduction of two stages to practice education known as Practice Educator Professional Standards (PEPS). The changes to the way practice educators are trained may mean you have two practice educators, with one being responsible for overseeing your day-to-day work and the other supervising the process. This model was designed to support quality assessment of practice, as well as worker progression (for further discussion, see Williams and Rutter, 2013). The core role of observing and assessing student social work practice has not changed. Stone (2016) outlines how practice learning is a less developed area of social work research and perhaps this explains the issues in bridging the gap between theory and practice within social work education. Domakin outlines how the role of the practice educator is integral to the learning experience and it is important you build a good working relationship with your practice educator (Domakin, 2014).

The relationship with your practice educator needs to be built on trust and clear communication. Finch discusses how practice educators are 'gatekeepers' for the profession and they therefore do need to ensure students are fit to practise and progress, and so assessment on placement is continuous (Finch, 2017). This can feel difficult when students are struggling with placement, and it is important you talk to your practice educator and your university tutor as soon as you feel any problems are arising within your practice placement.

Case study : Aamir

Aamir has found it difficult to settle into his placement. During his induction period, his practice educator had some sick leave and other staff seemed to be very busy. After Aamir had been in placement for about a month he was concerned that he was not beginning to hold cases independently and did not feel confident to do so. He had a chat with his tutor about this. Aamir agreed that he had not raised how he was feeling with his practice educator as he did not want to 'bother her'. However, following the discussion with his tutor, this issue was raised. His practice educator set an action plan with him to move towards more independent working and they agreed that the placement had not got off to a good start.

Reflective questions

- What actions does Aamir take here?
- Thinking about the PCF, what is Aamir doing in relation to his own learning?

Models of practice learning

Talking to your practice educator about how you learn is an essential part of your placement induction. There are several learning models that can support this process (e.g. Felder and Silverman, 1988; and Honey and Munford 1982). Learning styles models and questionnaires enable you to talk through with your practice educator about your preferred style of learning. Discussion also enables students to action plan development in areas which need developing – for example, confidence building. What your practice educator will be doing is encouraging you to look beyond an event or piece of work and examine your learning at a deeper level. Deeper learning encourages personal and professional growth (Williams and Rutter, 2013). This process will also support students to feel more competent and capable within the work environment. Your practice educator will have received training concerning work-based learning to support your assessment and progression. Work-based learning is a way of looking at practice placements to offer a staged process as to how students prepare for and then practice in the workplace (Williams and Rutter, 2013).

Domakin (2014) discusses a developmental pathway between student, educator and tutor, and your practice learning agreement meeting at the start of placement is integral to looking at a holistic approach to your practice learning. It has been seen as challenging for students to transfer their learning from university and readiness for practice into the practice setting (Tompsett et al., 2017). This appears to relate to the dual nature of the social work role in social justice versus care and control shaped by law and policy. Discussing ways of supporting practice learning is essential for student social workers and a core part of this is how supervision is used.

Using supervision

Supervision is a core component of professional development, enabling in-depth exploration of work through placement and beyond into qualified practice. Social work students report that the supervisory relationship with their educator or mentor is highly significant (Cleak et al., 2016). The ability of the practice educator to link theory to practice was also valued (ibid.). It is important to make a distinction between 'informal' supervision, which takes place 'in action' during the placement, and 'formal' supervision, which is pre-arranged, planned and minuted and supports evidence of progression. It may also be possible in your placement that a group supervision is arranged by your practice educator(s) with other students in a similar setting. This can be helpful in sharing and learning from each other's experiences. Supervision provides a number of functions: it provides support to discuss your work, it gives you the opportunity to reflect on your feelings about your work and it should provide you with opportunities for learning and development (Beddoe, 2010).

Because the supervisory relationship is integral to progression it is again important to discuss any concerns with your practice educator or tutor – for example, if regular supervision is not occurring. Field and colleagues (2014) point to the importance of the supervisory agreement in order to ensure that expectations for all parties are clear. Your supervisor may use a variety of tools and techniques within supervision to support reflection on practice and to enable your development throughout and beyond placement.

Consider this...

* What is your understanding of professional supervision?
* How would you see yourself as preparing for supervision?

Navigating your way between practice placements

At the time of writing, as discussed earlier, there are some changes to placements with the advent of the Teaching Partnerships initiative. This means, for some students, two placements within a local authority (or similar) setting may now be taking place. However, for others, Placement 1 may still be within the third sector. Additionally, some education providers may provide a placement with a third sector provider that fulfils 'statutory' tasks for Placement 1. The important distinction is that each placement requires that you achieve a different level of capability. Edmondson (2014) outlines how by the end of Placement 1 students should be using core knowledge and skills and working with situations that gradually increase in complexity. By the end of Placement 2 students should be working independently with more complex tasks. Social work education providers and practice placements will be able to provide further guidance on the differences between the two placements. There are a number of key issues here.

Firstly, working in statutory contexts has generally been seen as more challenging for social work students (Hill, 2010). By the end of Placement 2, students will have larger caseloads, be presenting information in professional forums and possibly attending court or other formal proceedings (e.g. a mental health tribunal). This requires the ability to work independently and to make decisions, while still receiving direction. It will also require a high level of written and verbal communication.

Secondly, the work undertaken may be with service users who are resistant or hostile to social work involvement. This may because the social worker is undertaking statutory duties which can seem oppressive or authoritarian to service users (Hill, 2015). Students within final placement particularly may experience dissonance between personal and professional values in the context of using social work power and authority and intervening in service users' lives. This means it is important that students work with their practice educators and tutors to reflect on these issues when they arise and seek support in managing their emotional responses to such situations.

Finally, within many placement settings, students will come to experience the challenges of working within large, complex and at times bureaucratic organisations. Jones talks about the challenges of working within organisational cultures where there may be hierarchical structures (Jones,S 2015). A further challenge may be around professional discourse and working with others. For example, in health settings, you may need to develop an understanding of medical terminology in order to be able to liaise and work more effectively with a range of health professionals. As a social worker, you will need to be able to challenge other professionals, as well as managing working in complex situations. The question we now ask is, how do students and qualified workers meet these challenges?

Managing your emotions

The debate about managing your emotions within social work practice is connected to examining the cost of the emotional labour that certain professions can demand of their employees. The work of Hochschild (1983) is seminal here. Hochschild's work developed from research in the 1960s concerning the emotional impact of the work of flight attendants. Her work looked at the links between care given to 'customers' and the feelings and emotions of the flight attendants. She discussed this process as 'emotional labour', as it focused on the individual suppressing their own emotions in order to preserve a public face within their workplace. As such, the cost of maintaining a public face could result in a dissonance between the public and the private worlds of individuals. This also relates to the reasons why it is important to work on your personal and professional identity to ensure such dissonance does not occur. It also requires social workers to be able to manage their emotions.

Howe (2008) agrees with the importance of managing emotions within the context of social work practice. Social workers engage with people in a complex and contradictory context, and the ability to manage emotions is integral to the job (Llewellyn et al., 2015). Morrison argues that the study of emotions and emotional intelligence enables social workers to cope with the current context of social work practice. Morrison's (2007) article can be seen as a critical point in advocating that social workers develop their voice, research and evidence in relation to this area of social work practice.

The emotionally intelligent practitioner should also be insightful of their own health and well-being (Grant and Kinman, 2013). It is important that we manage our emotions in terms of both thoughts and thought processes and feelings and emotions (Freshwater and Stickley, 2004). Finally, as discussed previously, the importance of reflective practice has been identified as important. Managing emotions can be seen as part of the reflective process in using a reflective framework to process feelings, thoughts and emotions. Grant (2014) argues within her study that social work students who are reflective are less likely to express an inaccurate or harmful empathic response. Ingram (2013: 999) offers a useful model of reflective practice adapted from Schon's work to connect with emotionally intelligent and resilient practice. Emotionally intelligent practice is at the heart of developing professional capabilities.

What does resilience mean in social work practice?

Being resilient has become a topical subject in the training of social workers. The need for resilient behaviours is seen as necessary to develop over the course of social work training, and as part of the transition to qualified practice and the Assessed and Supported Year in Employment (ASYE). Resilience training has also been advocated as part of pre-qualifying social work education in recent years (Napoli and Bonifas, 2011; Grant and Kinman, 2014). More recent reforms of social work have stressed the need for social workers to develop resilience (Munro, 2011).

Resilience can be seen as a complex concept related to how individuals manage stress and difficult events. The meaning of resilience is variable. For example, in psychological literature, resilience relates to the ability to be adaptable and resourceful in responding to difficult events (Klohen, 1996). Resilience can also be seen as a contested concept within political theory concerning the relationship between the individual and government (Chandler, 2014). Resilience can be seen to be advocated in a range of governmental policies, but the meaning can vary according to the context. For example, the notion of resilient communities has been suggested in relation to coping with adverse local events such as flooding (Chandler, 2014).

The key question is, do human beings have the capacity to cope and even thrive after dealing with traumatic events? This is significant within social work where individuals are often continually coping with difficult situations. It is also significant for organisations in terms of successful outcomes from staff that are able to manage and deal with a range of complex tasks and activities. Stress can also be a motivating factor and may motivate workers to develop within the workplace and help them learn to manage increasingly complex tasks (Kinman and Grant, 2011).

Rajan-Rankins offer a helpful view of how resilience relates to social workers in connection with 'the individual's adaptive response to adversity, stress-resistant personality traits and the ability to "bounce back"' (Rajan-Rakin, 2013: 1). As such the cost of maintaining a public face could result in a tension between your personal and professional life. Thinking back to earlier in the chapter, this is why it is important to think about the connections between personal and professional values. Where this stress becomes significant, then stress and fatigue can become significant factors for individuals leading to 'burn out' and patterns of sickness, absence from work and ultimately leaving a career in social work. Adams and Sheard (2013) discuss how patterns of stress can develop within social work, and offer ways of working with these to support your continued career in social work.

How you manage your emotions, anxieties and fears is important to consider throughout your placement journey and into qualified practice. This involves self-reflection and awareness and is something that you should be working on throughout the course. Grant and Kinman (2012) refer to this as the 'emotional curriculum' and urge that students and educators support students in self-managing emotions. The development of emotional intelligence is also seen as an important factor.

Goleman (1996) expanded the concept of emotional intelligence beyond a perceived narrow view of traits and abilities focused around IQ testing to include aspects of emotions such as hope and impulse control (Ingram, 2013). Goleman stated emotional intelligence related to the ability 'to motivate oneself and persist in the face of frustrations: to control impulse and delay gratification; to regulate one's moods and keep distress from swamping the ability to think; to empathise and to hope' (1996: 34). Goleman (1998) also focused on good communication skills as being related to emotional intelligence, which is also important within the caring professions and in relationship to leadership and the use of authority. For Ingram (2015), emotional intelligence is about how we identify and manage our responses to ourselves and to others. Your placement journey should enable you to work on your understanding of emotional intelligence and resilience.

Negotiating your first job – the Assessed and Supported Year in Employment (ASYE)

During Placement 2 it is likely you will start to think about applying for a social work newly qualified post. Literature and research have focused on the need for organisations to support the newly qualified social worker, and this has been supported by government through the ASYE programme. Hussain and colleagues (2014) review some of the literature in this area. They point to the fact that support for newly qualified social work staff has been seen as integral to improving retention within front-line social work. They also looked at how this was developed from final placement onwards, in terms of feeling prepared for the challenges of front-line social work.

It is also important to look for 'compassion satisfaction' within your career and this is not always highlighted in the same way as avoiding 'compassion fatigue' (Collins, 2008). Collins also discusses how a focus on the stressful nature of social work has in itself created a negative view of social work both for social workers and the wider public. Job satisfaction has also been linked to intention to continue within front-line social work (Tham, 2007). It is therefore important to consider carefully what you are looking for from your employer, as well as being prepared for the interview process.

Reflective questions

- What are you looking for in your first social work job?

- What do you think are the ingredients for a successful transition into qualified practice?

Chapter summary

This chapter has explored the core themes relating to the development of the student social worker from first placement to your first qualified role as a social worker. Key themes explored have included:

➢ An exploration of the changes to social work practice placement provision.

➢ Support and guidance needed to enhance your placement experience as a student social worker.

➢ Readiness for practice, values and ethics, and placement progression.

➢ The transition into qualified practice and the maintenance of resilience.

Reflecting on the placement journey, and the pressures that student social workers face in placement and their qualified practice, the theme of career longevity remains key. If we accept that the cost of emotional labour can be burnout, then we can perhaps begin to explain why social workers are leaving front-line social work after only a few years, particularly in the area of child protection (Nissly et al., 2005; Searle and Patent, 2012). Studies have identified this as significantly lower than other caring professions (Curtis et al., 2010). Because of this, many local authorities have started training and development around emotional resilience to support retention. This has emphasised the importance of self-care and emotional well-being (Grant and Kinman, 2014). Stone's (2016) research with practice educators identifies three areas that social workers need to work on in developing resilient behaviour throughout practice learning: firstly, in coping with hostile and challenging situations in practice; secondly, managing organisational pressures such as caseload; and finally, developing self-awareness about managing personal life and developing effective boundaries.

However, the literature also reveals that workers also report 'compassion satisfaction' within their social work role (Adamson et al., 2014). A strengths-based approach can be helpful in looking at how social workers can also thrive and develop within the context of stressful events, complex practice situations and the need to balance competing demands (Adamson et al., 2014). While studies have examined the negative factors associated with social work, there are also a range of studies which indicate that social workers do find their jobs rewarding and satisfying (Collins, 2008). Individual experiences therefore vary despite all the factors relating to stress and emotional labour within social work practice that have been explored.

The aim of your practice journey, from preparing to qualified practice, is that your practice learning journey can be transformational and support lifelong learning and career longevity. Sue Jones (2015) identifies this as developing critical thought, skilled reflection and the ability to manage yourself and the world around you. Such an approach will enable students and newly qualified workers to meet the challenges of social work practice.

7
Summary

In writing this text, we hope to have provided a foundation for your knowledge and learning within social work. This text is not the definitive archive for social work; in fact, it must be acknowledged that no one text could offer an 'opera omnia' of social work, such is the breadth and diversity of social work as a subject. At best, we hope to have orientated you, and positioned you, as the reader, to explore and further investigate the role, profession and institution of social work.

I hope that from reading the text you will have gathered that social work is not an isolated activity that exists in a fixed position; we have much to learn from our historical trajectory. The historical foundations of social work have shaped our contemporary practice and role, often for the better, sometimes for the worse. One of the key messages that we have articulated is that the global political and economic forces that shape our lived experience can be grounded and explored in local social work practice. We are not isolated individuals dealing with social crises; the world that we live, work and operate in is interconnected. Through exploring social work theory, we would like you to have gained a foundation for anchoring your student practice as well as an understanding that theory and practice are interlinked, and that by using theory we can begin to explore the complexity of the environment we operate within. We would like you, as reader, to understand that your student journey within placement is only one small part of your preparation – that the art of doing and the art of learning and reflecting are not isolated activities: they are one integrated system.

One of the essential messages of this text is the development of a sociopolitical context. Quite simply, social work is a political activity; our practice is defined and shaped through legislation and social policy. Beyond reading and enquiry, we would also like you, as the future of social work practice, to position yourself as an active agent of change in the development of contemporary and future social work service provision. One of the dominant themes that has emerged from the writing of this book is that social work as an activity can be considered a social construction. By social construction we mean to imply that social work is shaped and contingent on the wider social, political and economic forces that shape and order society.

The key message for you, as students and future practitioners, is that you have an active role in shaping the future and direction of social work. You have an active choice to make: Are we to continue with a social work system whose primary drive is the maintenance of social order and containment of social crises? Or do we want to be part of a social work movement that promotes social justice and reshapes the society we live within?

To redefine and become active participants within social work, we must step outside our professional role; it is often the demands of professionalism that create and support a silo-based limited thinking centred on individual casework. In moving beyond individual casework, we can begin to appraise our practice within a collective context. This poignant quote taken from the Case Con Manifesto, a key moment in social work history within the UK, has resonance for social workers past, present and yet to qualify:

> Every day of the week, every week of the year, social workers see the utter failure of social work to meet the real needs of the people it purports to help. Faced with this failure, some social workers despair and leave to do other jobs, some hide behind the facade of professionalism and scramble up the social work ladder regardless; and some grit their teeth and just get on with the job, remaining helplessly aware of the dismal reality. Of course, some do not see anything wrong in the first place.

> (Bailey and Brake, 1975: 145)

If we are to do more than reproduce the present political, social and material conditions that we live within, we must acknowledge that social work and social service provision are more than just an intervention or an agency. The primary motivation for prospective social work students and social workers is overwhelmingly the desire to help others overcome social crises and support them through complex periods within their lives. The desire to help and support change cannot be done through acts of individual solidarity alone; we need a broader structural framework that places emphasis on the equity of lived experience for all people within society. For us within our profession, this starts with the recognition that the present model of social work operation is limited, and at best, it acts as a social safety-valve mechanism for the worst excesses of political liberalism and economic capitalism. For social work to be meaningful and relevant, we need to move beyond the identity of professional individualism. One of the key messages we would like you to take from this book is the need to build a political, social and economic movement that seeks to challenge and shape our future based on a more positive model for society. To do this we, as social workers, must become politically active workers within our profession – using our professional associations and trade unions to advocate for systemic change. The experience of the social work service user and social work practitioner is interconnected. Through advocating for better social and material conditions for our service users, we are creating a sustainable social service provision that meets the needs of the communities we serve. Beyond our professional associations, we must become active citizens and use our democratic tools in the form of voting, canvassing and political lobbying to improve our social and material conditions. The ballot box may be a limited choice; however, the ability to shape social, political and economic policy has huge implications for our profession. Political control and a social policy based on solidarity and equity have the ability to reshape and redefine contemporary social work practice. We, as educators, practitioners and students, have a world to win. To socially construct our profession and society, on our terms, we must build a movement, a movement that is not based on competition, individualism or pragmatic moralism. We need to build a movement that sees a preferred vision of the future, and that seeks to improve the social and material conditions of our collective lived experience. As Clement Attlee, a former social worker and prime minister, highlighted:

> The social service movement of modern times is not confined to any one class, nor is it the preserve of a particular section of dull and respectable people. It has arisen out of a deep discontent with society as at present constituted, and among its prophets have been the greatest spirits of our time. It is not a movement concerned alone with the material, with housing and drains, clinics and feeding centres, gas and water, but is the expression of the desire for social justice, for freedom and beauty, and for the better appointment of all things that make a good life.

(Attlee, 1920: 3)

In developing better social and material conditions for all, we highlight that individuals within society are interconnected. It is our role, as social workers, to promote a better way of living; this cannot be done through an individual deficit reduction model of social work that isolates, individualises and compartmentalises complex social problems. We must remember that the end goal of social work on a micro and macro level is to make the social worker redundant. The redundancy of social work as an end goal is not a negative desire; it is a desire to see that freedom, beauty and social justice are ingrained within our economic, social and political system. The redundancy of social work is the realisation of ending poverty and inequality, of not having individuals, families and communities fall through safety nets. The end of social work is a desire to see the good life made a concrete reality for those that we serve.

References

Abrams, L. and Moio, J.A. (2009) Critical race theory and the cultural competence dilemma in social work education. *Journal of Social Work Education*, 45(2), (Spring/Summer), 245–261.

ACDS (2015) Age assessment guidance: Guidance to assist social workers and their managers in undertaking age assessments in England. [Online.] Available from http://adcs.org.uk/assets/documentation/Age_Assessment_Guidance_2015_Final.pdf (last accessed 10 September 2017).

Acquah, D., Selers, R., Stock, L. and Harold, G. (2017) *Inter-Parental Conflict and Outcomes for Children in the Contexts of Poverty and Economic Pressure*. London: The Early Intervention Foundation.

Adam, J. and Sheard, A. (2013) *Positive Social Work: The Essential Toolkit for NQSW*. St Albans: Critical Publishing.

Adamson, C., Beddoe, L. and Davys, A. (2014) Building resilient practitioners: Definitions and practitioner understandings. *British Journal of Social Work*, 44, 572–541.

The Adoption Act 1958. London: HMSO.

The Adoption and Children Act 2002 HMSO.

Age UK. (2017) Changes to the way you pay for residential care. [Online.] Available from https://www.ageuk.org.uk/information-advice/care/social-care-and-support-where-to-start/paying-for-care-support/changes-to-the-way-you-pay-for-residential-care/ (last accessed 10 September 2017).

Alden, P. (1929) Definition and progress of social work. In: *First International Conference of Social Work Proceedings*, Vol. 1, pp. 597–606. First Conference, Paris, 8–13 July 1928.

All Party Parliamentary Group for Children (2017) *No Good Options: Report of the Inquiry into Children's Social Care in England*. London: The National Children's Bureau.

Allen, G. (2011) *Early Intervention: The Next Steps. An Independent Report to Her Majesty's Government*. London: The Cabinet Office.

Anderson, K.M. (2013) Assessing strengths: Identifying acts of resistance to violence and oppression. In: D. Saleebey (ed.), *The Strengths Perspective in Social Work Practice, International*, 6th edition. London: Pearson.

Asquith, S., Clark, C. and Waterhouse, L. (2005) *The Role of the Social Worker in the 21st Century*. Edinburgh: Scottish Executive.

Attlee, C.R. (1920 [2016]) *The Social Worker*. London: G. Bell & Sons. Available from https://archive.org/stream/socialworker00attliala#page/22/mode/2up (last accessed August 2016).

Bailey, R. and Brake, M. (1975) *Radical Social Work*. London: Arnold.

Bamford, T. (2015) *A Contemporary History of Social Work: Learning from the Past*. Bristol: Policy Press.

Banks, S. (2004) *Ethics, Accountability and the Social Professions*. London: Palgrave.

Banks, S. (2009) From professional ethics to ethics in professional life: Implications for learning, teaching and study. *Ethics and Social Welfare*, 3(1), 55–63.

Banks, S. (2012) *Ethics and Values in Social Work* (Practical Social Work Series). Basingstoke: Palgrave Macmillan.

Barclay, P. (1982) *Social Workers: Their Role and Tasks*. London: National Institute for Social Work.

Barn, R., Sinclair, R. and Ferdinand, D. (1997) *Acting on Principle: An Examination of Race and Ethnicity in Social Services Provision to Children and Families*. London: BAAF.

Barnard, H., Kumar, A., Wenham, A., Smith, E., Drake, B., Collingwood, A. and Lees, D. (2017) *UK Poverty 2017*. London: Joseph Rowntree Foundation.

Barnett, H. (1918) *Canon Barnett: His Life Work and Friends by His Wife*. London: J. Murray.

Bartoli, A., Chopping, T., Douglas, V. and Tedam, P. (2015) *Embedding Equality and Diversity in the Curriculum: A Social Work Practitioners Guide*. Heslington: The Higher Education Academy.

BASW (British Association of Social Workers) (2012) *The Code of Ethics for Social Work*. Birmingham: BASW. Available from www.basw.co.uk/codeofethics/ (last accessed November 2017).

BASW (British Association of Social Workers). (2017) *Professional Capabilities Framework*. Birmingham: BASW.

Bate, A. (2017) *Delayed Transfers of Care in the NHS*. House of Commons Briefing Paper Number 7415, 20 June, House of Commons Library.

Bauman, Z. (1991) *Modernity and Ambivalence*. Ithaca, NY: Cornell University Press.

Bauman, Z. (2009) The absence of society. In: D. Utting (ed.), *Contemporary Social Evils*, pp. 147–150. Bristol: Policy Press and Joseph Rowntree Foundation.

Bebbington, A. and Miles, J. (1989) The background of children who enter local authority care. *British Journal of Social Work*, 19(5): 349–368.

Beck, U. (1992) *Risk Society: Towards a New Modernity*. London: Sage.

Beckett, C., Maynard, A. and Jordan, P. (2017) *Values and Ethics in Social Work*. London: Sage.

Beckett, J. (2009 [1830]) *Swing Riots*. Oxford: Oxford University Press.

Beddoe, L. (2010) Surveillance or reflection: Professional supervision in the 'Risk Society'. *British Journal of Social Work*, 40(4), 1279–1296.

Bell, E.M. (1942) *Octavia Hill: A Biography*. London: Constable.

Bellinger, A. (2010) Talking about (re)generation: Practice learning as a site of renewal for social work. *British Journal of Social Work* (40), 2450–2466.

Bernstein, S. (1960) Self-determination: King or citizen in the realm of values? *Social Work (US)* (5), January, pp. 3–8.

Bisman, C. (2004) Social work values: The moral core of the profession. *British Journal of Social Work*, 34, 109–123.

Boccagni, P. (2015) (Super)diversity and the migration–social work nexus: A new lens on the field of access and inclusion? *Ethnic and Racial Studies*, 38(4): 201.

Boddy, J; Cameron, C; Heptinstall, E; McQuail, S and Petrie, P. (2001) Working with Children: Social Pedagogy and Residential Child Care in Europe. Report to the Department of Health, 2001.

Bolger, J. (2014) Video self-modelling and its impact on the development of communication skills within social work education. *Journal of Social Work*, 14(2), 196–212.

Bradley, K. (2007) Creating Local Elites: The University Settlement Movement, National Elites and Citizenship in London, 1884–1940. [Online.] Available from https://kar.kent.ac.uk/7808/1/Bradley_CreatingLocalElites_2007.pdf (last accessed April 2017).

Brandon, M., Belderson, P., Warren, C., Howe, D., Gardner, R., Dodsworth, J. and Black, J. (2008) *Analysing Child Deaths and Serious Injury through Abuse and Neglect: What Can We Learn? A Biennial Analysis of Serious Case Reviews 2003–05*. London: Department for Children, Schools and Families.

Bronfenbrenner, U. (1979) *The Ecology of Human Development*. Cambridge, MA: Harvard University Press.

Brown, K. (2006) *Vulnerable Adults and Community Care*. Exeter: Learning Matters.

Burawoy, M. Blum, J.A. George, S. Gille, Z. Gowan, T. Haney, L. Klawiter, M. Lopez, S.H. Rian, S.O. & Thayer, M. (2000) *Global Ethnography: Forces, Connections, and Imaginations in a Postmodern World*. Berkeley: University of California Press.

Butler, J. (1990) *Gender Trouble: Feminism and the Subversion of Identity*. London: Routledge.

Butt, J. (2006) *Are We There Yet? Identifying the Characteristics of Social Care Organisations That Successfully Promote Diversity*. SCIE Race equality discussion paper 03, Social Care Institute for Excellence.

Bywaters, P., Brady, G., Sparks, T., and Bos, E. (2016) Inequalities in child welfare intervention rates: the intersection of deprivation and identity. *Child & Family Social Work*, 21: 452–463.

Bywaters, P., Bunting, L., Davidson, G., Hanratty, J., Mason, W., McCartan, C. and Steils, N. (2016b) *The Relationship between Poverty, Child Abuse and Neglect*. York: Joseph Rowntree Foundation.

Cameron, C. (2005) [Internet] With heart, head and hands. Community Care. Available from <http://www.communitycare.co.uk/2005/08/16/with-hearthead-and-hands/> [last Accessed April 2017]

Carers UK (2015) *Facts about caring policy briefing*. [Online.] Available from: https://www.carersuk.org/for-professionals/policy/policy-library/facts-about-carers-2015

Casey, L. (2013) Social workers 'collude' with problem families. *BBC*, 3 July [Online.] Available from http://www.bbc.co.uk/news/uk-politics-23158680 (last accessed 10 September 2017).

Chandler, D. (2014) *Resilience: The Governance of Complexity*. London: Routledge.

Chandler, J., Bell, L., Berg, E. and Barry, J. (2015) Social work in movement: Marketisation, differentiation and managerial performativity in Sweden and England. *International Journal of Social Work and Human Services Practice Horizon Research Publishing*, 3(3), 109–117.

Chase, M. (2007) *Chartism: A New History*. Manchester: Manchester University Press.

The Children Act 1989. London HMSO.

The Children and Young Persons Act 1963. London: HMSO.

Clapton, G., Cree, V., Allan, M., Edwards, R., Forbes, R., Irwin, M., MacGregor, C., Paterson, W., Paterson, W., Brodie, I. and Perry, R. (2008) Thinking 'outside the box': A new approach to integration of learning for practice. *Social Work Education*, 27, 334–340.

Clarity Social Enterprise. *Languages in Leeds*. Available from http://www.claritysocialenterprise.org/leeds-languages/ (last accessed December 2017).

Clarke, J., Huliaras, A. and Soteropoulos, D. (2015) *Austerity and the Third Sector in Greece: Civil Society at the European Frontline*. Farnham and Burlington, VT: Ashgate Publishing.

Cleak, H., Roulston, A. and Vreugdenhil, A. (2016) The inside story: A survey of social work students' supervision and learning opportunities on placement. *British Journal of Social Work*, 46, 2033–2050.

Clements, P. (2008) *Policing a Diverse Society*, 2nd edition. Oxford: Oxford University Press.

Cohen, J. (2008) Original communication: Safe in our hands?: A study of suicide and self-harm in asylum seekers. *Journal of Forensic and Legal Medicine*, 15, 235–244.

Collins, S. (2008) Statutory social workers: Stress, job satisfaction, coping, social support and individual differences. *British Journal of Social Work*, 38, 1173–1193.

Community Care. (2017) *A Quarter of Adult Social Care Workforce Leaving their Jobs, Report Says*. Available from http://www.communitycare.co.uk/2017/05/18/quarter-adult-social-care-workforce-leaving-jobs-year-report-says/ (last accessed December 2017).

Community Tool Box (2017): Building Culturally Competent Organizations. Available from http://ctb.ku.edu/en/table-of-contents/culture/cultural-competence/culturally-competent-organizations/main (last accessed December 2017).

Congress, E. (2015) The culturagram. In: A. Roberts and K. Corcoran (eds), *Social Workers Desk Reference*, 3rd edition, pp. 129–130. Oxford: Oxford University Press.

Constance-Huggins, M. (2013) Critical race theory in social work education: A framework for addressing racial disparities. *Critical Social Work*, 13(2), 1–16.

CQC (Care Quality Commission). (2016) *Building Bridges, Breaking Barriers: Integrated Care for Older People*. Newcastle upon Tyne: CQC.

Crawford, K. and Walker, J. (2017) *Social Work and Human Development*. London: Sage.

Cree, V. (1995) *From Public Streets to Private Lives: Changing Task of Social Work*. Aldershot: Avebury.

Cree, V. (ed.) (2003) *Becoming a Social Worker*. London: Routledge.

Crenshaw, K. (1989) Demarginalizing the intersection of race and sex: A black feminist critique of antidiscrimination doctrine, feminist theory and antiracist politics. *University of Chicago Legal Forum*, 140(1), 139–167.

Crisp, B. and Hosken, N. (2016) A fundamental rethink of practice learning in social work education. *Social Work Education*, 35(5), 506–517.

Crofts, P. (2013) Critical race theory and exploring 'whiteness'. In: A. Bartoli (ed.), *Anti-racism in Social Work Practice*. St Albans: Critical Publishing.

Croisdale-Appleby, D. (2014) *Re-visioning Social Work Education. An Independent Review*. London: Department of Health.

Curtis Committee. (1946) *Report of the Child Care Committee*. Cmd. 6922. London: HMSO.

Curtis, L., Moriarty, J. and Netten, A. (2010) The expected working life of a social worker. *British Journal of Social Work*, 40(5), 1628–1643.

CWIP (Child Welfare Inequalities Project). (2017) *Identifying and Understanding Inequalities in Child Welfare Intervention Rates: Comparative Studies in Four UK Countries* Briefing Paper England 1, Child Welfare Inequalities Project, Coventry University Research Centre, Innovative Research Across the Life Course.

Das, C. and Carter-Anand, J. (2016) 'Pushing theory': Critical cultural competence in social work practice: Case example from Northern Ireland. In: C. Williams and M.J. Graham (eds), *Social Work in a Diverse Society*, pp. 21–37. Bristol: Bristol Policy Press.

Davies, A. (2008) *Celebrating 100 Years of Social Work 1998–2008*. University of Birmingham. [Online.] Available from http://www.birmingham.ac.uk/ Documents/college-social-sciences/social-policy/IASS/100-years-of-social-work.pdf (last accessed October 2016).

DCSF (Department of Children Schools and Families). (2009a) *Building a Safe, Confident Future: The Final Report of the Social Work Task Force*. London: DCSF.

DCSF (Department of Children Schools and Families). (2009b) *The Protection of Children in England: Action Plan the Government Response to Lord Laming*. London: DCSF.

Delgado, R. and Stefanic, J. (2001) *Critical Race Theory: An Introduction*. New York: New York University Press.

Dennis, J. (2012) *Not a Minor Offence: Unaccompanied Children Locked Up as Part of the Asylum System*. Available from https://www.refugeecouncil. org.uk/assets/0002/5945/Not_a_minor_offence_2012.pdf (last accessed December 2017).

DfE (Department for Education). (2015) *Knowledge and Skills for Child and Family Social Work*. London: DoE.

DfE (Department for Education). (2016a) *Characteristics of Children in Need 2015 to 2016*. London: National Statistics Office. Available from https://www. gov.uk/government/uploads/system/uploads/attachment_data/file/564620/ SFR52-2016_Main_Text.pdf (last accessed December 2017).

DfE (Department for Education). (2016b) *Children Looked after in England Including Adoptions*. London: DfE.

DfE (Department for Education). (2016c) *Education Select Committee Memorandum on Social Work Reform January*. London: DfE.

DfE (Department for Education). (2016d) *Social Work Teaching Partnerships Programme Pilots: Evaluation*. London. DoE.

DfE (Department for Education). (2017) Children's social work workforce 2016. Staff employed by children's social services in England as at 30 September 2016. DfE.

DHSS (Department of Health and Social Security). (1975a) *Better Services for the Mentally Ill*. London: HMSO.

DHSS (Department of Health and Social Security). (1975b) *Better Services for the Mentally Handicapped*. London: HMSO.

Dilnot, A. (2011) *Fairer Care Funding for All: The Report on the Commission of Funding on Care and Support*. London: Commission of Funding on Care and Support.

Dinham, A. (2006) A review of practice of teaching and learning of communication skills in social work education in England. *Social Work Education*, 25(8), 838–850.

Doel, M. and Marsh, P. (1992) *Task Centred Social Work*. London: Ashgate.

DoH (Department of Health). (2001) *The Requirements for Social Work Training*. London: DoH.

DoH (Department of Health). (2003) *Fair Access to Care Services – Guidance on Eligibility Criteria for Adult Social Care*. London: DoH.

DoH (Department of Health). (2007) *Putting People First*. London: DoH.

DoH (Department of Health). (2010a) *A Vision for Adult Social Care: Capable Communities and Active Citizens*. London: HMSO.

DoH (Department of Health). (2010b) Prioritising need in the context of putting people first: A whole system approach to eligibility for social care. In: *Guidance on Eligibility for Adult Social Care*. London: HMSO.

DoH (Department of Health). (2013) *Integrated Care: Our Shared Commitment*. London: DoH.

DoH (Department of Health). (2015) *Knowledge and Skills Statement for Social Workers in Adult Services*. London: DoH.

DoH (Department of Health). (2017) *Social Work: Essential to Integration*. Advice note. Available from https://www.gov.uk/government/uploads/system/uploads/attachment_data/file/598910/Social_Work_Essential_to_Integration.pdf (last accessed 8 December 2017).

DoH (Department of Health), DoEE (Department for Education and Employment), and Home Office. (2000) *Framework for the Assessment of Children in Need and Their Families*. London: The Stationery Office.

Domakin, A. (2014) Are we making the most of learning from the practice placement?. *Social Work Education*, 33(6), 718–730.

Dominelli, L. (2008) *Anti-Racist Social Work*. Basingstoke: Palgrave.

Donovan, T. (2017) A fast-track future? What condensed social work training may mean for traditional courses. Available from http://www.communitycare.co.uk/2016/03/30/fast-track-future-condensed-social-work-training-may-mean-traditional-courses/ (last accessed 10 September 2017).

Douglas, A. and Philpot, T. (1988) *Caring & Coping*. London: Routledge.

Driscoll, J.J. (2009) Prevalence, people and processes: A consideration of the implications of Lord Laming's progress report on the protection of children in England. *Child Abuse Review*, 18(5), 333–345.

Dunk-West, P. (2013) *How to be a Social Worker: A Critical Guide for Students*. London: Palgrave.

Dupre, M. (2012) Disability culture and cultural competency in social work. *Social Work Education*, 31(2), 168–183.

Dustin, D. (2006) Skills and knowledge needed to practise as a Care Manager. *Journal of Social Work*, 6(3), 293–313.

Dutt, R. (2003) Introduction to Chapter 16. *The Victoria Climbie Inquiry: Report of an Inquiry by Lord Laming*. London:HMSO.

Edbrooke-Childs, J.H., Gondek, D., Deighton, J. et al (2016) When is sessional monitoring more likely in child and adolescent mental health services? *Administration Policy Mental Health*, 43, 316. [Online.] https://doi.org/10.1007/s10488-016-0725-6.

Edmondson, D. (2014) *Social Work Practice Learning*. London: Sage.

Egan, M., Neely-Barnes, S. and Combs-Orme, T. (2011) Integrating neuroscience into the lifespan. *Journal of Social Work Education*, 47(2), 269–282.

Eilers, K. (2003) Social policy and social work in 1928: The first international conference of social work in Paris takes stock. In: S. Hering and B. Waaldijk (eds), *History of Social Work in Europe (1900–1960): Female Pioneers*, pp. 119–28. Opladen: Leske & Budrich.

Englander, D. (1998) *Poverty and Poor Law Reform in Britain: From Chadwick to Booth, 1834–1914*. London: Longman.

Epstein, L. (1988) *Helping People: The Task Centred Approach*. Columbus, OH: Merrill.

Evans, M. and Jones, P. (2014) 'A stubborn, intractable body': Resistance to the workhouse in Wales, 1834–1877. *Family & Community History*, 17(2), 101–121.

Farlow, A. (2013) *Crash and Beyond: Causes and Consequences of the Global Financial Crisis*. Oxford: Oxford University Press.

Featherstone, B., Morris, K. and White, S. (2013) A marriage made in hell: Early intervention meets child protection. *British Journal of Social Work*, 10(1), 1–15.

Felder, R.M. and Silverman, L.K. (1988) Learning and teaching styles in engineering education. *Engineering Education*, 78, 674–681.

Ferguson, F. and Woodward, R. (2009) *Radical Social Work in Practice: Making a Difference*. Bristol: Policy Press.

Ferguson, H. (2011) *Child Protection Practice*. Basingstoke: Palgrave Macmillan.

Field, P., Jasper, C. and Littler, L. (2014) *Practice Education in Social Work*. London: Critical Publishing.

Finch, J. (2015) 'Running with the fox and hunting with the hounds': Social work tutors' experiences of managing failing social work students in practice learning settings. *British Journal of Social Work*, 45(7), 2124–2141.

Finch, J. (2017) *Supporting Struggling Students on Placement: A Practical Guide*. London: Policy Press.

Flaschel, P. and Greiner, A. (2012) *Marx: Socially Acceptable Capitalism?* Oxford: Oxford University Press.

Fook, J. (2016) *Social Work: A Critical Approach to Practice*, 3rd edition. London: Sage.

Forrester, D. and Hutchinson, A. (2012) A theoretical perspective on social work and substance use. In: M. Davies (ed.), *Social Work with Adults: From Policy to Practice*. Basingstoke: Palgrave Macmillan.

Foucault, M. (1979) *Discipline and Punish*. Harmondsworth: Penguin.

Francis, R. (2013) *Report of the Mid Staffordshire NHS Foundation Trust Public Inquiry*. London: The Stationery Office.

Freeden, M. (2015) *Liberalism: A Very Short Introduction*. Oxford: Oxford University Press.

Freshwater, D. and Stickley, T. (2004) The heart of the art: Emotional intelligence in nurse education. *Nursing Inquiry*, 11, 91–98.

Friedman, M. (2002) *Capitalism and Freedom*. London: University of Chicago Press.

Frost, N, Abbott, S. and Race, T. (2015) *Family Support*. Cambridge: Cambridge Polity Press.

Fulcher, J. (2015) *Capitalism: A Very Short Introduction*. Oxford: Oxford University Press.

Furness, S. (2005) Shifting sands: Developing cultural competence. *Practice*, 17(4), 247–56.

Furness, S. and Gilligan, P. (2010) *Religion, Belief and Social Work*. Bristol: Policy Press.

Gardenswartz, L. and Rowe, A. (1994) *Four Layers of Diversity*. Available from http://www.gardenswartzrowe.com/why-g-r/ (last accessed 10 September 2017).

Gaskell-Mew, E. and Lindsay, J. (2015) Working with resistance. In: R. Davies and K. Jones (eds), *Skills for Social Work Practice*, pp. 196–220. London: Palgrave.

Gaylard, D. (2008) Policy to practice. In A. Mantell and T. Scragg (eds), *Safeguarding Adults in Social Work*, pp. 9–34. Exeter: Learning Matters.

Gelman, C. (2004) Empirically-based principles for culturally competent practice with Latinos. *Journal of Ethnic and Cultural Diversity in Social Work*, 13(1), 83–108. [Online.] doi:10.1300/J051v13n01_05.

Gibbs, R. (1988) *Learning by Doing: A Guide to Teaching and Learning Methods*. London: Further Education Unit.

Giddens, A. (1998) *The Third Way: The Renewal of Social Democracy*. London: Polity Press.

Giddens, A. (2009) *Sociology*, 6th edition. London: Polity Press.

Gillborn, D. (2008) *Racism and Education: Coincidence or Conspiracy?* London: Routledge.

Gilligan, C. (1982) *In a Different Voice*. Cambridge, MA: Harvard University Press.

Gilligan, R. (2007) Adversity, resilience and education of young people in public care. *Emotional and Behavioural Difficulties*, 12(2), 135–145.

Gitterman, A. (2014) Social work: A profession in search of its identity. *Journal of Social Work Education*, 50(4), 599–607.

Goleman, D. (1996) *Emotional Intelligence: Why It Can Matter More Than IQ*. London: Bloomsbury.

Goleman, D. (1998) What makes a leader? IQ and technical skills are important, but emotional intelligence is the sine qua of leadership. *Harvard Business Review*, Nov/Dec, 93–102.

Goodwin, N. (2016) Understanding integrated care. *International Journal of Integrated Care*, 16(4), 6.

Grant, L. (2014) Hearts and minds: Aspects of empathy and wellbeing in social work students. *Social Work Education*, 33(3), 338–352.

Grant, L. and Kinman, G. (2012) Enhancing wellbeing in social work students: Building resilience in the next generation. *Social Work Education*, 31, 605–621.

Grant, L. and Kinman, G. (2013) *The Importance of Emotional Resilience for Staff and Students in the Helping Professions: Developing an Emotional Curriculum.* Southampton: Higher Education Academy Subject Centre for Social Policy and Social Work (SWAP).

Grant, L. and Kinman, G. (2014) *Developing Resilience for Social Work Practice.* London: Palgrave.

GSCC (General Social Care Council). (2008) *Evaluation of the New Social Work Degree Qualification in England.* London: Department of Health.

Hall, J., Eisenstadt, N., Sylva, K., Smith, T., Sammons, P., Smith, G., Evangelou, M., Goff, J., Tanner, E., Agur, M. and Hussey, D. (2015) A review of the services offered by English Sure Start Children's Centres in 2011 and 2012. *Oxford Review of Education*, 41(1), 89–104.

Hancock, G. (1991) *Lords of Poverty: The Power, Prestige, and Corruption of the International Aid Business.* New York: Grove Atlantic.

Harris, J. and White, V. (2013) *Beveridge Report 1942.* Oxford: Oxford University Press.

Harvey, D. (2007) *A Brief History of Neoliberalism.* Oxford: Oxford University Press.

Harvey, D. (2017) *RSA Animate – The Crises of Capitalism.* [Online.] Available from https://www.thersa.org/discover/videos/rsa-animate/2010/06/rsa-animate---crisis-of-capitalism (last accessed 10 September 2017).

HCPC (Health and Care Professions Council). (2016) *Standards of Conduct, Performance and Ethics.* London: HCPC.

Health and Care Professions Council. (2017)

Healy, K. (2005) *Social Work Theories in Context: Creating Frameworks for Practice.* Basingstoke: Palgrave Macmillan.

Healy, K. and Mulholland, J. (2012) *Writing Skills for Social Workers.* London: Sage.

Healy, M.L. (2008) Introduction: A brief journey through the 80 year history of the International Association of Schools of Social Work. *Social Work & Society*, 6(1) [Online]. Available from http://www.socwork.net/sws/article/view/98/387 (last accessed October 2016).

Hetzel, R.L. (2012) *The Great Recession: Market Failure Or Policy Failure?* Cambridge: Cambridge University Press.

Higgins, M. and Goodyer, A. (2015) The contradictions of contemporary social work: An ironic response. *The British Journal of Social Work*, 45(2), 747–760.

Hill, A. (2010) *Working in Statutory Contexts.* London: Polity Press.

Hill, D. et al (2015) *Working with Dual Diagnosis.* London: Macmillan.

Hill, D. Penson, W.J. and Charura, D. (2016) *Working with Dual Diagnosis: A Psycho Social Perspective.* London: Palgrave Macmillan.

Hill, D. and Frost, N. (2018) Social work in England: Regulation, competition and change. In: C. Nieto Morales and M. Solange de Martino Bermúdez (eds), *Trabajo Social en el Siglo XXI: Desafíos para la formación académica y profesional (Social Work in the Twenty-First Century: Challenges to Educational and Professional Training).* Madrid: Dykinson.

Hill, D. Penson, W.J. and Charura, D. (2016) *Working with Dual Diagnosis: A Psycho Social Perspective*. London: Palgrave Macmillan.

Hingley-Jones, H. and Ruch, G. (2016) Stumbling through?: Relationship based social work practice in austere times. *Journal of Social Work Practice*, 30(3), 235–248.

Hitchin, S. (2016) Role played interviews with service users in preparation for social work practice: Exploring students' and service users' experience of co-produced workshops. *Social Work Education*, 35(8), 970–981.

HM Government. (2003) *Every Child Matters*. Cm 5860. Norwich: The Stationery Office.

HMSO. (2003) *The Victoria Climbié Inquiry*.

Hobsbawn, E. (1999) *Age of Extremes*. London: Abacus.

Hobsbawn, E. (2004) *The Age of Capital*. London: Abacus.

Hochschild, A. (1983) *The Managed Heart: Commercialization of Human Feeling*. Berkeley: University of California Press.

Home Office. (1945) *Report by Sir William Monckton KCMG KCVO MC KC on the circumstances which led to the boarding out of Dennis and Terence O'Neill at Bank Farm, Minsterly and the steps taken to supervise their welfare, etc.* Cmd 6636. London: Home Office.

Home Office. (2007) *Asylum Claims under the New Asylum Model (NAM)*. [Online.] Available from https://www.gov.uk/government/publications/asylum-claims-under-the-new-asylum-model-nam (last accessed 10 September 2017).

Honey, P. and Mumford, A. (1982) *Manual of Learning Styles*. Maidenhead: Peter Honey.

Horner, N. (2006) *What is Social Work? Context and Perspectives*. Glasgow: Learning Matters.

Horner, N. (2009) *What is Social Work? Context and Perspectives*. London: Sage.

Howe, D. (1996) Surface and depth in social work practice. In: N. Parton (ed.), *Social Theory, Social Change and Social Work*. London: Routledge.

Howe, D. (2008) *The Emotionally Intelligent Social Worker*. Houndsmill: Palgrave Macmillan.

Howe, D. (2008) *The Emotionally Intelligent Social Worker*. London: Palgrave.

Howe, D. (2009) *A Brief Introduction to Social Work Theory*. London: Macmillan.

Howe, D. (2014) *The Compleat Social Worker*. London: Palgrave.

Humphrey, C. (2011) *Becoming a Social Worker: A Guide for Students*. London: Sage.

Humphries, B. (2004) An unacceptable role for social work: Implementing immigration policy. *British Journal of Social Work*, 34, 93–107.

Humphries, R., Thorlby, R., Holder, H., Hall, P. and Charles, A. (2016) *Social Care for Older People: Home Truths*. London: The Kings Fund.

Hussain, S., Moriarty, J., Stevens, M., Sharpe, E. and Manthorpe, J. (2014) Organisational factors, job satisfaction and intention to leave among newly qualified social workers. *British Journal of Social Work*, 33(3), 381–396.

Hylton, K. (2009) *'Race' and Sport: Critical Race Theory*. Milton Park: Taylor and Francis.

IASSW (International Association of the Schools of Social Work) & IFSW (International Federation of Social Workers). (2004) *Global Definition of Social Work*. [Online.] Available from http://cdn.ifsw.org/assets/ifsw_65044-3.pdf (last accessed 10 September 2017).

IASSW (International Association of the Schools of Social Work) & IFSW (International Federation of Social Workers). (2012) *Global Agenda for Social Work. International Association of the Schools of Social Work*. [Online.] Available from http://cdn.ifsw.org/assets/globalagenda2012.pdf (last accessed 10 September 2017).

IFS (Institute of Fiscal Studies). (2017) *Recessions, Income Inequality and the Role of the Tax and Benefit System*. [Online.] Available from https://www.ifs.org.uk/publications/10102 (last accessed 10 September 2017).

IFSW (International Federation of Social Workers). (2002) [Internet] Social Work and the. Rights of the Child. A Professional. Training Manual. <Available from http://cdn.ifsw.org/assets/ifsw_124952-4.pdf > [Last Accessed September 2017].

IFSW (International Federation of Social Workers). (2014) *Global Definition of Social Work*. [Online.] Available from http://ifsw.org/get-involved/global-definition-of-social-work/ (last accessed 10 September 2017).

IFSW (International Federation of Social Workers). (2017a) *What We Do*. [Online.] Available from http://ifsw.org/what-we-do/ (last accessed 10 September 2017).

IFSW (International Federation of Social Workers). (2017b) *Statement of Ethical Principles*. [Online.] Available from http://ifsw.org/policies/statement-of-ethical-principles/ (last accessed 10 September 2017).

IFSW (International Federation of Social Workers). (2017c) *IFSW History*. [Online.] Available from http://ifsw.org/tag/ifsw-history/ (last accessed 10 September 2017).

Ingram, R. (2013) Locating emotional intelligence at the heart of social work practice. *British Journal of Social Work*, 43(5), 987–1004.

Ingram, R. (2015) Exploring emotions within formal and informal forums: Messages from social work practitioners. *British Journal of Social Work*, 45(3), 1, 896–913.

Jack, G. and Donnellan, H. (2010) Recognising the person within the developing professional: Tracking the early careers of newly qualified child care social workers in three local authorities in England. *Social Work Education*, 29(3), 305–318.

Jack, G. and Gill, O. (2013) Developing cultural competence for social work with families living in poverty. *European Journal of Social Work*, 16, 220–234.

James, A. (1998) Supporting families of origin: An exploration of the influence of the Children Act 1948. *Child & Family Social Work*, 3(3), 173–181.

Jenson, T. and Tyler, I. (2015) 'Benefits broods': The cultural and political crafting of anti-welfare commonsense. *Critical Social Policy*, 35(4), 470–491.

Johnson, J., Rolph, S. and Smith, R. (2010) Uncovering history: Private care homes for older people in England. *Journal of Social Policy*, 39(2), 235–253.

Jones, J. (1983) *State Social Work and the Working Class*. London: Macmillan Press.

Jones, R. (2012) Child protection, social work and the media: Doing as well as being done to. *Research, Policy and Planning*, 29(2), 83–94.

Jones, R. (2015) The end game: The marketisation and privatisation of children's social work and child protection. *Journal of Critical Social Policy*, 35(4), 1–25.

Jones, S. (2015) *Social Work Practice Placements; Critical and Reflective Approaches*. London: Sage.

Jordan, B. (1984) *Invitation to Social Work*. Oxford: Robertson.

Jordan, B. and Drakeford, M. (2012) *Social Work and Social Policy Under Austerity*. Basingstoke and New York: Palgrave Macmillan.

Jütte, S., Bentley, H., Tallis, D., Mayes, J., Jetha, N., O'Hagan, O., Brookes, H. and McConnell, N. (2015) *How Safe Are Our Children?* London: NSPCC.

Katz, I. and Connolly, M. (2017) Disproportionality and risk decision-making in child protection. In: M. Connolly (ed.), *Beyond the Risk Paradigm in Child Protection Current Debates and New Directions*, pp. 63–76. London: Palgrave Macmillan.

Kinman, G. and Grant, L. (2011) Exploring Stress Resilience in Trainee Social Workers: The Role of Emotional and Social Competencies. *British Journal of Social Work*, 41(2), 261–275.

Kings Fund. (2014) *Volunteering in Health and Care; Securing a Sustainable Future*. London: Kings Fund.

Kirton, D. (2016) Neo-liberal racism: Excision, ethnicity and the Children and Families Act 2014. *Critical Social Policy*, 36(4), 469–488.

Klein, N. (2008) *The Shock Doctrine: The Rise of Disaster Capitalism*. London: Penguin.

Klohen, E. (1996) Conceptual analysis and measurement of the construct of ego resiliency. *Journal of Personality and Social Psychology*, 70(5), 1067–1079.

Kniephoff-Knebel, A. and Seibel, F. (2008) Establishing international cooperation in social work education: The first decade of the International Committee of Schools for Social Work (ICSSW). *International Social Work*, 51(6): 790–812.

Kohli, R. (2006) *Social Work with Unaccompanied Asylum-Seeking Children*. Basingstoke: Palgrave Macmillan.

Kolb, D. (1984) *Experiential Learning: Experience as the Source of Learning and Development*. Englewood Cliffs, NJ: Prentice Hall.

Koprowska, J. (2010) *Communication and Interpersonal Skills*. London: Sage.

Kowalski, R.I. (2006) *European Communism 1848–1991*. Basingstoke: Palgrave Macmillan.

Krugman, P.R. (2008) *The Return of Depression Economics and the Crisis of 2008*. London: Penguin.

KSS (Knowledge and Skills Statement). (2015) *Knowledge and Skills Statement for Social Workers in Adults Services*. London: DfE.

Kuilema, J. (2015) Lessons from the First International Conference on Social Work. *International Social Work*, Sage, pp. 1–13.

Laird, S. (2008) *Anti-Oppressive Social Work: A Guide for Developing Cultural Competence*. London: Sage.

Lavalette, M. (2017) Austerity, inequality and the context of contemporary social work. *Social Work & Social Sciences Review*, 18(1), 15–30.

Lee, M. and Greene, G.J. (2008) A teaching framework for transformative multi-cultural social work education. *Journal of Ethnic & Cultural Diversity in Social Work*, 12(3), 1–28.

Leece, J. (2012) The emergence and development of the personalisation agenda. In: M. Davies (ed.), *Social Work with Adults*, pp. 10–23. Basingstoke: Palgrave Macmillan.

Linton, D. (1992) The Luddites: How did they get that bad reputation? *Labour History*, 33(4), 529–537.

Llewellyn, A., Agu, L. and Mercer, D. (2015) *Sociology for Social Workers*. London: Polity Press.

Lomax, R., Jones, K., Leigh, S. and Gay, C. (2010) *Surviving Your Social Work Placement*. London: Palgrave.

London Edinburgh Weekend Return Group. (1980) *In and Against the State*. London: Pluto Press.

Lowe, P., Lee, E. and Macvarish, J. (2015) Biologising parenting: Neuroscience discourse, English social and public health policy and understandings of the child. *Sociology Health Illness*, 37(2), 198–211.

Luttwak, E. (1999) *Turbo Capitalism: Winners and Losers in the Global Economy*. London: Orion Business.

Lymbery, M. (2005) *Social Work with Older People*. London: Sage.

Lymbery, M. (2006) United we stand? Partnership working in health and social care and the role of social work in services for older people. *British Journal of Social Work*, 36(7), 1119–1134.

Lymbery, M. and Postle, K. (2010) Social work in the context of adult social care in England and the resultant implications for social work education. *British Journal of Social Work*, 8(1), 2502–2522.

McIntosh, M.K. (2005) Poverty, charity, and coercion in Elizabethan England. *Journal of Interdisciplinary History*, 35(3), 457–479.

McIntosh, M.K. (2014) Poor relief in Elizabethan English communities: An analysis of Collectors' accounts. *Economic History Review*, 67(2), 331–357.

McKenzie, L. (2015) *Getting By: Estates, Class and Culture in Austerity Britain*. Bristol: Policy Press.

MacLeavy, J. (2008) Neoliberalising subjects: The legacy of New Labour's construction of social exclusion in local governance. *Geoforum*, 39(5), 1657–1666.

MacNicoll. (2017) *Social Work England: A Quick Guide to the Regulator Set to Replace HCPC*. [Online.] Available from http://www.communitycare.co.uk/2016/11/04/social-work-england-quick-guide-regulator-set-replace-hcpc/ (last accessed 10 September 2017).

McPhatter, A.R. (2004) Modeling culturally competent practice. In M. Austin and K. Hopkins (eds), *Supervision as Collaboration in the Human Services*, pp. 47–58. Thousand Oaks, CA: Sage.

Macvarish, J., Lee, E. and Lowe, P. (2014) The 'first three years' movement and the infant brain: A review of critiques. *Sociology Compass*, 8, 792–804. [Online.] doi:10.1111/soc4.12183.

Maltby, J. and Rutterford, J. (2016) Investing in charities in the nineteenth century: The financialization of philanthropy. *Accounting History*, 21(2/3), 263–280.

Mann, J. (2005) *Out of Harm's Way: The Wartime Evacuation of Children from Britain*. London: Headline Publishing.

Marlow, J. (1969) *The Peterloo Massacre*. London: Rapp & Whiting.

Martin, A. (2011) Practitioners' experience of former World War Two child evacuees in therapy: A qualitative study. PhD thesis, University of Hertfordshire.

Martin, R. (2010) *Social Work Assessment*. London: Sage.

Marwick, A. (1976) *Home Front: British and the Second World War*. London: Thames & Hudson.

Marx, K. and Engels, F. (2016 [1848]) *The Communist Manifesto*. [Online.] Available from https://www.marxists.org/archive/marx/works/1848/communist-manifesto/ (last accessed October 2016).

Masocha, S. (2015) *Asylum Seekers, Social Work and Racism*. Palgrave Macmillan.

Meek, J. (2014) *Private Island: Why Britain Belongs to Someone Else*. London: Verso.

The Mental Health Act 1959. London: HMSO.

Michie, R. (2012) Too big to fail: UK financial services reform in history and policy. *Economic Affairs*, 32(3), 11–16.

Milne, S. (2004) *The Enemy Within: The Secret War Against the Miners*. London: Verso.

Milner, J. and O'Byrne. (2009) *Assessment in Social Work*, 3rd edition. Basingstoke: Palgrave Macmillan.

Milner, J., Myers, S. and O'Byrne, P. (2015) Assessment in Social Work, 4th edition. London: Palgrave.

Mohanty, C. (1992) Feminist encounters: Locating the politics of experience. In: M. Barrett and A. Phillips (eds), *Destabilising Theory*, pp. 74–92. Oxford: Polity Press.

Moloney, P. (2013) *The Therapy Industry: The Irresistible Rise of the Talking Cure, and Why It Doesn't Work*. London: Pluto Press.

Moriarty, J., Manthorpe, J., Stevens, M. and Hussein, S. (2015) Educators or researchers? Barriers and facilitators to undertaking research among UK social work academics. *British Journal of Social Work*, 45(6), 1659–1677.

Morrison, A. (2016 [1889]) "Whitechapel". *The Palace Journal*, 24 April 1889 [Online.] Available from http://www.library.qmul.ac.uk/sites (last accessed August 2016).

Morrison, T. (2007) Emotional intelligence, emotion and social work: Context, characteristics, complications and contribution. *British Journal of Social Work*, 37, 245–263.

Moss, B.R., Dunkerley, M., Price, B., Sullivan, W., Reynolds, M. and Yates, B. (2007) Skills laboratories and the new social work degree: One small step towards best practice? Service users' and carers' perspectives. *Social Work Education*, 26, 708–722.

Moulin, L. (1978) *La Vie quotidienne des Religieux au Moyen Age (X^e–XVe siècle)*. Hachette Littérature: Paris.

Munro, E. (2011a) *The Munro Review of Child Protection: Final Report: A Child Centred System*. London: Department for Education.

Munro, E. (2011b) *The Munro Review of Child Protection. Interim Report: The Child's Journey*. London: Department for Education.

Murdach, A.D. (2011) Mary Richmond and the image of social work. *Social Work*, 56(1), 92–94.

NAO (National Audit Office). (2012) *Enablers and Barriers to Integrated Care.* London: NAO.

NAO (National Audit Office). (2014) *The Impact of Funding Reductions on Local Authorities.* [Online.] Available from http://www.nao.org.uk/wp-content/uploads/2014/11/Impact-of-funding-reductions-on-localauthorities-Executive-Summary.pdf (last accessed 8 December 2017).

NAO (National Audit Office). (2017a) *Children and families – Children in Care.* [Online.] Available from https://www.nao.org.uk/report/children-in-care/ (last accessed October 2017).

NAO (National Audit Office). (2017b) *Health and Social Care Integration.* London: NAO.

Napoli, M. and Bonifas, R. (2011) From theory toward empathic self-care: Creating a mindful classroom for social work students. *Social Work Education,* 30(6), 635–649.

Narey, M. (2014) *Sir Martin Narey's Independent Review: Making the Education of Social Workers Consistently Effective.* London: Department for Education.

Nayak, A. (2007) Critical whiteness studies. *Sociology Compass,* 1, 737–755. [Online.] doi:10.1111/j.1751-9020.2007.00045.x.

Nersisyan, Y. (2015) The repeal of the Glass-Steagall Act and the Federal Reserve's extraordinary intervention during the global financial crisis. *Journal of Post Keynesian Economics,* 37(4), 545–567.

Neville. (2000) The construction and validation of the colour-blind racial attitudes scale (COBAS). *Journal of Counselling Psychology,* 47(1), 59–70.

NIESR (National Institute of Economic and Social Research). (2016) *National Evaluation of the Troubled Families Programme: Final Synthesis Report.* London: NIESR.

Nissly, J.A., Mor Barak, M.E. and Levin, A. (2005) Stress, social support and workers intentions to leave their jobs in public welfare. *Administration in Social Work,* 29 (1), 79–100.

No Deportations. (2017) *No-Deportations – Residence Papers for All.* [Online.] Available from http://www.no-deportations.org.uk/Media-6-4-2011/DeathInRemovalCentres.html (last accessed October 2017).

O'Connor, L., Cecil, B. and Boudioni, M. (2009) Preparing for practice: An evaluation of an undergraduate social work 'preparation for practice' module. *Social Work Education,* 28(4), 436–454.

Ofsted. (2012) *Right on Time: Exploring Delays in Adoption.* London: Ofsted.

Oliver, M. Sapey, B. and Thomas, C. (2012) *Social Work with Disabled People.* London: Palgrave.

Owen, C. and Statham, J. (2009) *Disproportionality in Child Welfare: The Prevalence of Black and Minority Ethnic Children within the 'Looked After' and 'Children in Need' Populations and on Child Protection Registers in England.* London: Department for Children, Schools and Families.

Parker, J. (2006) Developing perceptions of competence during practice learning. *British Journal of Social Work,* 36, 1017–1036.

Parker, M. (2009) *The Past, the Passion, the Potential: How the History of the Settlement Movement Informs Our Pursuit of Social Justice.* London: British Association of Settlements and Social Action Centres.

Parker, J. (2010) *Social Work Practice: Assessment and Intervention*. London: Sage. HYPERLINK "http://www.research.lancs.ac.uk/portal/en/publications/-(e8cfe834-4dc6-4011-b2f6-9e1b1dea929f).html" Social work and drug usePaylor, I. 2011 In: Social Work. Pearson Longman DoH (Department of Health). (2015) Knowledge and Skills Statement for Social Workers in Adult Services. London: DoH.

Parker, J. (2017) *Social Work Practice: Assessment, Planning, Intervention and Review*. London: Palgrave.

Parker, R. (2011) Getting started with the 1948 Children Act: What do we learn?. *Adoption & Fostering*, 35(3), 17–29.

Parker, S. (2005) *Mentor UK Coastal and Ex-mining Areas Project – A Review of the Literature*. London: Mentor.

Parliament. (2016) *Poor Law reform*. [Online.] Available from http://www.parliament.uk/about/living-heritage/transformingsociety/livinglearning/19thcentury/overview/poorlaw/ (last accessed October 2016).

Parrott, L. (2010) *Values and Ethics in Social Work Practice*. London: Palgrave.

Parrott, L. (2014) *Values and Ethics in Social Work Practice*. Exeter: Sage and Learning Matters.

Parton, N. (2017) Concerns about risk as a major driver of professional practice. In: M. Connolly (eds), *Beyond the Risk Paradigm in Child Protection*, pp. 3–14. Basingstoke: Palgrave Macmillan.

Parton, N. and Williams, S. (2017) The contemporary refocusing of children's services in England. *Journal of Children's Services*, 12(2), 85–96.

Pasini, A. (2016) How to make good choices? Ethical perspectives guiding social workers moral reasoning. *Social Work Education*, 35(4), 377–98.

Payne, M. (2005) *The Origins of Social Work: Continuity and Change*. Basingstoke: Palgrave.

Petrie, P; Boddy, J; Cameron, C; Heptinstall, E; McQuail, Susan & McQuail S; Wigfall, A; Wigfall, V. (2008) *Pedagogy-a holistic, personal approach to work with children and young people, across services European models for practice, training, education and qualification*. London: IOE-UOL.

Philip, A.F. and Timms, N. (1962) *The Problem of The Problem Family*. London: Family Service Units.

Ploesser, M. and Mecheril, P. (2012) Neglect – recognition – deconstruction: Approaches to otherness in social work, *International Social work*, 55(6), 794–808.

Pointon, B. (2011) *Integration in Dementia Care: A Carer's Perspective*. Alzheimer's Society. [Online.] Available from https://www.alzheimers.org.uk/download/downloads/id/1266/alzheimers_society_response_to_the_rcgp_consultation_on_integration_of_care.pdf (last accessed December 2017).

Porter, R. (1989) *A Social history of Madness: Stories of the Insane*. London: Weidenfeld & Nicolson.

Porter, R. (2002) *Madness: A Brief History*. Oxford: Oxford University Press.

Postle, K. (2002) Working 'between the idea and the reality': Ambiguities and tensions in care managers' work. *British Journal of Social Work*, 32(3), 335–351.

Prochaska, J. and DiClemente, C. (1982) Transtheoretical therapy: Towards a more integrative model of change. *Psychotherapy: Theory, Research and Practice*, 19, 276–288.

PSA (Professional Standards Authority). (2017) *Review of Professional Regulation and Registration with Annual Report and Accounts 2016/2017*, https://www. professionalstandards.org.uk/docs/default-source/publications/annual-reports/ professional-standards-authority-review-of-professional-regulation-amp-registration(annual-report-amp-accounts-english).pdf?sfvrsn=10 (last accessed 23 July 2018).

Race, T. and O'Keefe, R. (2017) *Child-Centred Practice*. London: Palgrave.

Rajan-Rankin, S. (2013) Self identity, embodiment and the development of emotional resilience. *British Journal of Social Work*, 44(8), 1–17.

Rajan-Rankin, S. (2015) Anti-racist social work in a 'post-race society'? Interrogating the amorphous 'other'. *Critical and Radical Social Work*, 3(2), 207–220.

Rees, P., Wohland, P., Norman, P. et al. (2012) Ethnic population projections for the UK, 2001–2051. *Journal of Population Research*, 29(1), 45–89.

Refugee Council. (2017a) *The Truth about Asylum*. [Online.] Available from https://www.refugeecouncil.org.uk/policy_research/the_truth_about_ asylum?gclid=CjwKCAiA6qPRBRAkEiwAGw4SdqKqC6kSdhF6MYoMdN02prMt-A2TRv60iFOMdogG-mukMWBteQSfZ8xoCZxEQAvD_BwE (last accessed October 2016).

Refugee Council. (2017b) *I am Seeking Asylum*. [Online.] Available from https:// www.refugeecouncil.org.uk/how_can_we_help_you/i_am_seeking_asylum (last accessed October 2016).

Reid, W.J. and Epstein, L. (1972) *Task-Centred Social Work*. New York: Columbia University Press.

Richardson, G. (2001) A tale of two theories: Monopolies and craft guilds in medieval England and modern imagination. *Journal of The History of Economic Thought*, 23(2), 217–242.

Rogowski, S. (2010) *Social Work, the Rise and Fall of a Profession*. Bristol: Policy Press.

Rogowski, S. (2011) Managers, managerialism and social work with children and families: The deformation of a profession? *Practice*, 23(3), 157–167.

Rosenthal, R. (1977) The PONS Test: Measuring sensitivity to nonverbal cues. In: P. McReynolds (ed.), *Advances in Psychological Assessment*. San Francisco, CA: Jossey-Bass.

Rubinstein, W.D. (1998) *Britain's Century: A Political and Social History, 1815–1905*. London: Arnold.

Ruch, G. (2005) Relationship-based and reflective practice in contemporary child care social work. *Child and Family Social Work*, 10, 111–123.

Ruch, G. (2010) Theoretical frameworks informing relationship based practice. In: G. Ruch, D. Turvey and A. Ward (eds), *Relationship Based Social Work: Getting to the Heart of Practice*. London: Jessica Kingsley.

Sargant, S. (2014) Trapped in legal discourse: Transracial adoption in the United States and England. *Denning Law Journal*, 23, 131–162.

Sargant, S. (2015) Transracial adoption in England: A critical race systems theory analysis. *International Journal of Law in Context*, 11, 412–425.

Sayer, S. (2008) *Critical Practice in Working with Children*. Basingstoke: Palgrave.

Scheuer, J. (1985) *Legacy of Light: University Settlement's First Century*. New York: University Settlement Society of New York. [Online.] Available from http://

socialwelfare.library.vcu.edu/settlement-houses/origins-of-the-settlement-house-movement/ (last accessed May 2017).

Scourfield, P. (2007) Are there reasons to be worried about the 'cartelisation' of residential care? *Critical Social Policy*, 25(2), 155–180.

Searle, Rosalind & Patent, Volker. (2012) Recruitment, Retention and Role Slumping in Child Protection: The Evaluation of In-Service Training Initiatives. *British Journal of Social Work*, 43, 1111–1129. doi:10.1093/bjsw/bcs.

Seebohm, F. (1968) *Report of the Interdepartmental Committee on Local Authorities and Allied Personal Social Services*. London: HMSO.

Seebohm, F. (1989) *Seebohm: Twenty Years On, Three Stages in the Development of the Personal Social Services*. London: Policy Studies Institute.

Sernau, S. (2013) *Social Inequality in a Global Age*, 4th edition. Thousand Oaks, CA: Sage.

Seymour, R. (2014) *Against Austerity: How We Can Fix the Crisis They Made*. London: Pluto Press.

SfC (Skills for Care). (2015) *The Social Work ASYE: Guidance for NQSWs Completing the ASYE in Adults and Child and Family Settings*. London: SfC.

SfC (Skills for Care). (2017) *State of the Adult Social Care Sector and Workforce in England*. London: SfC.

Shardlow, Steven and Mark Doel. (1996) *Practice Learning and Teaching* (British Association of Social Workers). London: Macmillan Press Ltd.

Shardlow, S. (2012) Learning and teaching in practice learning. In: J. Lishman (ed.), *Social Work Education and Training*, pp. 102–115. London: Jessica Kingsley.

Shennan, G. (2015) BASW statement on the closure of the College of Social Work. [Online.] Available from https://www.basw.co.uk/news/article/?id=980 (last accessed December 2017).

Silva, D.M.D. (2017) The othering of Muslims: Discourses of radicalization in the *New York Times*, 1969–2014. *Sociology Forum*, 32, 138–161. [Online.] doi:10.1111/socf.12321.

Singh, G. and Cowden, S. (2009) The social worker as intellectual. *European Journal of Social Work*, 12(4), 479–493.

Sked, A. and Cook, C. (1979) *Post-War Britain: A Political History*. London: Penguin.

Skeggs, B. (2004) *Class, Self, Culture*. London: Routledge.

Skidelsky, R.A. (2010a) *Keynes: The Return of the Master*. London: Penguin.

Skidelsky, R.A. (2010b) *Keynes: A Very Short Introduction*. Oxford: Oxford University Press.

Smale, G. and Tuson, G., with Brehal, N. and Marsh, P. (1993) *Empowerment, Assessment, Care Management and the Skilled Social Worker*. London: National Institute for Social Work.

Smith, D. and Craft, R. (2011) Mapping the great recession: A reader's guide to the first crisis of 21st century capitalism. *New Political Science*, 33(4), 577–601.

Smith, M.K. (2002) *Casework and the Charity Organization Society*. [Online.] Available from http://www.infed.org/socialwork/charity_organization_society.htm (last accessed October 2016).

Smith, R. (2008) *Social Work and Power*. London: Palgrave.

Standing, G. (2011) *The Precariat: The New Dangerous Class*. London: Bloomsbury Academic.

Statham, J. Cameron, C. and Mooney, A. (2006) *The Tasks and Roles of Social Workers: A Focused Overview of Research Evidence*. [Online] Available from https://www.kcl.ac.uk/sspp/policy-institute/scwru/pubs/2007/blewettetal-2007changing.pdf (last Accessed October 2017).

Stevenson, L. (2015) Doncaster's Children's Trust 'inadequate' but shows signs of improvement, Ofsted finds. *Community Care* [Online.] Available from http://www.communitycare.co.uk/2015/11/27/doncasters-childrens-trust-inadequate-shows-signs-improvement-ofsted-finds/ (last accessed October 2016).

Stone, C. (2016) The role of practice educators in initial and post qualifying social work education. *Social Work Education*, 35(6), 706–718.

Strauss, P. (1929) Definition and progress of social work. In: *First International Conference of Social Work Proceedings*, Vol. 1, pp. 595–6. First Conference, Paris, 8–13 July 1928.

Sutton, C. (1999) *Helping Families with Troubled Children*. Chichester: Wiley.

Swaine, J. (2008) *Gordon Brown Hails £500 billion Bank Rescue Plan*. London: The Telegraph. 8 October, 2008.

Taliadoros, J. (2013) Law, theology, and morality: Conceptions of the rights to relief of the poor in the twelfth and thirteenth centuries. *Journal of Religious History*, 37(4), 474–493.

Taylor, B. (2017) *Decision Making, Assessment and Risk in Social Work*. London: Sage.

Tedam, P. (2013) Developing cultural competence. In: A. Bartoli (ed.), *Anti-racism in Social Work Practice*, pp. 48–65. St Albans: Critical Publishing.

Tew, J. (2012) Theory in mental health social work. In M. Davies (ed.), *Social Work with Adults: From Policy to Practice*, pp. 123–40. Basingstoke: Palgrave Macmillan.

Tham, P. (2007) Why are they leaving? Factors affecting intention to leave among social workers in child welfare. *British Journal of Social Work*, 37, 1225–1246.

Tham, P. and Lynch, D. (2014) Prepared for practice? Graduating social work students' reflections on their education, competence and skills. *Social Work Education*, 33, 704–717.

The Royal Society. (2010) 'Learning it's all in your head' http://invigorate.royalsociety.org/ks5/learning-its-all-in-your-head.aspx (Last accessed August 20–18).

Thompson, N. (1992) *Existentialism and Social Work*. London: Routledge.

Thompson, N. (2003) *Communication and Language: A Handbook of Theory and Practice*. Basingstoke: Palgrave Macmillan.

Thompson N. (2009) *Promoting Equality, Valuing Diversity: A Learning and Development Manual (Learning for Practice)*. Lyme Regis: Russell House Publishing.

Thompsons, N. (2016) *Anti-Discriminatory Practice: Equality, Diversity and Justice*, 6th edition. Basingstoke: Palgrave.

Thorpe, A. (2008) *A History of the British Labour Party*. Basingstoke: Palgrave Macmillan.

Titmuss, R.M. (1958) The social division of welfare. In: *Essays on the Welfare State*. London: Unwin University Books.

TMO (The Migration Observatory). (2017) *Briefing: Immigration Detention in the UK*. [Online.] Available from http://www.migrationobservatory.ox.ac.uk/wp-content/uploads/2016/04/Briefing-Immigration_Detention-2.pdf (last accessed October 2017).

Toarna, A. and Cojanu, V. (2015) The 2008 crisis: Causes and future direction for the academic research. In: *Procedia Economics and Finance, 27, 22nd International Economic Conference of Sibiu 2015, IECS 2015 'Economic Prospects in the Context of Growing Global and Regional Interdependencies'*, pp. 385–393.

Tompsett, H. Henderson, K., Mathew Bryne, J., Gaskell Mew, E. and Tompsett, C. (2017) On the learning journey: What helps and hinders the development of social work students' core pre-placement skills. *Social Work Education*, 36(1), 6–25.

Trevelyan, G.M. (1944) *English Social History*. London: Longmans, Green & Co.

Tunstill, J. and Willow, C. (2017) Professional social work and the defence of children's and their families' rights in a period of austerity: A case study. *Social Work & Social Sciences Review*, 19(1), 40–65.

UNHCR (United Nations Refugee Agency) (2015) *Global Trends: Forced Displacement in 2015*. [Online.] Available from http://www.unhcr.org/uk/statistics/unhcrstats/576408cd7/unhcr-global-trends-2015.html (last accessed October 2016).

UNISON. (2017) *Cuts to local services*. [Online.] Available from https://www.unison.org.uk/at-work/local-government/key-issues/cuts-to-local-services/ (last accessed December 2017).

Valutis, S., Rubin, R. and Bell, M. (2012) Professional socialization and social work values: Who are we teaching? *Social Work Education*, 31(8), 1046–1057.

Van Horn, C. and Schaffner, H. (eds) (2003*) Work in America, An Encyclopaedia of History, Policy, and Society*, Vol. 1. Oxford: ABC-CLIO.

Vertovec, S. (2007) Super-diversity and its implications. *Ethnic and Racial Studies*, 30(6), 1024–1054.

Walker, S. (2005) Towards culturally competent practice in child and adolescent mental health. *International Social Work*, 48(1), 49–62.

Washington, D. (2008) *The Concept of Diversity*. [Online.] Available from http://dwashingtonllc.com/images/pdf/publications/the_concept_of_diversity.pdf, (last accessed 8 December 2017).

Wastell, D. and White, S. (2012) Blinded by neuroscience: Social policy, the family and the infant brain. *Families Relationships and Societies*, 1(3), 397–414.

Watson, D. and West, J. (2006) *Social Work Process and Practice: Approaches, Knowledge and Skills*. London: Palgrave.

Weaver, H.N. (1999) Culture and professional education the experiences of native American social workers. *Journal of Social Work Education*, 36(3), 217–225.

Weick, A., Rapp, C., Sullivan, W.P. and Kisthardt, W. (1989) A strengths perspective for social work practice. *Social Work*, 34(4), 350–354.

Welbourne, P. and Dixon, J. (2016) Child protection and welfare: Cultures, policies and practices. In: C. Williams and M.J. Graham (eds), *Social Work in a Diverse Society*, pp. 139–169. Bristol: Bristol Policy Press.

Williams, S. and Rutter, L. (2013) *The Practice Educator Handbook*. London: Sage.

Wilson, G. and Kelly, B. (2010) Evaluating the effectiveness of social work education: Preparing students for practice learning. *British Journal of Social Work*, 40, 2431–2449.

Woods, T. (2015) 'Practice educators' experiences of facilitating and assessing student values and ethics learning: Constructing dialogue. *Social Work Education*, 34(8), 936–951.

Wright, E.O. (1994) *Interrogating Inequality: Essays on Class Analysis, Socialism and Marxism*. New York: Verso.

Yan, M. and Wong, Y.L. (2005) Rethinking Self-Awareness in Cultural Competence: Toward a Dialogic Self in Cross-Cultural Social Work. Families in Society; April–June 2005; 86, 2; Research Library. 181–188

Young, A.F. (1956) *British Social Work in the Nineteenth Century*. London: Routledge and Kegan Paul.

Younghusband, E. (1959) *Younghusband Report. Ministry of Health/Department of Health for Scotland Report of the Working Party on Social Workers in the Local Authority Health and Welfare Services*. London: HMSO.

Younghusband, E. (1978) *Social Work in Britain: 1950–1975: A Follow Up Study*, Vol. 2. London: Allen & Unwin.

Index

www.ingramcontent.com/pod-product-compliance
Lightning Source LLC
Chambersburg PA
CBHW062027270326
41929CB00014B/2351